"A major contribution to pronunciation research, this engaging volume is packed with clear explanations of key concepts, along with detailed practical advice on the special issues that frequently arise in data collection and analysis. Essential reading for new and seasoned researchers alike."

Murray J. Munro, *Professor Emeritus, Simon Fraser University*

"I cannot praise this book enough. Charlie Nagle's *Guide to Research Methods* is a state-of-the-art overview and an engaging primer to research design and data analysis that will inspire both novice and seasoned scholars. Writing with candor, clarity, and flair, Nagle mentors the reader, through personal insight and examples of best research practice, on how to be a conscientious, caring, and creative researcher."

Pavel Trofimovich, *Professor, Concordia University (Montreal, Canada)*

"Charlie Nagle has produced a superb resource, which will be valuable for anyone interested in research methods in SLA, not only pronunciation. The message that 'absence of evidence is not evidence of absence' rings true: consequently, choosing the right methods for the research questions posed is essential. The meticulous and accessible nature of the writing and analyses make this an excellent text for applied linguistics programs. In a clear, step-by-step manner, Charlie outlines every stage of the design of experiments, but this is much more than a how-to manual. Drawing on literature from several disciplines within SLA, Charlie has created an informative volume that is likely to be a classic in the years to come."

Tracey Derwing, *Professor Emeritus, University of Alberta*

"*A guide to quantitative research methods in second language pronunciation* provides 8 accessible chapters that serve as the authoritative introduction to this growing field of research. It provides relevant examples of some of the current analytic techniques used by pronunciation researchers, all of which are described in a clear manner and complemented with R code. Importantly, this definitive guide makes some of the new analytic tools of open science and reproducible research accessible to students and early career researchers and serves as a foundational reference for anybody interested in learning and teaching open science practices in second language pronunciation research."

Joseph Casillas, *Associate Professor, Rutgers University*

A GUIDE TO QUANTITATIVE RESEARCH METHODS IN SECOND LANGUAGE PRONUNCIATION

This book offers a comprehensive resource on the state-of-the-art in L2 pronunciation, surveying the most up-to-date theoretical and methodological developments to highlight the multidimensional nature of pronunciation scholarship and directions for future research. The volume examines both speech perception and production, including the perception-production link. The book explores production from a range of perspectives, including acoustic analysis of specific features and listener-based ratings of global dimensions of pronunciation. Each chapter spotlights a different dimension of pronunciation through a consistent structure, including a summary of the latest research, a critical appraisal of methods, and an overview of data analysis procedures with recommendations for practical implementation. The innovative interconnected structure allows readers to build on their knowledge with each successive chapter while also allowing the flexibility to use chapters as standalone units depending on individual interests. A concluding chapter outlines a research agenda for future scholarship, spotlighting the methods and approaches that are most likely to advance the field. This book is an invaluable resource for graduate students and researchers, at all stages of their careers, looking to expand their knowledge base in SLA and L2 pronunciation and related fields such as phonetics and phonology.

Charlie Nagle is Associate Professor in the Department of Spanish and Portuguese at The University of Texas at Austin, USA. As a quantitative research methodologist working in the areas of second language learning, phonetics and phonology, and speech perception and production, he is especially interested in longitudinal research methods and the statistical modeling of speech data. His work has been supported by the Fulbright Program and the National Science Foundation.

Second Language Acquisition Research Series

Susan M. Gass and Alison Mackey, Series Editors

Kimberly L. Geeslin, Associate Editor

The *Second Language Acquisition Research Series* presents and explores issues bearing directly on theory construction and/or research methods in the study of second language acquisition. Its titles (both authored and edited volumes) provide thorough and timely overviews of high-interest topics, and include key discussions of existing research findings and their implications. A special emphasis of the series is reflected in the volumes dealing with specific data collection methods or instruments. Each of these volumes addresses the kinds of research questions for which the method/ instrument is best suited, offers extended description of its use, and outlines the problems associated with its use. The volumes in this series will be invaluable to students and scholars alike, and perfect for use in courses on research methodology and in individual research.

Theories in Second Language Acquisition
Researching Incidental Vocabulary Learning in a Second Language
Edited by Mark Feng Teng and Barry Lee Reynolds

Second Language Speech Processing
A Guide to Conducting Experimental Research
Isabelle Darcy

Research Methods in Generative Second Language Acquisition
Roumyana Slabakova, Tania Leal and Laura Domínguez

For more information about this series, please visit: www.routledge.com/Second-Language-Acquisition-Research-Series/book-series/LEASLARS

A GUIDE TO QUANTITATIVE RESEARCH METHODS IN SECOND LANGUAGE PRONUNCIATION

Charlie Nagle

NEW YORK AND LONDON

Designed cover image: Panuwat Srijantawong

First published 2025
by Routledge
605 Third Avenue, New York, NY 10158

and by Routledge
4 Park Square, Milton Park, Abingdon, Oxon, OX14 4RN

Routledge is an imprint of the Taylor & Francis Group, an informa business

© 2025 Charlie Nagle

The right of Charlie Nagle to be identified as author of this work has been asserted in accordance with sections 77 and 78 of the Copyright, Designs and Patents Act 1988.

All rights reserved. No part of this book may be reprinted or reproduced or utilised in any form or by any electronic, mechanical, or other means, now known or hereafter invented, including photocopying and recording, or in any information storage or retrieval system, without permission in writing from the publishers.

Trademark notice: Product or corporate names may be trademarks or registered trademarks, and are used only for identification and explanation without intent to infringe.

ISBN: 9781032245560 (hbk)
ISBN: 9781032245553 (pbk)
ISBN: 9781003279266 (ebk)

DOI: 10.4324/9781003279266

Typeset in Galliard
by codeMantra

To my mom, Nancy Nagle

CONTENTS

Acknowledgments   *xiii*

1 Introduction   1

    Rationale for the Book 1
    Intended Audience, Features, and Structure 2
    A Note on Style 5
    Approach to Data Analysis 6
    Mixed-Effects Modeling 8
    Statistical Significance and Modeling 11
    Summary 13
    Analysis Software 13
    R Packages and Coding Conventions 15
    Getting Started 17

2 Researching Speech Perception   22

    Introduction 22
    Theoretical Models 27
    Research Topics 29
    Measuring Perception 31
    Designing the Perception Task 34
      Designing the Stimuli 34
      Recording and Preparing the Stimuli 39

x Contents

Designing the Procedure 41
Analyzing Perception Data 44
Statistical Analysis 47
   Example 1: Stop Consonant Perception over Time 47
   Example 2: Vowel Perception over Time 59
Summary and Recommendations 63

3   Researching the Production of Specific Features   68

Introduction 68
Target Structures 71
Speech Production Tasks and Stimuli 77
Collecting, Coding, and Analyzing Production
   Data 79
   Collecting the Data 79
   Coding and Analyzing the Data 80
Statistical Analysis 82
   Example 1: Stop Consonant Production over
     Time 84
   Example 2: Vowel Intelligibility over Time 97
Summary and Recommendations 103

4   Researching the Perception-Production Link   110

Introduction 110
Current Approaches to the Link 113
Perception-Production Measurement Issues 116
A Systematic Approach to the Link 118
Statistical Analysis 122
   Example 1: Mixed-Effects Model 122
   Example 2: Multivariate Latent Growth Curve
     Model 126
Summary and Recommendations 130

5   Researching the Production of Global Features   134

Introduction 134
Sampling Speakers 137
Sampling Speech for Evaluation 139
Preparing Speech for Evaluation 142
Sampling Listeners 143

Designing the Rating Task 146
Validating L2 Speech Ratings Data 149
Statistical Analysis 150
  Example 1: Development of Comprehensibility,
    Fluency, and Accentedness 150
  Example 2: The Effect of Study Abroad on
    Comprehensibility Development 157
Summary and Recommendations 163

6 Researching Pronunciation Training and Instruction   169

Introduction 169
Researching Perception Training 171
  Picking a Topic 171
  Measuring Learning 176
  Developing the Training Procedure 179
  Perception Summary 181
  Statistical Analysis: The Shape of Learning during
    HVPT 182
Researching Production Training 187
  Picking a Topic 187
  Designing the Intervention 193
  Selecting Variables for Experimental
    Manipulation 194
  Measuring Learning 198
  Production Summary 200
  Statistical Analysis: Visual Feedback Training:
    Retention Over Time 201
Integrated and Complex Designs 211
Learning beyond Training 212
Summary and Recommendations 213

7 Researching Individual Differences   219

Introduction 219
Mechanisms and Timelines in Individual Differences
  Research 222
Motivation 227
  Motivation in Pronunciation Research 230
Experience 232

Connecting the Dots 237
Statistical Analysis 238
  Example 1: Language Use and
    Comprehensibility 238
  Example 2: Motivation, Learning Behavior,
    and Comprehensibility 242
Summary and Recommendations 246

8 Conclusion   252

Index   *259*

ACKNOWLEDGMENTS

In high school, while studying Spanish at a summer honor's program, one of my classmates made an offhand comment that I spoke Spanish well but with an American accent. I didn't know what that meant, so I asked Carla, a friend in the program who was studying art and had grown up speaking Spanish. She explained to me that the Spanish tap /ɾ/ was produced like the English /d/ in words like "ladder." That was the first time I thought about pronunciation and accents, and that conversation and many others like it laid the basis for my interest in language and linguistics. I never got the chance to properly thank Carla, so I wanted to take the opportunity to acknowledge her. In my undergraduate studies, Bill Prince, one of my Spanish professors, was extremely generous with his time and expertise. I was probably insufferable during his office hours, but Bill always made time to talk to me. It was in his class on contrastive grammatical analysis that I first began my journey into linguistics, a journey that would become my career.

The writing of this book has been over two years in the making, but its conceptualization has been a far longer process. In many ways, that process started in graduate school, when I first became interested in the means by which we generate knowledge and use that knowledge to guide practice. It takes a village, and in the case of research, the village is large indeed, encompassing colleagues, mentors, reviewers, conference participants, and research assistants and participants. To everyone who has taken the time to help with my research, attend my talks, provide feedback on my work, and serve as a sounding board for conceptual and methodological questions, thank you.

xiv Acknowledgments

Many people have been especially instrumental to the writing of this book and deserve special recognition. To Tracey Derwing and Murray Munro, whose work initially captured my interest and inspired me to work in this area. Thank you for paving the way for me and countless other speech researchers. To Pavel Trofimovich, a constant source of support and encouragement. Without you, I would never have had the confidence to pursue several projects, especially my projects on the perception-production link. To John Levis, Chad Gasta, Julia Domínguez, and Megan Myers. You were all instrumental to my success and well-being during my time at Iowa State. To Mari Sakai and Germán Zárate Sández, who have enriched my personal and professional life beyond measure. Thank you for your unflagging willingness to workshop research concepts and methods with me. To my collaborators, especially Amanda Huensch and Melissa Baese-Berk. It has been an absolute pleasure to work with you and learn from you, and I look forward to our future projects. I would also like to thank Nick Pandža and Joseph Casillas, who have been fonts of statistical knowledge and support. Thank you for always taking the time to respond to my questions about statistical modeling in R. I'm certain that I wouldn't know half of what I know now if it weren't for you. I am also indebeted to Keith Goldfeld and Lisa DeBruine, whose guidance on data simulation was invaluable. Thank you to Pavel Trofimovich, Kelsey Bergeson, and Shelby Bruun for reading and providing feedback on drafts of this book. Your expertise and guidance have sharpened both my thinking and my writing.

To my friends and family, to whom I owe everything. To Katie Vater, for the countless hours of conversation, laughter, and joy we have shared. To Sonya Parpart Li, a brilliant scientist and an unfailingly kind and thoughtful friend. Most importantly, to Peter Cruz. Without your support, this book would not have been possible.

1

INTRODUCTION

Rationale for the Book

Second language (L2) pronunciation research is flourishing. At the time of writing, the field has already accumulated research syntheses on a range of key topics, such as the effectiveness of various forms of L2 speech perception and production training (Lee et al., 2015; McAndrews, 2019; Saito & Plonsky, 2019; Sakai & Moorman, 2018; Thomson & Derwing, 2015; Zhang et al., 2021) and relationships among listener-based dimensions of pronunciation and their linguistic predictors (Chau & Huensch, 2021; Saito, 2021). The Speech Learning Model (Flege, 1995) has also been revised (Flege & Bohn, 2021), and several other state-of-the-art articles have scrutinized prominent subdomains of L2 pronunciation research, including high variability phonetic training (Barriuso & Hayes-Harb, 2018; Thomson, 2018) and the perception–production link (Nagle & Baese-Berk, 2021). Book-length publications also abound. Derwing and Munro's (2015) *Pronunciation fundamentals*, Levis's (2018) book on intelligibility, and Levis, Derwing, and Sonsaat-Hegelheimer's (2022) edited volume on bridging the gap between pronunciation research and pronunciation teaching are noteworthy examples. There are also many books dealing with pronunciation learning and teaching in specific languages. Signs of disciplinary progress are not limited to publications. There are more professional conferences on pronunciation than ever (e.g., Pronunciation in Second Language Learning and Teaching, the International Symposium on the Acquisition of Second Language Speech), and the American Association of Applied Linguistics has

DOI: 10.4324/9781003279266-1

2 Introduction

a dedicated Phonology and Oral Communication Strand. Last but certainly not least, the *Journal of Second Language Pronunciation* is nearly a decade old at the time of publication of this book.

This disciplinary growth makes now the perfect time to delve into the research topics and methods that are central to L2 pronunciation research and, indeed, to cross-linguistic pronunciation research more generally: L2 speech perception (Chapter 2), L2 speech production, which encompasses the production of both specific pronunciation features (Chapter 3) as well as global, listener-based dimensions of pronunciation (Chapter 5), the perception–production link (Chapter 4), training and instruction (Chapter 6), and individual differences and pronunciation learning (Chapter 7). One of the most exciting aspects of L2 pronunciation is that it draws upon concepts and methods from many neighboring disciplines. As a result, L2 pronunciation research is uniquely positioned to contribute to those fields. By researching the processes by which individuals learn and become proficient in the pronunciation of another language, L2 pronunciation studies can illuminate the nature of sound representations in the bilingual mind, provide insight into language learning and bilingualism as an engine of sound change, and of course shed light on how to support the millions of L2 learners and users worldwide.

Intended Audience, Features, and Structure

I have made every effort to write this book to appeal to a wide readership of speech and pronunciation scholars. In each chapter, I provide an overview of the historical development and state of the art of the area, focusing on the main topics, questions, and hypotheses that have defined the research agenda. I then turn to methodological and analytical issues. In discussing the methodological features of research, I comment on broad conceptual considerations such as how to pick a target structure or a training paradigm for examination. I also comment on granular issues like designing, creating, and counterbalancing stimuli and designing a rating task when eliciting listener-based judgments of the global dimensions of pronunciation. I have found that doing research involves making many small decisions that don't always appear in research reports, and these small decisions, taken in the aggregate, can be overwhelming. They're the hidden side of methodology that needs to be brought to light. These decisions can also render conceptually similar studies quite different in terms of their experimental methods and procedures. In commenting on these two facets of methodology, I intend this book to be useful to graduate students and novice researchers who are interested in learning more about L2 pronunciation research as well as seasoned scholars seeking an overview of quantitative research methods in the field.

A focus on data analysis is an important feature of the book. This is the area of research methods where I receive the most questions. In my experience, researchers are often concerned about how they can apply specific analytical techniques, such as mixed-effects modeling, to their own data. Certainly, there are many resources available on mixed-effects modeling and other techniques, but those resources do not often focus on pronunciation data, so it falls to researchers to bridge the gap between the analysis they want to run and how to run it on their data. I aim to bridge this gap in this book so that researchers with diverse quantitative backgrounds will find the analytical sections useful and approachable. In each chapter, I have included two worked examples using simulated data. I have written the chapters to function as standalone units, but I have designed and implemented the analysis examples in a scaffolded manner. Researchers will benefit from reading the analytical portions of the book in sequence, but individuals who are interested in specific research topics can also read individual chapters without consulting previous ones. In the few cases where reference to a previous chapter is essential, I have made a note, directing the reader to the relevant section. For this same reason, some of the analytical concepts and steps are reiterated throughout the book.

With respect to analytical topics, in the first two chapters, I present analysis of variance (ANOVA) and mixed-effects modeling so that readers comfortable with ANOVA can see how it can be translated into a mixed-effects model. I also revisit ANOVA in the chapter on researching training (Chapter 7), given that factorial designs are often analyzed using that technique. I gradually build up the complexity of analyses by increasing the number of variables, integrating interaction terms, and working with incomplete data sets (i.e., data sets with some missing data). In the chapters on the perception–production link and individual differences, I discuss multivariate latent growth curve modeling, part of the structural equation modeling family, as a promising analytical technique that could prove useful for answering some of the most pressing questions guiding the field at this time. Though a more advanced topic, I believe this type of analysis will appeal to more seasoned scholars who are already comfortable with some of the basic analytical tools used in the field.

Longitudinal research methods, including longitudinal data analysis, are a prominent feature of the book. In fact, all of the data sets analyzed in this book are longitudinal. In my view, longitudinal research has the greatest potential to advance the state of the art, but it can also be conceptually, methodologically, and logistically challenging. Doing longitudinal research entails making complex decisions about the number, timing, and spacing of data collection sessions, which also means thinking about developmental windows, rates of change, and end states. As I have

4 Introduction

argued elsewhere, longitudinal design choices must also be coordinated with other aspects of research methodology (Nagle, 2021). Furthermore, when time is a central variable in the analysis, it can be integrated into interactions with many other predictors. Crucially, if enough data points are included, then appropriate forms of longitudinal change beyond simple linear growth can also be examined and modeled. By centering longitudinal approaches in this book, I hope to illustrate the ways in which researchers can conceptualize and design longitudinal studies that can shed light on pronunciation learning as a complex, time-sensitive process. I also hope to dispel any fears or anxieties researchers might have about longitudinal work.

I don't assume prior knowledge on any of the research topics. By the end of each chapter, readers should have gained a solid command of the concepts, methods, and analyses carried out in work addressing the target area. At the same time, there are some fundamental concepts, models, and methods that readers should be familiar with to get the most out of this book. For instance, I expect most readers to have some understanding of the basic scope of phonetics and phonology research, including notions such as phonological contrast, phonetic cues, and so on. Readers might also profit from reviewing the major models of pronunciation learning that are routinely invoked in the field, especially the Speech Learning Model (Flege, 1995; Flege & Bohn, 2021). Readings on that model could be paired with the chapters on speech perception (Chapter 2), the production of specific features (Chapter 3), or the perception–production link (Chapter 4).

Likewise, I suspect it will be helpful for readers to have a reference manual on quantitative data analysis, such as Larson-Hall's (2016) book. I assume that most readers will be familiar with basic statistical concepts like means, standard deviations, and so on. If not, I suggest reading Chapters 2–4 of Larson-Hall (2016), which cover "Some preliminaries to understanding statistics," "Describing data numerically and graphically and assessing assumptions for parametric tests," and "Changing the way we do statistics: The new statistics." Whenever I introduce statistical concepts relevant to the data analysis sections presented in the book, I have tried to provide a brief overview, but admittedly, I haven't written the book assuming no statistical knowledge. This book can, therefore, serve as an overview and introduction to quantitative research methods, and for those with some background in statistics and statistical analysis, it can serve as a guide for carrying out robust and appropriate analyses.

The primary statistical software I use in this book is R, which I use with the RStudio interface (both of which I describe in detail below). I have

Introduction **5**

annotated and explained my code as extensively as possible, given space limitations, but I assume some basic familiarity with R and/or coding conventions. That being said, all of the code in the R markdown files accompanying each chapter can be run without modification, so readers with limited to no experience in R can still reproduce the analyses reported in the book.

Last but certainly not least, I would like to address instructors who teach pronunciation and research methods courses. I have conceptualized this book as a comprehensive introduction to quantitative pronunciation research, so this book could be used as the primary book in a course dedicated to similar topics. This is the primary reason I have incorporated questions for discussion at the end of each chapter. Alternatively, individual chapters from the book can be selected and integrated into more focused graduate coursework (e.g., a course on listener-based assessments) or into general research methods courses (e.g., to give students a sense of the types of studies and methods carried out in pronunciation research). The data analysis sections and accompanying R markdown can also be used in courses dealing with quantitative methods and statistical analysis.

In summary, I have tried to weave together the conceptual, methodological, and analytical dimensions of pronunciation research. I have also interwoven R code into the book, discussing the primary packages and functions I use, how I use them, and the information they output. I then interpret the statistical output in plain language. I hope that I have brought the distinct elements that make up this book into balance in a way that is comprehensive, informative, and approachable.

A Note on Style

I use the first person throughout this book for several reasons. First, I have taken inspiration from Field et al.'s (2012) *Discovering statistics using R* and Larson-Hall's (2016) *A guide to doing statistics in second language research using SPSS and R*, both of which have a more informal style that I find engaging. Second, sometimes we get the impression that there is an objectively "correct" decision in research, especially with respect to methodology. In my view, that's rarely the case. Thus, using the first person is my attempt to remind myself and you that the recommendations I'm making are based on my own perspective and expertise. Certainly, I think these recommendations are well founded, but I'm also aware of the fact that there are many profitable and methodologically sound ways to approach research. In this book I present one way, which I hope you will approach openly but critically. Finally, I'm also a member of the field, so it seems fitting that I should use the first person to describe my place in it and the work I have

6 Introduction

carried out up to this point. In the remainder of the introduction, I spend some time discussing my approach to data analysis and interpretation and the statistical software I use.

Approach to Data Analysis

I have made data analysis a central feature of this book for several reasons. For one, we tend to think of research as a linear progression from an idea, to study design and piloting, to data collection and processing, and finally to data analysis. It has been my experience that this linear progression rarely holds true. Instead, research tends to be iterative and reflexive, moving forward and backward, flowing from research questions to design to data but also from data back into research questions. In some cases, researchers design a study around a specific set of questions or hypotheses, and in that case, the traditional flow is sensible. However, it's equally true that the data from that study could spark interest in topics that the researcher did not originally intend to address, or an intriguing pattern could come to light, inviting the researcher to use the data for another purpose. In short, there are many ways to approach research, and the field is now beginning to acknowledge these possibilities and create opportunities for clear and consistent reporting of results obtained through non-linear research.

If new analyses are conducted that are conceptually linked to the original analyses that the researcher formulated, then a separate results section can be created for exploratory (i.e., unplanned) analysis. And if the analyses lead to a new set of questions altogether, questions that may be rather distant from the original intent despite the shared data set, then researchers could publish another article, making it clear to readers why and how the data have been repurposed. Such a manuscript, which would likely be smaller in scope than the original study, could be published as a short form manuscript, such as a research report. When I approach a research topic, the statistical model is the first thing that appears in my mind's eye. To be clear, I don't see this as a better or worse way of approaching research, but rather one way among many. But because it's my way, and because I find data fascinating, I decided it was important to emphasize data analysis. A second reason is because data analysis is growing more and more complicated. ANOVA, once the dominant analytical technique, is slowly making its exit, and mixed-effects models, generalized additive mixed models, and Bayesian analysis are becoming common. Of these, mixed-effects models are now relatively common in the literature, but the fact that they are common does not mean that researchers are comfortable using them, nor does it mean that the field has arrived at an accepted set of standards regarding how models should be fit, evaluated, and reported.

As Meteyard and Davies observed in their synthesis of reporting practices, mixed-effects models require a different analytical mindset altogether:

> The key issue is that since [Linear Mixed-Effects Models] are an explicit modelling approach, they require a different attitude than has been ingrained, perhaps, through the long tradition of the application of ANOVA to the analysis of data from factorial design studies.
>
> *(2020, p. 9)*

Thus, although mixed-effects models offer several crucial advantages over ANOVA, and although there are several tutorials (Cunnings, 2012; Cunnings & Finlayson, 2015; Gries, 2021; Linck & Cunnings, 2015) and textbooks (Winter, 2019) on how to use them to analyze linguistic data, they still intimidate many researchers. Why? Several reasons come to mind. One is the "attitude" problem that Meteyard and Davies (2020) pointed out. Another is the evolving nature of the state of the art in modeling and the fact that best practices are in flux. Thus, rather than a single gold standard, there are sets of principles that researchers can follow in accordance with their research goals. Finally, as I mentioned previously, it can be difficult to envision how to apply a mixed-effects model to a different data set, even if that data set is also linguistic. In short, pronunciation researchers may find themselves wondering how to fit models to pronunciation data, where speakers, items/trials, and listeners can all be conceptualized as meaningful and important sampling units.

In the book, I use simulated data. Although open research practices are expanding in applied linguistics (Marsden & Morgan-Short, 2023), open, well-annotated data sets are not easy to find, and data sets that are well-suited to the types of analyses I highlight in this book are, to my knowledge, not available at all. For practical reasons, then, it was necessary to simulate data. Second, simulated data offers the crucial advantage of determining beforehand what the effect will be. Thus, even if an effect does not emerge as statistically significant and robust in the models we fit, we know that the effect is there. This scenario—where we know an effect is there, but we fail to detect it—is informative, insofar as it provides insight into the amount of data needed to achieve the statistical power that makes the effect detectable. This isn't a book about statistics, so I don't delve into this issue deeply in each chapter, but the simulated data reminds us that absence of evidence is not evidence of absence. In other words, just because we can't detect the effect doesn't mean it doesn't exist. And, on the flip side, just because we detect an effect doesn't mean that it is a true effect. After all, we might have detected it due to chance. Knowing what we simulated in the data allows us

8 Introduction

TABLE 1.1 Classification Scheme Based on Simulated and Detected Effects

	Effect Simulated	*Effect Not Simulated*
Effect detected	Hit	Type 1 error (False positive)
Effect not detected	Type 2 error (False negative)	Hit

to classify what we have found, as shown in Table 1.1. The bottom line is that some effects may arise due to chance, whereas other effects may be real but go undetected.

Mixed-Effects Modeling

I don't have the space to give a comprehensive overview of mixed-effects modeling, the primary analytical technique I use in the book. However, before we get started, I want to synthesize some important literature on fitting and evaluating models and describe the principles I follow. A mixed-effects model, as its name implies, involves two types of effects: fixed and random. Fixed effects are the independent or predictor variables that we enter into the model. These could be variables we manipulate (e.g., experimental group) or ones that we observe (e.g., age of onset, language aptitude). The levels of these variables are fixed and consistent across studies, even if we don't observe all potential levels. For example, the meaning of age of onset does not change from one study to the next, or, more precisely, an age of onset of ten in one study means the same thing as an age of onset of ten in another study. Of course, there may be operational differences in how researchers define age of onset, but the principle remains the same: the possible levels are known, fixed, and do not change from one study to the next.

Random effects, however, change. Random effects are essentially sampling units. The most common sampling unit in pronunciation research is participants. We sample participants from a target population, and those participants became the sample in our study. Inferential statistics then allow us to generalize from that sample to the population if the sample is random and representative and if the statistical assumptions of the inferential test are upheld. Beyond participants, there are several other potential sampling units in pronunciation, namely items and listeners. Just as we sample participants from a larger population of potential participants, so too do we sample items from an item population and listeners from a listener population. Here, population refers to all relevant members of the group. Thus, if we are studying the production of stop consonants or vowels, we don't ask participants to produce all L2 words containing stop consonants or vowels. Rather, we sample words that conform to a set of characteristics, use those words in the study, and then use tests that allow us to generalize from that sample of items to the population of items. The same is true of listeners. If we label these units "participant 1," "item 1," and "listener 1," the randomness becomes clear: "1" in one study refers to a completely different unit than "1" in another study.

It bears mentioning that there are many other possible random effects. For instance, a classic example of a hierarchical model is students nested in classes, and classes in schools. Each of these groupings can be conceptualized and modeled as a random effect. Yet, as Judd et al. (2012) argued, beyond what can be modeled as a random effect on conceptual grounds, there is the empirical reality of trying to fit random effect models to a particular data set. In some cases, if there aren't enough units in the group, it will simply be impossible to model any random effects at all, despite the fact that we know that there is random variation within the group. For example, if we ask participants to respond to the same five items, then we could model item as a random effect. However, with five levels, the amount of item-level variance (i.e., the amount of variation in participants' responses attributable to item-level characteristics) is likely to be very small.

Recommendations for minimum sample size vary considerably, with researchers suggesting a minimum sample size of 10 (Raudenbush & Bryk, 2002) or 16 (Westfall et al., 2014) units per random effect grouping (e.g., 10 subjects, 10 items per condition). However, to model random effects reliably, and to ensure that error rates for fixed effects are not inappropriately inflated (e.g., because random variation has not been properly estimated), a larger sample size may be required. Meteyard and Davies (2020) recommended a minimum of 30–50 participants and 30–50 items for typical designs in psychology where participants respond to items across experimental conditions, and Luke (2017) showed that in small sample sizes (<40–50 sampling units), Type 1 error rates may be slightly inflated for certain tests of statistical significance in mixed-effects models. In pronunciation research, we rarely reach such sample sizes for participants and items and listeners, but there is no need to panic. One of the advantages of using mixed-effects modeling is that it controls Type 1 error rates reasonably well even in small sample sizes, whereas in ANOVA, where one type of random effect must be ignored for the purpose of analysis, Type 1 error rates can soar as high as 0.381 for designs with ten participants and ten items (i.e., a 38% chance of a false positive, see Judd et al., 2012). I therefore subscribe to Meteyard and Davies' (2020) sensible advice "to have as many sampling units as possible" (p. 17). As with any analysis, an important step, both conceptual for the researcher and necessary for publication, is acknowledging the limitations

10 Introduction

of the data, which could include somewhat underpowered effects when the number of sampling units is small. As we, as a field, collect larger data sets through multisite studies and data aggregation, then we can fit more robust models, leading to estimates that are appropriately powered and precise.

If we have fewer than ten levels of a random effect, we may still be able to model it. However, the fewer the levels, the less likely it is that the model will be able to estimate the variance components for the random effects, which in very small samples or samples involving highly homogenous units may approach zero. This is why, Judd et al. (2012) distinguished between the conceptual and empirical basis of random effects. Conceptual random effects cannot always be modeled, and even if they can be, depending on the size and homogeneity of the sample, variance may be zero. Worth noting is that in discussing the number of items needed for research on the production of specific features, Flege (1987) advocated for a minimum of 5–10 per category/condition. Thus, the upper limit of his suggestion aligns well with the minimum number of levels required for random effects to be estimated.

Assuming we have the numbers to model the effects, we need to decide what random effects to model. Random intercepts capture random variation in baseline performance across sampling units. To put it plainly, some participants will perform better than others, and some items will be more difficult than others. Random intercepts capture this variation. More interesting are random slopes for within-unit variables. Imagine a perception study in which we ask learners to identify L2 words that are known to be challenging for L2 listeners. These words vary in frequency from very high frequency to very low frequency. We hypothesize that learners' identification accuracy depends on frequency. We predict that the higher the frequency of the word, the more likely they will be to identify it correctly. We can estimate the overall effect of frequency on the likelihood of identifying the target correctly via a fixed effect. We can also test whether the strength of that effect varies across participants. Some individuals may respond to frequency in a very strong way, whereas for others frequency may not make much of a difference at all. We test for this by including a by-participant random slope for frequency. I'll illustrate this important point with a couple more examples.

Assume that we collect production data from participants over several data points to examine how their pronunciation of the target feature changes over time. We fit a fixed effect for time, and we also include by-participant random slopes for time. The fixed effect estimates the overall effect of time on production, and the random slopes capture participant-level variation around that effect. Random effects can also be fit to other grouping units. Many studies have examined the grammatical, lexical, and phonological features that make speech more or less intelligible, comprehensible, and accented. In these studies, L2 speakers are recorded, and their speech is transcribed and coded for a range of variables. Listeners are also asked to transcribe and rate the samples. In this design, the features are within-listener variables, which means that we can fit a fixed effect to estimate, for instance, the overall effect of grammatical errors on intelligibility and a by-listener random effect to examine the extent to which that effect varies across listeners. As with the frequency example, some listeners may be more sensitive to grammatical errors than others, so for some, the effect may be larger than average, whereas for others, it may be smaller than average.

There has been substantial debate about how to model random effects (Barr et al., 2013; Matuschek et al., 2017). Despite this debate, "most experts agree that the final [model] needs to contain the random slope(s) for the predictor that is the focus of the researchers' hypothesis, regardless of the variance of this (these) random slope(s)" (Brauer & Curtin, 2018, p. 406). Notice that Brauer and Curtin state that the random slope needs to be included even if the variance is empirically very small (and therefore may not improve the fit of the model relative to a model without the random slope). Random effects need to be included to ensure that fixed effect estimates are reliable. Not including random effects can dramatically increase Type 1 error rates (i.e., false positives).

Statistical Significance and Modeling

We can't talk about data analysis and statistical models without addressing statistical significance, that is, without addressing p values. In a famous article on statistical errors, Nuzzo discussed the "surprisingly slippery nature of the P value, which is neither as reliable nor as objective as most scientists assume" (2014, p. 150). As Nuzzo explained, p values were never intended to be treated as ironclad evidence for the presence of an effect. In fact, treating them as such has had some deleterious effects on science at large. For one, p values seem to cluster around 0.05, the most common cutoff used for determining statistical significance even though that cutoff is arbitrary. Another unintended consequence is p-hacking, where researchers search for statistically significant $p < 0.05$ effects, at times disregarding common sense. When p is the only piece of evidence brought to bear on a hypothesis, small changes in data analysis can push or pull p values above or below alpha, which means that even well-intentioned researchers may end up engaging in some form of p-hacking. In a field such as ours, where we are beginning to explore more complex, nuanced effects, "such practices have the effect of turning discoveries from exploratory studies — which should be treated with skepticism — into what look like sound confirmations but vanish on replication" (Nuzzo, 2014, p. 152).

12 Introduction

Since Nuzzo's publication, there have been several other prominent "policy" pieces on the topic of p values and null hypothesis significance testing. In another commentary appearing in the journal *Nature*, a group of researchers took aim at several problematic practices related to privileging one piece of statistical information above all others. In their opener, they stated: "Let's be clear about what we must stop: we should never conclude there is 'no difference' or 'no association' just because a P value is larger than a threshold such as 0.05 or, equivalently, because a confidence interval includes zero" (Amrhein et al., 2019, pp. 305–306). As the authors explained, "an interval that contains the null value will often contain non-null values of high practical importance" (p. 307). They also recommended renaming confidence intervals to "compatibility intervals," encouraging researcher to interpret the full range of values within the interval. The American Statistical Association published an editorial on statistical significance and p values in which they observed that "statistical significance is not equivalent to scientific, human, or economic significance" (Wasserstein & Lazar, 2016, p. 132). In that publication, they encouraged researchers to draw upon multiple sources of evidence when evaluating hypotheses. They also explained why p values have become so entrenched in the scientific mind: researchers and editors use them, so journals expect them, and for that reason, they continue to be taught, which in turn reinforces their use. I agree with the sentiment of these editorial pieces: p values are one piece of evidence among many, and they probably aren't the most important piece. Thus, rather than doing away with p values altogether, it seems fruitful to situate them within the body of evidence available for the presence or absence of an effect and, importantly, its magnitude or practical significance.

Statistical significance is challenging in mixed-effects modeling. Mixed-effects models do not output p values because it's unclear what the denominator degrees of freedom should be given the multidimensional nature of the data to which they are fit. Set against a backdrop of serious concerns about the use of p values, this seems felicitous, but the reality is that many journals and researchers expect p values to be reported. Researchers have relied on three approaches to generate p values for mixed-effects models: t-to-z, likelihood ratio tests, and Satterthwaite and Kenward-Rogers approximations. In the t-to-z approach, $t > 1.96$ (or >2, adopting a slightly more conservative standard) is treated as statistically significant for an alpha of .05 because in large data sets, as the degrees of freedom increase, the t distribution approaches the standard normal distribution (z). Likelihood ratio tests involve stepwise model comparisons where one model is tested against another nested model. That is, a model with $x + 1$ effects is tested against a simpler model with x effects, and if the bigger model is a better fit to the data (if the Chi-squared test is statistically significant), then the added effect is deemed statistically significant (i.e., the effect has significantly improved the fit of the model). Both methods have been shown to be somewhat anti-conservative, leading to inflated Type 1 error rates (Luke, 2017). On the other hand, the Satterthwaite and Kenward-Rogers approximations perform well for a range of data sets and should therefore be preferred. I therefore adopt this standard in the book, using the *lmerTest* (Kuznetsova et al., 2017) package to implement the Satterthwaite approximation for degrees of freedom, which will then allow for a p value to be computed.

Summary

In summary, in the mixed-effects models presented in this book, I adhere to the reporting standards and principles that Meteyard and Davies (2020) have put forth. With respect to random effects, I follow Brauer and Curtin's (2018) three rules, but I take a pragmatic approach to addressing random effect convergence issues. Brauer and Curtin (2018) provided a useful list of 20 potential remedies for resolving convergence problems, but discussion and exposition of many of those techniques (e.g., dropping covariances) is beyond the scope of this book, which I aim to keep as accessible as possible. Long story short, I attempt to model at least the by-subject random effects for all primary fixed effects. I take a flexible approach to fitting and evaluating fixed effects, again in line with Meteyard and Davies' (2020) recommendations. To assess the significance of effects, I use the Satterthwaite approximation, but I take a balanced approach, prioritizing all statistical evidence rather than relying solely on p values. I therefore interpret confidence intervals, following Amrhein et al. (2019). For the limited other types of analysis included for the purpose of comparison (ANOVA) or extension (structural equation models; SEM), I follow standard conventions, which I discuss as relevant.

Analysis Software

In this book, I use R for data analysis. For each chapter, I provide a description of the data and notes on simulation for accompanying data sets in an R markdown file. I have made every effort to annotate my R code thoroughly so that it's easy to understand. In the book, I provide explanations and chunks of code so that you can link the markdown and the book. I prefer to use R because it's a free and open source, which in my view makes it more appealing than for-purchase software such as IBM SPSS Statistics (SPSS). Second, whereas SPSS and similar software are mostly point and click, in R, you author the code. I see this as advantageous because it brings you closer to the data and the analysis. Simply put, to create the analysis code, you must have a firmer understanding of what's in the data file and what you're trying to do with it. Third, R and its packages have a large and supportive community, which means that if you have problems with a package, get an error message that you don't understand, and so on, you can almost always find a solution online. Finally, and perhaps most critically, because R is open-source software, once you have authored code, you can make it publicly available. During the review process, reviewers can provide helpful feedback on your code, feedback that can shore up and enhance your analysis and interpretation. In the long term, publishing code as a supplementary file with the manuscript and/or making it available on a platform such as the Open Science Framework (OSF; https://osf.io/) supports open science, allowing future researchers to learn from and reproduce your analysis. Making code publicly available can be a nerve-racking endeavor at first—anything new can be—but as I have described elsewhere (Nagle, 2023), my experience has been overwhelmingly positive.

I'd like to take the opportunity to describe my experience with R so that you understand my background. I began using R in 2015 when completing my dissertation. Over the years, and with the help of many skilled colleagues, I have become a more proficient R user. I have learned how to troubleshoot problems and how to annotate and format code in markdown. I have also learned data simulation, a skill I continue to develop, and I have cultivated my personal annotation style. Although I have taken several courses on data analysis, I never took a course on R. Instead, I learned it independently, partly out of necessity because the types of models I wanted to fit (polynomial growth models) were much easier to fit in R than in SPSS. Now, many graduate programs offer courses on R, and similar courses are offered online through professional organizations, institutes, and so on. The point is: there are many pathways into data analysis using R, so I hope you don't feel intimidated to work in R in this book. The bottom line is if I can do it, you certainly can too. Learning R is like learning a language, an incremental process of knowledge creation and refinement, so don't be afraid to dive in.

Although I cannot introduce R itself in this book, I have done my best to explain what code does and how it can be manipulated and repurposed. In fact, one of the advantages of working in R is that you can look at other researchers' code, experiment with it, and repurpose it for your own analysis, which means that you don't need to produce everything completely on your own. R also offers many tutorials and vignettes for individual packages, with sample code, that you can access. There are many ways to accomplish the same task in R, so in the next section, I describe my approach to R, the primary packages I use, and some basic R functions that you will likely find helpful.

R Packages and Coding Conventions

I use R with the RStudio interface. I predominantly work within the tidyverse (Wickham et al., 2019; https://www.tidyverse.org/). I use the following packages for data analysis and plotting:

- *afex* (Singmann et al., 2023) for ANOVA
- *lme4* (Bates et al., 2015) for mixed-effects modeling
- *lavaan* (Rosseel, 2012) for structural equation modeling
- *lmerTest* (Kuznetsova et al., 2017) for significance testing in mixed-effects models
- *DHARMa* (Hartig, 2017) to simulate residuals and check assumptions for logistic models
- *emmeans* (Lenth, 2023) to create pairwise estimates for multi-level factors and interactions
- *sjPlot* (Lüdecke, 2022) to obtain summary information for model objects
- *ggplot2* (Wickham, 2016) to create plots

A combination of these packages appears in every chapter. I use several other packages for specific analyses, and when I do, I describe and cite them. I have structured analyses similarly throughout the book: (1) read and inspect the data, (2) preliminary steps, including plotting and descriptive statistics, and (3) inferential analyses. I principally use the *dplyr* (Wickham et al., 2023) package to manipulate the data structure and compute descriptive statistics, and I use *ggplot2* (Wickham, 2016) for plotting. I also make extensive use of piping, which is a method of chaining pieces of code together using the %>% operator. For instance, the following chunk of code appears at the outset of the perception data analysis markdown.

```
Data_stopid_summary <- data_stopid %>%
    group_by(participant, session, target_sound) %>%
    summarize(accuracy = mean(correct))
```

In this code, I ask R to create a new object called "data_stopid_summary" by taking the "data_stopid" data frame, grouping data by three variables (participant, session, and target_sound) and then returning mean accuracy. Each of these steps appears on one line of code followed by %>%, the piping operator. Some of the chunks of code can get quite long due to chaining many operations together, but the bottom line is that each line of code represents one step in a series of operations, linked by the piping operator. The *ggplot2* package is an exception because it takes the + operator. To add elements to a plot, rather than using piping, + is used. In the following chunk

16 Introduction

of code, piping is used to create a summary data frame, and that summary is then piped into *ggplot2* code to create the plot. Notice that %>% switches to + once we move from manipulating the data to making the plot.

```
Data_stopid %>%
    mutate(session = as.factor(session)) %>%
    group_by(participant, session, target_sound) %>%
    summarise(mean = mean(correct)) %>%
    ggplot(aes(x = session, y = mean, fill = target_sound)) +
    geom_boxplot() +
    theme_bw() +
    theme(legend.position = "bottom")
```

Table 1.2 provides a list of common R operators and what they do. These will appear throughout the book and R markdown files. Of the R operators given in the table, I want to draw your attention to the ? operator. This operator can be used to get information on any R function or package. For instance, ?lme4 returns information on the *lme4* package, and ?lmer returns information on the lmer() function. The first portion of the help information lists the usage and arguments for the function. While useful, I find it more helpful to scroll directly to the bottom of the help information and look at the sample code.

In this book, when I refer to code, I use indentation and Calibri font to set it off from prose, which appears in Times New Roman. In the data sets and R markdown documents, I only use lower case to avoid coding errors,

TABLE 1.2 Summary of Common R Operators and Their Functions

Operator	Meaning	What Does It Do?
<-	Make this	Creates an object in R
$	Look within	Looks inside a data frame for something, usually a column
?	Get help	? + package or function pulls up the help window
#	Ignore	Tells R that anything that follows # are notes
%>%	Piping	Goes to the next line of code and runs it
::	Load from	Use this to load a function from a specific package (e.g., "dplyr::select()" when two or more packages are loaded that use the same syntax or function (e.g., dplyr and MASS both use "select()")
~	By Is predicted by Is regressed onto	Operator for creating models in R; the dependent variable goes to the left and the independent, or predictor, variables to the right.

Introduction **17**

but when I refer to variables in text, I use capital letters. For instance, in the code, the variable may be named "session" but in text, when I discuss it, I may use "Session" or "Time." I also use periods in the code to make object names more readable (e.g., "stopid.anova"). Some people use underscores or a combination of periods and underscores, but I prefer to keep the code as streamlined as possible.

Getting Started

Before you begin using this book, I recommend that you download and install the latest versions of R and RStudio. When you open R, it will automatically open in RStudio, which is a user-friendly interface for reading and writing R code. As you progress through the book, if you have not installed the R packages, you will need to do so using the install.packages("package name") function, such as install.packages("lme4"). Once installed, the package needs to be loaded using the library() function, such as library(lme4). If you can't get code to work, make sure that you have installed and loaded the necessary package. Installed packages are saved and only need to be updated periodically (or reinstalled once you install a new version of R), so you don't need to install them every time you use R. You do, however, need to load them each session.

There are many ways to set up a workflow in R (and many tutorials available online for how to work with R and RStudio; see, e.g., http://www.sthda.com/english/wiki/r-basics-quick-and-easy), but one essential step is setting the working directory, which tells R where to look for files (e.g., CSV data files) and where to save objects (e.g., markdown files, plots). You can set your working directory two ways: (1) use the setwd() function and provide the file path or (2) in the bar at the top of the RStudio interface, click on "Session," then on "Set Working Directory," and then on "Choose Directory," and select the folder that you want to use. When you're ready to work with code, make sure the markdown file and data files are stored in that folder. To give you an idea of how I work, I have a folder called "R," and within that folder I have many subfolders for each project. Each of those folders is a working directory for one R project. For instance, for this book, you could have the following structure:

- R

  - A guide to quantitative research methods in second language pronunciation

    - Perception
    - Production Specific
    - Perception-Production

18 Introduction

- Production Global
- Training and Instruction
- Individual Differences

You could then set up a new RStudio project for each chapter, storing chapter data and markdown files in the corresponding folder. I recommend that you don't agonize too much over your workflow. Instead, I suggest getting started and then allowing your workflow to evolve over time as you determine what works best for you, what you like and don't like, and so on.

References

Amrhein, V., Greenland, S., & McShane, B. (2019). Scientists rise up against statistical significance. *Nature, 567*, 305–307. https://doi.org/10.1038/d41586-019-00857-9

Barr, D. J., Levy, R., Scheepers, C., & Tily, H. J. (2013). Random effects structure for confirmatory hypothesis testing: Keep it maximal. *Journal of Memory and Language, 68*(3), 255–278. https://doi.org/10.1016/j.jml.2012.11.001

Barriuso, T. A., & Hayes-Harb, R. (2018). High variability phonetic training as a bridge from research to practice. *The CATESOL Journal, 30*(1), 177–194.

Bates, D., Maechler, M., Bolker, B., & Walker, S. (2015). Fitting linear mixed-effects models using lme4. *Journal of Statistical Software, 67*(1), 1–48. https://doi.org/10.18637/jss.v067.i01

Brauer, M., & Curtin, J. J. (2018). Linear mixed-effects models and the analysis of nonindependent data: A unified framework to analyze categorical and continuous independent variables that vary within-subjects and/or within-items. *Psychological Methods, 23*(3), 389–411. https://doi.org/10.1037/met0000159

Chau, T., & Huensch, A. (2021, June). *Measuring the strengths of the relationships among global L2 speech dimensions: A meta-analysis* [Conference presentation]. Pronunciation in Second Language Learning and Teaching, Brock University in St. Catharines Ontario Canada.

Cunnings, I. (2012). An overview of mixed-effects statistical models for second language researchers. *Second Language Research, 28*(3), 369–382. https://doi.org/10.1177/0267658312443651

Cunnings, I., & Finlayson, I. (2015). Mixed effects modeling and longitudinal data-analysis. In L. Plonsky (Ed.), *Advancing quantitative methods in second language research* (pp. 159–181). Routledge.

Derwing, T. M., & Munro, M. J. (2015). *Pronunciation fundamentals: Evidence-based perspectives for L2 teaching and research.* John Benjamins.

Field, A., Miles, J., & Field, Z. (2012). *Discovering statistics using R.* Sage.

Flege, J. E. (1987). The instrumental study of L2 speech production: Some methodological considerations. *Language Learning, 37*(2), 285–296. https://doi.org/10.1111/j.1467-1770.1987.tb00569.x

Flege, J. E. (1995). Second language speech learning: Theory, findings, problems. In W. Strange (Ed.), *Speech perception and linguistic experience: Issues in cross-language research* (pp. 233–277). York Press.

Flege, J. E., & Bohn, O.-S. (2021). The revised Speech Learning Model. In R. Wayland (Ed.), *Second language speech learning: Theoretical and empirical progress* (pp. 3–83). Cambridge University Press.

Gries, S. T. (2021). (Generalized linear) Mixed-effects modeling: A learner corpus example. *Language Learning, 71*(3), 757–798. https://doi.org/10.1111/lang.12448

Hartig, F. (2017). DHARMa: Residual Diagnostics for Hierarchical (Multi-Level / Mixed) Regression Models. R package version 0.1.5. <http://florianhartig.github.io/DHARMa/>.

Judd, C. M., Westfall, J., & Kenny, D. A. (2012). Treating stimuli as a random factor in social psychology: A new and comprehensive solution to a pervasive but largely ignored problem. *Journal of Personality and Social Psychology, 103*(1), 54–69. https://doi.org/10.1037/a0028347

Kuznetsova, A., Brockhoff, P. B., & Christensen, R. H. B. (2017). lmerTest Package: Tests in linear mixed effects models. *Journal of Statistical Software, 82*(13), 1–26. https://doi.org/10.18637/jss.v082.i13.

Larson-Hall, J. (2016). *A guide to doing statistics in second language research using SPSS and R*. Routledge.

Lee, J., Jang, J., & Plonsky, L. (2015). The effectiveness of second language pronunciation instruction: A meta-analysis. *Applied Linguistics, 36*(3), 345–366. https://doi.org/10.1093/applin/amu040

Lenth, R. (2023). _emmeans: Estimated Marginal Means, aka Least-Squares Means_. R package version 1.8.4-1, <https://CRAN.R-project.org/package=emmeans>.

Levis, J. M. (2018). *Intelligibility, oral communication, and the teaching of pronunciation*. Cambridge. https://doi.org/10.1017/9781108241564

Levis, J. M., Derwing, T. M., & Sonsaat-Hegelheimer, S. (Eds.). (2022). *Second language pronunciation: Bridging the gap between research and teaching*. Wiley-Blackwell.

Linck, J. A., & Cunnings, I. (2015). The utility and application of mixed-effects models in second language research. *Language Learning, 65*(S1), 185–207. https://doi.org/10.1111/lang.12117

Lüdecke, D. (2022). _sjPlot: Data Visualization for Statistics in Social Science_. R package version 2.8.11, <https://CRAN.R-project.org/package=sjPlot>.

Luke, S. G. (2017). Evaluating significance in linear mixed-effects models in R. *Behavioral Research Methods, 49*(4), 1494–1502. https://doi.org/10.3758/s13428-016-0809-y

Marsden, E., & Morgan-Short, K. (2023). (Why) Are open research practices the future for the study of language learning? *Language Learning*. Advance online publication. https://doi.org/10.1111/lang.12568

Matuschek, H., Kliegl, R., Vasishth, S., Baayen, H., & Bates, D. (2017). Balancing Type I error and power in linear mixed models. *Journal of Memory and Language, 94*, 305–315. https://doi.org/10.1016/j.jml.2017.01.001

McAndrews, M. (2019). Short periods of instruction improve learners' phonological categories for L2 suprasegmental features. *System, 82*, 151–160. https://doi.org/10.1016/j.system.2019.04.007

Meteyard, L., & Davies, R. A. I. (2020). Best practice guidance for linear mixed-effects models in psychological science. *Journal of Memory and Language, 112*, 104092. https://doi.org/10.1016/j.jml.2020.104092

20 Introduction

Nagle, C. L. (2021). Assessing the state of the art in longitudinal L2 pronunciation research. *Journal of Second Language Pronunciation, 7*(2), 154–182. https://doi.org/10.1075/jslp.20059.nag

Nagle, C. (2023). From an individualistic to a collectivistic mindset in open research: A commentary on "(Why) Are open research practices the future for the study of language learning?". *Language Learning*. Advance online publication. https://doi.org/10.1111/lang.12578

Nagle, C. L., & Baese-Berk, M. M. (2021). Advancing the state of the art in L2 speech perception-production research: Revisiting theoretical assumptions and methodological practices. *Studies in Second Language Acquisition, 44*(2), 580–605. https://doi.org/10.1017/s0272263121000371

Nuzzo, R. (2014). Scientific method: Statistical errors. *Nature, 506*(7487), 150–152. https://doi.org/10.1038/506150a

Raudenbush, S. W., & Bryk, A. S. (2002). *Hierarchical linear models: Applications and data analysis methods* (2nd ed.). Sage.

Rosseel, Y. (2012). lavaan: An R Package for Structural Equation Modeling. *Journal of Statistical Software, 48*(2), 1–36. https://doi.org/10.18637/jss.v048.i02.

Saito, K. (2021). What characterizes comprehensible and native-like pronunciation among English-as-a-second-language speakers? Meta-analyses of phonological, rater, and instructional factors. *TESOL Quarterly, 55*(3), 866–900. https://doi.org/10.1002/tesq.3027

Saito, K., & Plonsky, L. (2019). Effects of second language pronunciation teaching revisited: A proposed measurement framework and meta-analysis. *Language Learning, 69*(3), 652–708. https://doi.org/10.1111/lang.12345

Sakai, M., & Moorman, C. (2018). Can perception training improve the production of second language phonemes? A meta-analytic review of 25 years of perception training research. *Applied Psycholinguistics, 39*(1), 187–224. https://doi.org/10.1017/s0142716417000418

Singmann, H., Bolker, B., Westfall, J., Aust, F., & Ben-Shachar, M. (2023). _ afex: Analysis of Factorial Experiments. R package version 1.2-1, <https://CRAN.R-project.org/package=afex>.

Thomson, R. I. (2018). High Variability [Pronunciation] Training (HVPT). *Journal of Second Language Pronunciation, 4*(2), 208–231. https://doi.org/10.1075/jslp.17038.tho

Thomson, R. I., & Derwing, T. M. (2015). The effectiveness of L2 pronunciation instruction: A narrative review. *Applied Linguistics, 36*(3), 326–344. https://doi.org/10.1093/applin/amu076

Wasserstein, R. L., & Lazar, N. A. (2016). The ASA statement on p-values: Context, process, and purpose. *The American Statistician, 70*(2), 129–133. https://doi.org/10.1080/00031305.2016.1154108

Westfall, J., Kenny, D. A., & Judd, C. M. (2014). Statistical power and optimal design in experiments in which samples of participants respond to samples of stimuli. *Journal of Experimental Psychology General, 143*(5), 2020–2045. https://doi.org/10.1037/xge0000014

Wickham, H. (2016). *ggplot2: Elegant graphics for data analysis*. Springer-Verlag.

Wickham, H., Averick, M., Bryan, J., Chang, W., McGowan, L. D., François, R., Grolemund, G., Hayes, A., Henry, L., Hester, J., Kuhn, M., Pedersen, T. L.,

Miller, E., Bache, S. M., Müller, K., Ooms, J., Robinson, D., Seidel, D. P., Spinu, V., Takahashi, K., Vaughan, D., Wilke, C., Woo, K., & Yutani, H. (2019). Welcome to the tidyverse. *Journal of Open Source Software, 4*(43), 1686. https://doi.org/10.21105/joss.01686

Wickham, H., François, R., Henry, L., Müller, K., & Vaughan, D. (2023). _dplyr: A grammar of data manipulation_. R package version 1.1.0, <https://CRAN.R-project.org/package=dplyr>

Winter, B. (2019). *Statistics for linguists*. Routledge.

Zhang, X., Cheng, B., & Zhang, Y. (2021). The role of talker variability in non-native phonetic learning: A systematic review and meta-analysis. *Journal of Speech, Language, and Hearing Research, 64*(12), 4802–4825. https://doi.org/10.1044/2021_JSLHR-21-00181

2

RESEARCHING SPEECH PERCEPTION

Introduction

Speech perception is a complex cognitive skill that involves mapping acoustic information onto representations stored in long-term memory. These representations emerge shockingly quickly as the infant is exposed to their native language(s) (L1s) during the prenatal period and first year of life (for a review, see Chládková & Paillereau, 2020). Shifting from a language-general mode of perception to language-specific perception is advantageous because it allows the listener to deal with the tremendous variation present in everyday speech. The precise characteristics of a particular word, including exactly how phonological contrasts are produced, depend on the speaker, speech style, and speaking context. A speaker who is involved in a casual conversation with a friend while waiting in line for coffee may undershoot phonetic targets, leading to a blending or blurring of phonological categories, especially when information is known or shared between the two interlocutors. In another context, when giving a talk or a presentation, the same speaker may adopt a more careful style, producing more phonetically robust contrasts for the sake of clarity. Even when the same speaker produces the same word in the same context multiple times, that word will not be produced in the exact same way. Thus, the perceptual system needs to be able to cope with this variability, mapping phonetically disparate targets onto a single, stable mental representation. Early and rapid perceptual attunement and the refinement that continues thereafter enable the listener to do that, making L1 speech processing fast and efficient. Without such efficiency,

DOI: 10.4324/9781003279266-2

communication would be impossible because processes that occur on the order of milliseconds would take far longer, impeding fluid conversation.

But what is the listener actually learning when they learn to perceive L1 contrasts? In other words, what are phonological categories actually made of? This is a complex and challenging question that continues to stimulate much debate. One view is that the L1 listener learns to pay attention to the phonetic cues that are most meaningful and informative in the L1 (Strange, 2011). Phonological contrasts (e.g., *pet* vs. *bet, pit* vs. *pet*) are often implemented through several phonetic cues, but some cues are more reliable than others and therefore serve as the primary cue to contrast. The primary phonetic cue that distinguishes the /p/ and /b/ in *pet* and *bet* is known as voice onset time (VOT), which is a temporal cue that relates the timing of two events: the onset of voicing and the release gesture of the stop consonant (see, e.g., Lisker & Abramson, 1964). However, there are many other secondary cues to stop consonant voicing in English, such as pitch, and some of these cues covary with VOT. When an English listener creates representations for /p/, /b/, and other stop consonants, they are creating those representations based on the phonetic distribution of the input, that is, based on differences in VOT and, to a lesser extent, based on differences in other secondary cues. The point is that VOT is the most reliable and robust cue and therefore the cue that native English listeners pay the most attention to, perceptually speaking. Other languages also use this cue, but they may use it in different ways, and some languages may not exploit this cue at all. L1 perception thus involves learning which cues are relevant (think of a light switch, where the cue could be turned on or off) and how relevant they are (think of a light switch with a dimmer, where the intensity of the light can be controlled). As L1 categories take shape, they begin to warp perception, acting as perceptual magnets that effectively draw in a range of sounds that are phonetically distinct but phonologically invariant (Kuhl, 1991; Kuhl et al., 2008). That is, targets that may be phonetically quite different from one another are nonetheless categorized as instances of a single category. While advantageous for L1 speech perception, this process sets up a potential problem for learning to perceive the sounds and contrasts of another language (L2), especially if this language is learned after the L1 (i.e., after the perceptual system has become attuned to the cues used to create and distinguish L1 phonological categories).

Eighty years ago, Nikolai Trubetzkoy, a Russian linguist, described the L1 as a phonological sieve, affecting the perception of additional languages:

Each person acquires the system of his mother tongue. But when he hears another language spoken, he intuitively uses the familiar "phonological sieve" of his mother tongue to analyze what has been said. However, since this sieve is not suited for the foreign language, numerous mistakes and misinterpretations are the result. The sounds of the foreign language receive an incorrect phonological interpretation since they are strained through the "phonological sieve" of one's own mother tongue.

(1939, p. 52)

In modern terms, Trubetzkoy's "phonological sieve" encompasses the learned patterns of attention to L1 phonetic cues. These patterns may cause the L2 listener to misinterpret one L2 phonological category for another. For instance, if the L1 and L2 use the same phonetic cue but make use of it in different ways, then applying the "rules" of the L1 to the L2 may lead the listener to hear one word when another was intended. Both English and Spanish have phonologically voiced and voiceless stops, and in both languages, the primary phonetic cue to stop consonant voicing is VOT. However, each language maps its phonological categories onto the VOT phonetic continuum differently. In English, phonologically voiced stops are produced with a slight delay between the release gesture of the stop and the onset of voicing, and phonologically voiceless stops are produced with a more substantial delay. For instance, English /b/ may be produced with approximately 10 ms VOT, whereas /p/ might be produced with 60 ms VOT on average. In Spanish, on the other hand, in voiced stops, voicing begins before the release gesture, which is recorded as negative VOT, and voiceless stops are produced with a slight delay. Thus, Spanish /b/ may be produced with a VOT of –80 ms and Spanish /p/ with a VOT of 10 ms on average. Both English and Spanish listeners are accustomed to paying attention to VOT, which is critical for distinguishing between minimal pairs such as *bet* and *pet* or *beso* and *peso* ("a kiss" or "I kiss" vs. "weight" or "I weigh," respectively). However, an English speaker is used to processing stops produced with short or negative VOT as voiced, which means that they might perceive all Spanish stops as voiced, or at least they would interpret some voiceless stops in Spanish as voiced. Likewise, a Spanish speaker is used to processing stops produced with voicing delay as voiceless, which means that they might interpret most, if not all, English stops as voiceless. English speakers who are L2 learners of Spanish, and Spanish speakers who are L2 learners of English, need to adjust their perceptual "definition" of stop consonant voicing to perceive L2 stop consonants accurately.

In this case, English and Spanish both have phonologically voiced and voiceless stop consonants, and both use VOT, even though the "definition" of voiced and voiceless depends on VOT distributions in each language. What about when the L2 has more phonological categories than the L1, and what if those phonological categories involve different and/or additional phonetic cues? In Thai, like Spanish and English, VOT is the primary cue to stop consonant voicing, but Thai has three voicing categories, whereas Spanish and English only have two. To learn Thai, then, Spanish and English speakers would need to add a new phonological category using a familiar phonetic cue. This is like creating a new category from the same phonetic cloth. Korean is more complex still. Korean, like Thai, has three stop consonant categories, and like all the languages discussed thus far, Korean also makes use of VOT. However, the three-way Korean contrast also involves another phonetic cue, fundamental frequency or pitch (F0). Remember that in English F0 is a secondary cue to stop consonant voicing and covaries with VOT, so an English (or Spanish or Thai) speaker learning Korean needs to learn to pay attention to a new phonetic cue, while simultaneously adjusting the way they process VOT. This is like creating new categories from multiple bolts of phonetic cloth, one similar to the one the listener has worked with before and another entirely new one. Moreover, both cues (or bolts of cloth) must be used together.

Thus far, we have considered cases where both languages contain multiple categories, that is, cases where both languages have one or more phonological contrasts. What about when the L1 contains only one phonological category? This is conceptually, if not empirically, different than the multi-category scenarios we have discussed because when the L1 contains only one category, there is no contrast. In other words, the learning task involves creating a contrast where none previously existed, which necessarily involves learning to pay attention to a new phonetic cue. This is the case for L1 Japanese speakers of L2 English. Japanese speakers often have trouble distinguishing between English /l/ and /ɹ/, which means that words like *wrist* and *list* sound very similar to, if not indistinguishable from, one another. In this case, Japanese contains one phonological category, a tap /ɾ/, that falls somewhere between the English categories. Furthermore, the degree of correspondence between the Japanese phoneme and its English counterparts depends on where the English phonemes occur in the word. Phonetically, L1 English speakers rely on spectral differences, specifically differences in the third formant (F3), to discriminate /l/-/ɹ/, but Japanese speakers, who are unaccustomed to paying attention to that phonetic cue because it is not relevant to any L1 contrasts, pay more attention to duration and to spectral differences in the second formant (F2). In other words, they are not attending to the most informative phonetic cue to the English contrast. English vowels are another good example. Many L2 English speakers struggle to perceive English tense-lax vowel contrasts, such as the /i/-/ɪ/ contrast in the pair *leave-live*, if those vowels do not occur in their L1. Phonetically, because Spanish speakers are not accustomed to paying attention to the subtle spectral differences that L1 English speakers use to discriminate tense and lax vowels, they rely on duration, a secondary phonetic cue that is useful but far less reliable in most varieties of English.

One other type of perception issue that deserves attention is crosslinguistic differences in the status and distribution of L2 sounds. In one language, a sound may have phonemic status—it serves to differentiate words—whereas in another, it may be allophonic, which means that it is not used contrastively. For instance, in English, /ð/ is phonemic, but in Spanish, it is an allophone of /d/. Thus, English-speaking learners of Spanish need to learn the new status and distribution of [ð], which entails recognizing the contexts in which [d] and [ð] would occur. It's important to carefully consider the nature of the learning task to develop appropriate perceptual tests that tap into the hypothesized learning process. Different tasks are needed to measure sensitivity to phonological contrast versus sensitivity to allophonic distributions.

Perception researchers are interested in understanding the effect of the L1 "phonological sieve" on L2 perception for a range of target structures that represent diverse crosslinguistic scenarios. Crosslinguistic differences in phonetic and phonological structure are a necessary ingredient and, indeed, a necessary starting point for perception research. Crucially, though researchers in nearly all cases focus on a particular crosslinguistic scenario (e.g., English speakers' perception of Spanish stop consonants, Japanese speakers' perception of English liquids, Mandarin speakers' perception of Korean stop consonants), their goal in investigating that scenario is to obtain data that can shed light on perceptual learning as a general phenomenon. Put another way, the goal is to generalize beyond the target structure, considering what the target structure represents on a more abstract level. It also bears mentioning that perception research can be driven by theory, practice, or both. On the practical side, researchers may be interested in examining perception to identify targets that would be good candidates for intervention (i.e., to help learners improve their perception of challenging L2 sounds). Being clear about what your objectives are when undertaking perception research is an important first step toward designing a study.

All the examples I have discussed involve crosslinguistic segmental differences. Certainly, there has been important work on tonal languages and the perception of tonal contrasts, as well as work on the perception of prosodic features, including lexical stress and intonation (the latter often rooted in a pragmatic framework, where differences in intonation signal differences in information structure and pragmatic intent). Yet, it is the case that most perception research has focused on L2 sounds and thus most perception tasks have been developed and validated for that purpose. Likewise, the theoretical models I review in the next section are entirely focused on L2 sounds. I do not discount the important work taking place in other areas of perception research. Rather, my focus on the perception of L2 sound categories is a reflection of the field itself and my position within it.

Theoretical Models

Researchers typically work with two models: the Speech Learning Model (SLM; Flege, 1995; Flege & Bohn, 2021) and the Second Language Perceptual Assimilation Model (PAM L2; Best & Tyler, 2007). While I don't have the space to present both models in full detail and compare them to one another, it's worthwhile to review some of their basic predictions (for a detailed comparison, see, e.g., Chang, 2019). The basic idea guiding the SLM is that L1 and L2 sound categories exist in a common mental space and therefore interact with one another. The central issue is how the L2 listener perceives L2 sounds. Upon encountering an L2 sound, the listener may assimilate that sound to an L1 category, judging the L1 and L2 sounds to be equivalent even if they aren't. In this case, the L2 sound will be perceived (and produced) according to the phonetic norms of the L1. Alternatively, the listener may notice that the L2 sound is not quite like its L1 counterpart. In that case, the listener gradually creates a new category for the L2 sound, enabling but not guaranteeing accurate perception and production in the L2. The original SLM (Flege, 1995) was focused on ultimate attainment in highly proficient bilinguals, who were compared to age-matched monolingual speakers to see how closely bilinguals performed like monolinguals in each of their languages. The revised model (Flege & Bohn, 2021) no longer emphasizes ultimate attainment, but rather is anchored in examining longitudinal changes in perception and production throughout the learning process. It's also concerned with doing so at the level of the individual participant: "Working within the SLM-r framework requires obtaining enough data from each participant to permit treating each individual as a separate experiment. Meeting this condition makes it possible to determine if an individual has or has not achieved specific L2 speech learning 'milestones'" (Flege & Bohn, 2021, p. 59). This point is important because the SLM(-r) proposes a three-stage process for L2 category formation: differences between the L1 and L2 sounds are discerned, L2 sounds are grouped into a functional class, and the link between the L2 functional class and the L1 sound is broken (cf. Flege & Bohn, pp. 40–41). This is a gradual process rather than an abrupt one. Age was critical to the original model, but age was never conceptualized as an indicator of a potential critical period for language development. Rather, age was a proxy for the developmental state of the L1, under the view that the more advanced L1 development was at the onset of L2 learning, the less likely it was that

28 Researching Speech Perception

the listener would detect subtle crosslinguistic differences in phonetic realization. The revised model discusses age while taking into consideration a wider range of individual differences that could affect L2 speech learning (e.g., individual differences in perceptual acuity, L1 category compactness). Overall, in the SLM, the initial perceptual judgments that learners make are critical because sounds that are judged to be crosslinguistically similar are predicted to be more difficult to learn. Put another way, the greater the perceived crosslinguistic dissimilarity between the L2 sound and its closest L1 counterpart, the more likely it is that learning will take place (or, more precisely, that more learning will take place, compared to the amount of learning shown for sounds judged to be more similar).

PAM L2 (Best & Tyler, 2007) also places critical importance on initial perceptual assimilation patterns. According to this model, these patterns determine how discriminable L2 contrasts are and, by extension, how easily they might be learned. There are two basic considerations to this model for sounds that can be categorized (in some cases, L2 sounds may be uncategorizable). The first consideration is how the two sounds making up an L2 contrast are assimilated to L1 categories. Sounds may be assimilated to a single category or to two separate categories. If the sounds are mapped onto separate categories (two category assimilation), discriminability is predicted to be good, and the L2 contrast should be comparatively easy to learn. If, on the other hand, the two L2 sounds are mapped onto the same category, then discriminability depends on how similar the L1 and L2 sounds are perceived to be. If both L2 sounds are deemed to be similar in terms of their goodness of fit to the L1 category (single category assimilation type), then discriminability is predicted to be poor and learning difficult. If goodness of fit is variable, with one L2 sound showing a better fit to the L1 category than the other (category goodness assimilation), then discriminability may be better and learning of that L2 contrast easier. These predictions are relative, in the sense that two category > category goodness > single category. Thus, a category goodness assimilation should be easier to discriminate and easier to learn than a single-category assimilation, but that does not mean that a category goodness assimilation should be easy to learn in an absolute sense.

These models have been the impetus for a large body of research on crosslinguistic speech perception and production, but they have also been misunderstood, overgeneralized, and even misapplied, so before I turn to perception research topics, I'd like to comment on a few salient aspects of the models. First, the SLM-r is centered on crosslinguistic comparisons of position-specific allophones (e.g., word-initial stops in L1 and L2, word-final stops in L1 and L2). This means that crosslinguistic similarity is determined by asking participants to evaluate stimulus pairs consisting of an

L1 sound and its L2 counterpart(s). Stimulus pairs consisting of two L2 sounds can also be tested, but L1-L2 pairs are fundamental to the postulates of the SLM-r. In contrast, PAM L2 is centered on L2 contrasts and how those contrasts are assimilated to L1 categories, which means that methods related to PAM L2 must take into account pairs of L2 sounds and their relationship to the L1. Second, these models were designed to account for L2 speech learning in individuals living in an environment in which the L2 is spoken and used extensively. Neither model was intended to cover formal instruction in the language classroom, as Best and Tyler made clear in their characterization of the intended population for PAM L2: "[Foreign Language Acquisition] is a fairly impoverished context for L2 learning, and perceptual findings for FLA listeners should not be conflated with those for L2 listeners (SLA)" (2007, p. 19). At the same time, they recognized that "FLA conditions do provide a potentially useful (though not tightly controlled) basis of comparison to SLA" (2007, p. 19). Certainly, the models can be extended to cover populations that were not part of the original formulation, but in doing so, it is important to explicitly recognize that the models are being extended (for more discussion, see Nagle & Baese-Berk, 2022). In short, if these models are taken as a point of departure, they must be applied in ways that are theoretically and methodologically consistent.

Research Topics

L2 perception researchers are interested in how the L2 system develops, how the L1 and L2 systems interact throughout L2 learning, and how L2 learning affects the L1 (Dmitrieva et al., 2022). In other words, they are interested in how perceptual systems develop and interact throughout L2 learning. A related issue is identifying the learner and contextual variables that affect L2 perception learning and the extent of crosslinguistic interaction, both L1-to-L2 and L2-to-L1. Thus, from a methodological standpoint, it is not uncommon for perception research to test participants in L1 and L2. Furthermore, in terms of analysis, two types of comparisons have been made. First, bilinguals have been compared to age-matched groups of monolinguals in both languages. This is a between-subjects comparison, and the goal is to determine the extent to which bilinguals show monolingual-like behavior in L1 and L2. Second, when bilinguals are tested in both languages, their performance in one language is often compared to their performance in the other. This is a within-subjects comparison (because the same person has provided two points of data, data in the L1 and data in the L2), and the goal is to determine if bilinguals show different patterns in each language. If they do, then they likely have independent, language-specific representations, and if they don't, then representations are likely highly interdependent if not completely merged. Acknowledging the types of comparisons made provides insight into how the field has developed and can serve as a heuristic for interpreting and synthesizing research.

Flege and Eefting (1987) is an excellent example of early work involving both types of comparisons. In that study, the authors compared Spanish-English bilinguals to age-matched Spanish and English monolinguals, and they also compared bilinguals' performance in English to their performance in Spanish. Stop consonants were the target structure, and the goal was to understand the relationship between the participants' age of onset of L2 learning and their perception (and production) of L1 and L2 stops. As such, the researchers recruited several groups of bilinguals differing in age of onset of L2 learning, linguistic experience, and biological age at the time the study was conducted (one of the groups was bilingual children). Flege and Eefting adopted a fine-grained phonetic approach to crosslinguistic influence and L2 attainment. Perception was measured using a crossover boundary task, where the bilinguals heard stop-consonant-initial syllables varying in VOT (–60 ms to 90 ms in 10-ms steps) and labeled them as /da/ or /ta/. This task was repeated in each language, and to encourage a Spanish-like or English-like processing mode, instructions were given in Spanish and English. Using this task, the authors were able to determine the precise crossover boundary in each language (i.e., the point at which /da/ became /ta/), comparing the bilingual groups' boundaries to the age-matched monolinguals'. They also compared the bilingual groups' boundaries in English to their boundaries in Spanish.

Another fine-grained approach to understanding L2 perception (and production) is through cue weighting studies. In this type of study, a grid of stimuli is constructed where the stimuli vary systematically along two or more phonetic cues. For instance, Schertz et al. (2015) constructed a complex grid involving three phonetic cues, VOT, F0, and closure duration, to examine L1 Korean speakers' perception and production of L1 Korean and L2 English stops. Just like Flege and Eefting (1987), Schertz et al. used a labeling task, where participants heard and labeled each stimulus. The authors focused on within-subjects contrasts, comparing participants' stop consonant perception and production in Korean to their stop consonant perception and production in English. They also reported on data for individual participants, which aligns with approaches prioritizing the individual L2 learner-user (Flege & Bohn, 2021). Kim et al. (2018) is another cue-weighting study. In this case, the authors examined longitudinal changes in Korean speakers' use of two phonetic cues, duration and spectrum, in the perception of two challenging L2 English vowel contrasts: /i/-/ɪ/ and /ɛ/-/æ/. Although they included a group of L1 English speakers for comparison, the focus of the study was on within-subjects changes in cue weights.

Researchers have also investigated perception accuracy from a more global, holistic perspective, asking how accurately L2 listeners discriminate L2 contrasts and identify L2 sounds, irrespective of the phonetic cues they use to do so. For instance, MacKay et al. (2001) examined Italian speakers' identification of English consonants. Their aim was theoretical, insofar as they sought to understand how participants' age of arrival and amount of L1 Italian use affected their identification accuracy in the L2. However, the results could also be interpreted in a more practical sense, in terms of the likely areas of difficulty Italian speakers might have in the perception of English consonant contrasts. It's important to reflect on the ways in which discrimination and identification data may or may not align with cue-weighting data. Participants may discriminate and identify L2 sounds accurately even if they do not rely on the same cues native listeners do or rely on them to the same extent.

What variables have perception researchers targeted in their work? Age has been a mainstay and continues to generate interest in terms of pinpointing exactly when age effects (L1-to-L2 effects) emerge (e.g., Darcy & Krüger, 2012). Language use and exposure variables have also been important in perception research. In one impactful study, Escudero and Boersma (2004) examined L1 Spanish speakers' perception of English /i/-/ɪ/. Participants were living in two different English dialect regions: Scottish English and Southern English. Crucially, L1 Scottish English listeners predominantly rely on spectral cues, whereas L1 Southern English listeners use a combination of duration and spectrum. The goal of the study was to see if the Spanish speakers aligned their perception with the cues present in each dialect. Beyond age, experience, and use, researchers have examined diverse cognitive variables, often integrating the two sets of variables into a single study to paint a more complete picture of the regulators of L2 perception achievement (e.g., Saito et al., 2022) and learning (Sun et al., 2021). Methodologically, there has been a broadening of the types of learners recruited and the language pairs examined (e.g., Japanese learners of Korean, Holliday, 2019), and researchers have also investigated the relationship between perception ability and other linguistic processes such as lexical encoding (e.g., Darcy et al., 2012). Overall, the scope of L2 perception research continues to expand, but there remains a notable lack of longitudinal research examining changes in perception over time (but see, e.g., Kim et al., 2018; Sun et al., 2021).

Measuring Perception

Perception can be measured in a variety of ways depending on the goals of the research. In some cases, researchers are interested in perceptual accuracy and thus turn to tasks such as discrimination and identification. In others,

32 Researching Speech Perception

they are interested in measuring the precise characteristics of the perceptual system, examining crossover boundaries and cue weights.

Perception tasks can be divided into two broad categories: discrimination and identification. Discrimination tasks present multiple stimuli to the listener for judgment. The simplest version of a discrimination task is AX, where A represents a category and X a stimulus, and the listener must decide if the two stimuli are the same (i.e., if X is an exemplar of category A). Another common discrimination task is AXB or ABX. On this task, the speaker hears two anchor stimuli, A and B, each of which represents a different phonological category, and a stimulus, X. The speaker is then asked to decide if the target stimulus X matches A or B. Although both AX and AXB are discrimination tasks, they are not necessarily interchangeable because they involve somewhat different cognitive processes. For AX, the listener only needs to decide if the sounds match one another, that is, if they belong to the same category. In contrast, AXB involves categorization, insofar as the listener must select the category that the stimulus belongs to. A third discrimination task is an oddity or categorial discrimination task. On this task, three stimuli are played, and the listener must decide if all three belong to the same phonological category or if one of the stimuli belongs to a different category. If one of the stimuli belongs to a different category, the listener must indicate its position in the series. This task blends aspects of both AX and AXB. Like AX, it involves a global same versus different judgment because all stimuli could represent the same category, and like AXB, it requires categorization, insofar as the listener has to determine which sounds belong together. However, unlike AXB, there is no clear indication of what the categories are. Instead, the listener must group the stimuli together in some way (e.g., 1 and 3 represent the same phonological category but 2 is different; 1 and 2 belong to the same category but 3 is different).

The other basic type of perception task is an identification task. On this task, the listener hears a single stimulus (e.g., a word) and is asked to map it to an underlying category. As a result, there is no comparison among stimuli, but rather a comparison between the stimulus and the listener's representation in long-term memory. For instance, on this task, the participant might hear /ʃɪp/ and be asked to identify the word they heard. Response options could be presented orthographically, or images could be given if the stimuli are imageable (e.g., *sheep* vs. *ship*). Table 2.1 gives an example of discrimination and identification tasks for the English /i/-/ɪ/ contrast using words as stimuli. For an extensive discussion of perception tasks, see also Flege (2003).

In discussing perception research, Strange observed that "the precise units being investigated in particular experimental designs are not always made clear or explicit" (2011, p. 459). She further explained that there are

Researching Speech Perception 33

TABLE 2.1 Example of Perception Tasks for the English /i/-/I/ contrast

	AX	*AXB*	*Oddity*	*Identification*
Possible responses	same, different	A, B	none, 1, 2, 3	*sheep, ship*
Example trial	[ʃip]₁-[ʃɪp]₂	[ʃip]₁-[ʃɪp]₂-[ʃip]₁	[ʃip]₁-[ʃɪp]₂-[ʃɪp]₃	[ʃɪp]
Correct response	different	B	1	*ship*

Note. Subscripts indicate that each stimulus was produced by a different talker. For the identification task example, responses are given in standard orthography, but images could also be used.

two general perceptual modes, phonetic and phonological, which listeners can access depending on the characteristics of the task and stimuli. Listeners are generally sensitive to finer-grained phonetic distinctions when stimuli are presented in quiet conditions, when the length of the interstimulus interval is short, and when the stimuli are simple syllables or monosyllabic words. Conversely, when stimuli are presented in noise, when the interstimulus interval is long, and when the stimuli themselves are more complex, listeners may use a more phonological, that is, categorical, processing mode. To my knowledge, these variables have not been extensively explored using a consistent experimental design, but the length of the interstimulus interval is one variable that has been examined. Werker and Tees (1984) tested English speakers on their ability to discriminate two nonnative contrasts using an AX task with two interstimulus interval conditions: 500 ms and 1,500 ms. Their study involved a between-subjects design, where distinct but comparable groups of participants took part in the 500 ms and 1,500 ms versions of the AX task. Performance was significantly better in the 500 ms version than in the 1,500 ms version, suggesting that participants were better able to access a more gradient, phonetic processing mode when the interstimulus interval was shorter. Research has also shown that while all listeners struggle to perceive sounds in noise, bilinguals' perception shows greater deterioration in noisy conditions (MacKay et al., 1997).

Discrimination and identification tasks are useful for examining how L2 listeners perceive L2 contrasts. Another important task is a labeling task, which is a special variant of an identification task. On this task, rather than presenting a naturally produced stimulus for identification, natural stimuli are manipulated (or stimuli are synthesized) to create a phonetic continuum ranging from one sound to the other. This type of task is used when the goal is to gain fine-grained insight into the characteristics of listeners' L2 perceptual system. Here, fine-grained means information on the precise location of a category boundary along the target phonetic continuum (or continua) or perceptual cue weights. Escudero and Boersma (2004) generated a continuum from English /i/ to /ɪ/ using seven duration steps and seven spectral steps, which they combined into 37 stimuli. In their study on L1 Korean speakers' perception of Korean and English stops, Schertz et al. (2015) generated two sets of 147 stimuli varying in VOT (seven steps), F0 (seven steps), and closure duration (three steps), choosing values that would reflect the phonetic characteristics of Korean and English.

Importantly, perception tasks are not in and of themselves good or bad, but rather should be evaluated in terms of the research goals. Whether or not a perception task is methodologically appropriate depends on your research questions. No single perception task, no matter how well designed, can illuminate all aspects of perceptual performance and learning, which is why it often makes sense to use several perception tasks that provide complementary information on different aspects of L2 perception and to report on those tasks in full detail. As this brief survey of tasks makes clear, "perception research" is an umbrella term that includes studies that may be methodologically quite diverse and whose findings, therefore, may not be as comparable as they, at first, seem. One means of achieving transparency in research practices, in addition to accurate reporting, is by unambiguously labeling the type of research carried out. For instance, rather than titling a potential study "Perception of L2 English vowels," a more accurate title could name the task used: "Identification of L2 English vowels" or "Discrimination of L2 English vowels."

Designing the Perception Task

Once you select a perception task that is appropriate for your research, you have to design it, which entails making a range of decisions about the characteristics of the stimuli, the number of trials, and how those trials will be structured. In this section, I therefore move from theoretical issues related to perception research topics and tasks to practical issues of task design and implementation procedure.

Designing the Stimuli

It is impossible to divorce perception stimuli from the task into which they are embedded. Thus, many, but not all, stimulus decisions flow from the task itself. For instance, in research involving identification tasks, the stimuli tend to be real words, and if the task is designed with images as response options, then the real words must be imageable. In contrast, in research focusing on learners' ability to discriminate sounds from one another, real words, nonsense words, or syllables can be used. In fact, in research into perceptual sensitivity to contrast, it may be advantageous to avoid words altogether because the lexical characteristics of the words could influence the response the listeners give, which means that the data will represent both their baseline perceptual ability and their lexical knowledge. Simply put, in this case, using lexical items could introduce a confounding variable into the design, leading to imprecise insight into participants' true discrimination ability.

Regardless of the type of stimuli used, one central issue is their representativeness. Like participants, stimuli are sampled from a larger population of potential stimuli, which means that you must consider the stimulus population that you expect your results to generalize to. There are many different considerations for generalization, but here I focus on two major ones: phonological environments and voices. Perception is at least partially context-/environment-specific, which means that if you test learners using stimuli that represent a narrow range of environments in which the target structure occurs, results may not generalize to other environments. Simply put, don't assume that performance in one environment generalizes to performance in another. Practically speaking, for studies involving the perception of consonant categories and contrasts, target consonants should be paired with a range of vowels, and for studies involving vowel categories and contrasts, target vowels should be paired with a range of preceding and following consonants. Other variables, such as syllable structure and lexical stress, are often controlled. For example, in Spanish, stop consonants could be presented in disyllabic words stressed on the first syllable, and in English, vowels could be presented in monosyllabic words.

Another consideration is ensuring that the stimuli are produced by several talkers, which serves multiple purposes. For one, including multiple talkers guarantees adequate coverage of the diverse ways in which individual speakers may implement a category or contrast. In other words, although there are certainly group-level trends in terms of how, for instance, English speakers implement tense-lax vowel contrasts, there is also substantial individual variation in cue use and weighting. This means that an important dimension of L2 perception is learning to cope with this variation, that is, learning to discriminate and identify the sounds produced by many different L1 (and possibly L2) talkers. Another reason is purely methodological. If only a single talker is included, then the listener may become attuned to that individual's speech patterns over the course of the experiment. As a result, their performance does not necessarily represent their ability to perceive the L2, but rather talker-specific adaptation. In the case of discrimination tasks where two or more stimuli are presented for evaluation, stimuli are typically combined in such a way that the stimuli included in a trial are produced by different talkers. For instance, on ABX, A and B may be produced by one talker and X by another, and on an oddity task, each stimulus would be produced by a distinct talker.

The number of trials must also be determined. A good general recommendation is to include at least 10 trials per target structure per condition. If the study involves word-initial stop consonants in stressed and unstressed syllables, then at least ten trials could be included for each stop consonant in

36 Researching Speech Perception

each stress condition. To bring the number of trials into balance with other facets of generalization, such as phonological environments, there could be two trials each for five vowels. This task is not as daunting as it may seem. The first step is to determine the variables relevant to stimulus design, that is, the variables that will become part of your statistical analysis (e.g., perception of stops in stressed and unstressed syllables, where stress is a target variable), and then you can create a grid that allows you to control and account for other important but non-experimental variables. In the first example in Table 2.2 focusing on the English /i/-/ɪ/ contrast, I have created a grid to select 10 items per vowel per frequency band (in this hypothetical study, I am interested in the effect of word frequency on perception accuracy), or 60 items total (2 vowels × 3 frequency bands × 10 items/vowel/band). If these items are recorded by two speakers, one male and one female, then there are 120 items total for potential inclusion in the task. If they are recorded by four speakers, then there are 240 possible items. The second example, given in Table 2.3, shows a configuration for a study on stop consonants. In this case, each stop is paired with five different vowels, such that there are five items per stop. An item-indexing column is not necessary because there is exactly one stimulus per stop per vowel. If there were more stimuli per stop per vowel, then an item-indexing column would be needed. One advantage of making these grids, other than maintaining oversight over all aspects of stimulus creation, is that the grids can be included with publications as supplementary materials for the sake of transparent reporting.

The grids shown in Tables 2.2 and 2.3 focus on individual stimuli, but for discrimination tasks in particular, stimuli need to be combined into trials, which means thinking about how stimuli produced by different talkers should be combined. The goal in creating trials is to ensure that all talkers are equally represented and, additionally, that the location of the correct response is counterbalanced across trials and with respect to talkers. Grids can also be useful for that purpose. I recommend creating a comprehensive list of trials and how they were formed using, for instance, color coding to signal stimuli produced by different talkers. Table 2.4 gives an example of what this could look like for a categorial discrimination (i.e., oddity) task involving stop consonant contrasts. In this table, the trial type is shown in the first column, followed by the target response and the phone. Each type of trial/response has one set of trials with /p/ as the target category or odd item and one set of trials with /b/ as the target category or odd item. This information is given in the "Phone" column. For "different" trials, the odd item is shown in bold, and its serial position should correspond to the number shown in the "Response" column.

To map talkers onto this design, we would need to have a multiple of three because each stimulus within the trial should be produced by a different talker. We could have six talkers, three male and three female. In that

Researching Speech Perception 37

TABLE 2.2 Example of Stimulus Creation Grid for the English /i/-/ɪ/ Vowel Contrast

Vowel	Item	Frequency Band 1	Frequency Band 2	Frequency Band 3
/i/	1	word 1	word 21	word 41
/i/	2	word 2	word 22	word 42
/i/	3	word 3	word 23	word 43
/i/	4	word 4	word 24	word 44
/i/	5	word 5	word 25	word 45
/i/	6	word 6	word 26	word 46
/i/	7	word 7	word 27	word 47
/i/	8	word 8	word 28	word 48
/i/	9	word 9	word 29	word 49
/i/	10	word 10	word 30	word 50
/ɪ/	1	word 11	word 31	word 51
/ɪ/	2	word 12	word 32	word 52
/ɪ/	3	word 13	word 33	word 53
/ɪ/	4	word 14	word 34	word 54
/ɪ/	5	word 15	word 35	word 55
/ɪ/	6	word 16	word 36	word 56
/ɪ/	7	word 17	word 37	word 57
/ɪ/	8	word 18	word 38	word 58
/ɪ/	9	word 19	word 39	word 59
/ɪ/	10	word 20	word 40	word 60

TABLE 2.3 Example of Stimulus Creation Grid for Stop Consonant Contrasts

Stop	/i/	/e/	/a/	/o/	/u/
/p/	word 1	word 7	word 13	word 19	word 25
/b/	word 2	word 8	word 14	word 20	word 26
/t/	word 3	word 9	word 15	word 21	word 27
/d/	word 4	word 10	word 16	word 22	word 28
/k/	word 5	word 11	word 17	word 23	word 29
/g/	word 6	word 12	word 18	word 24	word 30

38 Researching Speech Perception

TABLE 2.4 Example of Trial Creation Grid for Stop Consonant Contrasts

Trial Type	Response	Phone	/i/	/e/	/a/	/o/	/u/
Same	N	p	pi-pi-pi	pe-pe-pe	pa-pa-pa	bo-bo-bo	bu-bu-bu
Same	N	p	pi-pi-pi	pe-pe-pe	pa-pa-pa	bo-bo-bo	bu-bu-bu
Same	N	b	bi-bi-bi	be-be-be	ba-ba-ba	bo-bo-bo	bu-bu-bu
Same	N	b	bi-bi-bi	be-be-be	ba-ba-ba	bo-bo-bo	bu-bu-bu
Different	1	p	**pi**[1]-bi-bi	**pe**[2]-be-be	**pa**[3]-ba-ba	**po**[1]-bo-bo	**pu**[2]-bu-bu
Different	1	b	**bi**[3]-pi-pi	**be**[1]-pe-pe	**ba**[2]-pa-pa	**bo**[3]-po-po	**bu**[1]-pu-pu
Different	2	p	bi-**pi**[2]-bi	be-**pe**[3]-be	ba-**pa**[1]-ba	bo-**po**[2]-bo	bu-**pu**[3]-bu
Different	2	b	pi-**bi**[1]-pi	pe-**be**[2]-pe	pa-**ba**[3]-pa	po-**bo**[1]-po	pu-**bu**[2]-pu
Different	3	p	bi-bi-**pi**[3]	be-be-**pe**[1]	ba-ba-**pa**[2]	bo-bo-**po**[3]	bu-bu-**pu**[1]
Different	3	b	pi-pi-**bi**[2]	pe-pe-**be**[3]	pa-pa-**ba**[1]	po-po-**bo**[2]	pu-pu-**bu**[3]

case, we would need to counterbalance with respect to talker gender. Alternatively, all trials could be produced by male or female talkers. This would simplify counterbalancing but raises questions about the generalizability of the results. If we assume that we have three talkers, then the simplest way of distributing them symmetrically across the trials is to focus on the target response, rotating through speakers. In Table 2.4, I have used superscripts to indicate the talker who produced the correct response on the "different" trials. Because we have three talkers and ten trials per location, for each location, two talkers will produce the correct response on three trials and one talker will produce it on four trials. However, across the entire set of trials, each talker will produce ten correct responses. If we wanted to include six talkers, three male and three female, then we could double the number of trials from 50 to 100, distributing talkers in the same way. Note that this design is not completely symmetrical in terms of its counterbalancing because talkers are not equally represented at the lowest level of the trial structure (e.g., phone within response location within different trials). The only way to create a symmetrical design would be to ensure that all levels of the trial structure were a multiple of three, but doing so could lead to a large and unwieldy trial set that would not be feasible for administration. Thus, counterbalancing to the extent possible is important, but perfect counterbalancing may be logistically impractical, if not impossible.

Once we have completed this process, we can check our work by computing summary information, as shown in Table 2.5. This may seem like a lot of work, and it can be, but creating these summary tables at the outset drastically reduces time, confusion, and potential mistakes for trial creation, and it makes reporting straightforward.

TABLE 2.5 Summary of Talker Balancing with Respect to the Location of the Correct Response on "Different" Trials

	Talker 1	*Talker 2*	*Talker 3*
Total	10 (5 /p/, 5 /b/)	10 (5 /p/, 5 /b/)	10 (5 /p/, 5 /b/)
Correct = 1	4 (2 /p/, 2 /b/)	3 (2 /p/, 1 /b/)	3 (1 /p/, 2 /b/)
Correct = 2	3 (1 /p/, 2 /b/)	4 (2 /b/, 2 /p/)	3 (2 /p/, 1 /b/)
Correct = 3	3 (2 /p/, 1 /b/)	3 (1 /p/, 2 /b/)	4 (2 /b/, 2 /p/)

One other aspect of stimulus/trial creation that merits discussion here is statistical: how many trials are needed for statistical power? The general recommendation is that researchers include 10–30 items per condition, where condition refers to a variable that the researcher is interested in modeling. In the examples given above, frequency band would be a variable of interest for the vowel contrast study, which means that ideally the researcher would include at least ten trials per band per vowel. For the stop contrast study, place of articulation (bilabial, alveolar/dental, velar) would be a variable of interest, but the following vowel would not be because the following vowel has been rotated for the sake of creating a diverse, representative sample of stimuli and trials. Therefore, for the stop study, the trials we have built would be sufficient for achieving statistical power. It also bears mentioning that the recommendation of 10–30 trials was conceptualized for psychology studies where the primary outcome measure is reaction time, a variable that is relatively noisy (i.e., there is substantial variability within- and between subjects in response time). Thus, in perception research where the outcome is accuracy, fewer trials may be needed to achieve adequate power. If, however, reaction time is to be analyzed, then the more trials the better, as long as the task remains feasible for participants (for detailed discussion, see, e.g., Judd et al., 2012).

Recording and Preparing the Stimuli

As I have reviewed in the previous sections, you should think carefully about the phonetic characteristics of the stimuli, aligning those characteristics with the goals of the research and other elements of the methodology. Once you are clear about what the stimuli should look like, you need to record them. Researchers seeking absolute control over audio quality will want to record in a sound-attenuated space such as a recording booth. If a booth is not available, recording in a quiet space with few hard surfaces will generally yield a high recording quality. Using a high-quality microphone is also beneficial (e.g., a Shure head-mounted microphone, a stand microphone

40 Researching Speech Perception

that has a cardioid recording pattern, which means that it captures sound in front of, or facing, the microphone while limiting capture from behind the microphone), but recording devices have progressed remarkably, and I have achieved excellent recording quality from cell phones as well.

Researchers typically create reading or picture naming lists that are presented to the talkers who produce the stimuli. I have found reading lists to be a better elicitation option than picture naming because target words may not be imageable, and words that are imageable may not be named unambiguously. For researchers using nonsense words, a word-reading task will be the only option, but researchers interested in avoiding orthography can consult resources such as LinguaPix database (Krautz & Keuleers, 2022), the Multilingual Picture Database (Duñabeitia et al., 2022), and the International Picture-Naming Project (Székely et al., 2003) for images with detailed information on naming ambiguity, latency, and so on. To elicit the stimuli, I recommend presenting one word or image per screen using a program that automatically advances after a fixed interval (e.g., three seconds) to avoid participant clicking. If participants click to advance, then they may click before they are done producing the target item, which means that the click will distort the recording of that item. They might also accidentally skip items if they click through too quickly, and if they develop a rhythm while clicking, they may transfer it to their production, leading to listing intonation and other intonation patterns that could introduce non-trivial prosodic differences into the stimulus set. Typically, the recording remains in progress throughout the entire task, such that after the stimuli are recorded, the researcher must then tag and extract them using Praat or Audacity and then normalize them to a consistent volume. In practice, this process is not very difficult because Praat scripts can be used to automatically identify and label voiced portions, greatly reducing the need for manual tagging. However, if each participant reads the items in a randomized order, automatic segmentation of voiced portions remains possible, but automatic labeling will not be (i.e., because the items have not been presented in a fixed order). This practical consideration is important to keep in mind depending on the volume of items to be recorded. More complex recording paradigms that allow individual sound files to be captured are possible, but at the time of writing of this book most of those paradigms require programming skills to set up.

Once the stimuli files have been recorded and extracted, they need to be normalized to a consistent volume. There are two options in Praat which in most cases produce similar results: scaling the peak amplitude or scaling the average intensity. Peak amplitude should be scaled to 0.98 or 0.99, and intensity should be set to 70 decibels, which is a comfortable listening volume. I typically scale intensity unless doing so produces a substantial amount of clipping. The scale intensity Praat function produces a report of the number of intervals that were clipped out of the total number of intervals. If the stimuli sound natural and only a small amount of clipping has occurred (e.g., <1%), then no additional manipulation is needed. If, however, a larger percentage of intervals are clipped, then the alternative, scaling peak amplitude, is likely a better option.

For identification tasks, the normalized files are ready for presentation, but for discrimination tasks, the files must be combined into trials. This involves creating a silent period in Praat, which serves as the interstimulus interval (e.g., 1,500 ms), and then combining the files and silences in order to create the trial using the concatenate function. For instance, for an AX task, you would combine A, the silent interval, and X to create a trial, and for an AXB task, you would combine A, the silent interval, X, the silent interval, and B. It is worth mentioning that it is important to normalize the individual sound files before combining them because if they are normalized with the silent intervals, then the sound level of the stimuli could be distorted.

Designing the Procedure

Designing, obtaining, and preparing the stimuli is not the end of the story. Once the stimuli are prepared, they must be put into the task. Decisions must be made about how the stimuli will be presented to participants and the instructions that will be given. For experiments involving a small number of trials (e.g., <100), all trials can be randomized and presented in a single block. However, it is often the case that stimuli must be blocked for conceptual or practical reasons. On the conceptual side, if there are multiple stimulus conditions (e.g., words in isolation and words in utterances, words presented auditorily and words presented with audiovisual cues), then it makes sense to block by condition because each of those conditions may impose different processing requirements on the listener. In other cases, it may be more sensible to intermix trials (e.g., for stops at different places of articulation, for stimuli of varying frequency). On a practical level, as the number of trials grows larger, it is important to give participants a short break to prevent fatigue, distraction, and other extra-experimental variables from introducing noise into the data. The number of trials that participants can complete consecutively depends on the nature of the task and is best determined through pilot testing.

When blocks are created to give participants short breaks throughout the task, stimuli must be distributed symmetrically into blocks. This means thinking about the variables that are the object of study and ensuring that these variables are equally represented in all blocks. If the focus is on

42 Researching Speech Perception

participants' ability to discriminate stops at varying places of articulation, then each place of articulation should be equally represented within blocks. Talkers and the location of the correct response would also need to be counterbalanced across blocks. In short, when creating blocks, it is important to make them as comparable as possible. This means creating blocks that mirror the trial structure (i.e., making sure blocks conform to the structure given in Table 2.4). Randomization is an important feature of any perceptual study. Stimuli should be presented in a random order within blocks, but the order of blocks should also be counterbalanced across participants in a Latin square design. Randomizing mitigates any effects that could arise due to the order in which participants complete blocks and move through trials.

One of the most important decisions to be made when designing the task is selecting the response options. For discrimination, this process is relatively straightforward because responses tend to be keys labeled according to the experimental task (e.g., "same" or "different," "the first and second word match" or "the second and third word match"). Identification tasks require more thought because labels could be orthographic words, keywords, International Phonetic Alphabet (IPA) transcription, or images, and the decision to use one or the other must be coordinated with other design elements, including the participant profile. For instance, novice learners have a smaller vocabulary than intermediate or advanced learners, which means that it is unlikely that the researcher would be able to use the same stimulus set with learners of varying proficiency, at least for an identification task using images. If orthographic labels are used, then researchers must be sensitive to another set of concerns. Novice and intermediate learners may not have a full understanding of phoneme-to-grapheme mappings, which means that an incorrect response may be due to incomplete knowledge of orthography rather than a true perceptual error. Advanced learners may be able to work with labels, but even then, orthography could trigger certain forms of bias if labels are shared across languages (e.g., is used in both English and Spanish, but the way /b/ is phonetically realized in those languages is different).

Last but certainly not least, instructions should be drafted and piloted so that participants have a clear understanding of what they are asked to do. If participants are asked to indicate the stimulus that is different from the others on a discrimination task, then they need to know what "different" means. One way of preventing misunderstanding is administering a small number of practice trials in the participant's L1, if possible. Giving appropriate instructions is not a trivial step because the instructions participants receive can affect how they perform on the task, and instructions should be piloted and evaluated.

Once you have all of these pieces (see Table 2.6 for a worksheet), where do they go? In other words, how do you pull them all together to run the

Researching Speech Perception **43**

TABLE 2.6 Perception Task Design Worksheet

Discrimination

- Target structure(s)?
- AX, AXB, or oddity?
- Syllables, nonsense words, real words?
- Syllable structure?[1]
- Stressed syllable?[1]
- Phonological environments?
- Length of the interstimulus interval?
- Number of talkers?
- Number of trials per condition?
- Total number of trials?
- Counterbalancing?

Identification

- Target structure(s)?
- Nonsense or real words?
- Syllable structure?
- Stressed syllable?
- Phonological environments?
- Number of talkers?
- Number of trials per condition?
- Total number of trials?
- Counterbalancing?
- Response options?

Labeling

- Target phonetic cue(s)?
- Endpoint labels (response options)?
- Number of steps per cue?
- Distance between steps for each cue?
- Number of repetitions of the continuum?
- Total number of trials?

[1] If applicable (if nonsense or real words are used).

experiment? Most researchers use experiment design and management software such as SuperLab, PsychoPy, or Gorilla to build the architecture of the study and then funnel trials into that architecture. For instance, to create an identification task, you might create a response screen "shell" and upload a Comma Separated Values (CSV) file with stimuli, response options, and the correct response into the experiment management software. The software

44 Researching Speech Perception

would then pull the information from the CSV into the response screen, such that participants would hear a stimulus, see response options, and click to select their response. This would repeat until the end of the experiment. In other words, using experiment design software, you do not create all of the individual trials. Instead, you create template pages and load the stimuli, and the software pairs the pages with the stimuli based on the parameters you have specified.

Analyzing Perception Data

The first thing to think about when approaching analysis is the nature of the data. What type of data do perception tasks generate? When a participant responds to a trial on a discrimination task, their response is either correct or incorrect. For instance, on an AX trial where A and X are different, the participant either detects that difference or they don't. Likewise, on an AXB trial where X matches A, the participant either correctly assigns X to A or they don't. The same is true for identification tasks. When the participant hears the stimulus and selects a response, their selection is either correct or incorrect. What about labeling tasks? Here, responses are not correct or incorrect because on labeling tasks the focus is on the labels themselves and how the phonetic cues that have been manipulated affect what the participant hears. Nonetheless, labeling tasks generate the same type of binary data as other perception tasks: upon hearing the stimulus, the participant assigns it to one label or the other. Thus, on all these tasks, the trial-level data, that is, a participant's response to a single trial, are always binary: correct versus incorrect, label 1 versus label 2. This trial-level data can be analyzed in a variety of ways.

Sometimes, researchers don't analyze the trial-level data at all. Instead, they combine the data for all trials into a participant-level mean. For example, if the participant responds to 12 AX trials, then those 12 responses can be pooled into an average that represents overall percent correct. Assuming that the participant responds correctly to nine of the 12 trials, then that participant's overall score would be .75 (75%). This difference can be hard to conceptualize, but it's easy to see. Table 2.7 shows what the data would look like for a hypothetical participant, contrasting by-trial and by-participant approaches. This table also makes clear that the trial-level data are long-format data, with one row per trial (i.e., 12 rows per participant, in our hypothetical example). I have coded correct responses as 1 and incorrect responses as 0 based on the correspondence between the Type and Response columns. In this table, I have listed the by-participant score 12 times, but if we were creating participant-level averages, then there would only be one row per participant.

Researching Speech Perception **45**

TABLE 2.7 Example of Trial-Level Data versus Pooled Data for an AX Task

Participant	Trial	Stimulus	Type	Response	By-Trial	By-Participant
1	1	pe-pe	same	same	1	0.75
1	2	pa-pa	same	same	1	0.75
1	3	po-po	same	different	0	0.75
1	4	be-be	same	same	1	0.75
1	5	ba-ba	same	different	0	0.75
1	6	bo-bo	same	same	1	0.75
1	7	pe-be	different	different	1	0.75
1	8	be-pe	different	same	0	0.75
1	9	pa-ba	different	different	1	0.75
1	10	ba-pa	different	different	1	0.75
1	11	po-bo	different	different	1	0.75
1	12	bo-po	different	different	1	0.75

Note. Notice that in this example, I have created a symmetrical, counterbalanced design for the stimuli. There are six same trials and six different trials, and within these categories, there are two trials each per vowel: /e/, /a/, and /o/. For the different trials, I have alternated the stop that occurs as the first stimulus. For instance, for different trials with /o/, on one trial, /po/ occurs first, and on the other trial, /bo/ occurs first.

Creating by-participant averages is perfectly fine (and necessary) for the purpose of descriptive statistics, but it's problematic for statistical analysis because it does not account for response bias and trial-level variance, which refers to the fact that some trials will simply be more difficult than others. If this trial-level property is not modeled, Type 1 error rates (false positives) may be dramatically inflated, making estimates inaccurate (Judd et al., 2012; Luke, 2017). Let me address response bias first. On a discrimination task such as AX, the goal is to minimize error by detecting a difference when one is actually present (the stimuli are different) and rejecting a difference when there is none (the stimuli are the same). An appropriate outcome measure must therefore encompass these two dimensions of task performance. For instance, on a discrimination task, there are four possible outcomes. A hit occurs when the stimuli are different and the participant correctly detects the difference, and a miss occurs when the participant fails to detect a difference when one is present. A correct rejection occurs when the stimuli are the same and the participant indicates as much, and a false alarm is the opposite, when the participant detects a difference that is not there. Thus, this four-way distinction crosses the type of trial with the participant's response, as shown in Table 2.8.

Using this information, a signal detection theory outcome like *d* prime can be computed. *d* prime is computed by (1) calculating the hit and false

46 Researching Speech Perception

TABLE 2.8 Signal Detection Theory Approach to Discriminability

	Response = Different	*Response = Same*
Stimuli = Different	Hit	Miss
Stimuli = Same	False alarm	Correct rejection

alarm rates, (2) taking the z score of those rates, and (3) subtracting the standardized false alarm rate from the standardized hit rate: $d' = z(H) - z(F)$. For instance, if there are 20 different trials and 20 same trials, and the participant responds correctly to 14 of the different trials, then the hit rate is 14/20 (0.70), and by extension the miss rate is 6/20 (0.30). If that participant responds incorrectly to 5 of the same trials, then the false alarm rate is 5/20 (0.25), and the correct rejection rate must therefore be 15/20 (0.75). For this participant, $d' = z(0.70) - z(0.25)$, which works out to $d' = 1.20$ (for more information, see Macmillan & Creelman, 2005).

These measures can be analyzed like any other average using analysis of variance (ANOVA) to examine within- and between-subjects contrasts. However, if you use aggregate measures like averages or d prime, it's important to bear in mind that you have moved away from the trial-level data. Put another way, using aggregate measures makes it impossible to consider any characteristics of the trials themselves. My recommendation is therefore to analyze the trial-level data rather than aggregating the data.

Trial-level data can be analyzed through logistic mixed-effects models. This type of model allows the researcher to predict the likelihood of a correct response. One of the principal advantages of using a logistic mixed-effects model is that it avoids a double analysis by items and participants. When perception data are collected, there are two levels of random sampling: participants and items (or trials). Participants are randomly sampled from the larger population to which results should be generalized, and items are also randomly sampled from a larger pool of potential items. Traditionally, researchers have used two ANOVAs to analyze this type of data, one applied to participants, averaging over items/trials, and another applied to items/trials, averaging over participants. These two F statistics can then be combined into an aggregate F statistic that avoids Type 1 error inflation (false positives) in each analysis. I do not often see this aggregate statistic reported. Instead, researchers may run the two analyses, assuming that if an effect is statistically significant in both analyses, then it generalizes to new participants and new items/trials. While intuitively appealing, this logic is flawed because neither analysis accounts for the variance associated with the other grouping unit (Judd et al., 2012). Mixed-effects models are a better approach that explicitly models the multiple sources of variance in the data.

I don't have the space to discuss reaction time, which is another important measure that is often analyzed. Reaction time data are not binary, but continuous, and thus would be analyzed using a linear (as opposed to a logistic) mixed-effects model. Readers interested in learning more about analyzing reaction time data can refer to Baayen and Milin (2010) for detailed discussion.

Statistical Analysis

In this section, we're going to talk about and work through two data analysis examples. I have structured each section similarly. First, I describe the data and the variables we'll be working with. Then, I go through descriptive statistics, plotting, and preliminary data checking. Finally, I turn to the inferential analyses: repeated measures ANOVA and mixed-effects modeling. I discuss both approaches in the first couple chapters so that you have a sense of how they differ and what the advantages of mixed-effects modeling are. Even though I strongly advocate for mixed-effects modeling, it's important that we also consider ANOVA because historically this has been the technique that many researchers have used to analyze longitudinal data sets. For each analysis, I provide information on interpretation, and throughout this section, I have incorporated notes on data analysis in R and relevant chunks of code, shown in Calibri font. For the complete analysis, please refer to the R markdown file, which also has notes on how I simulated the data.

Example 1: Stop Consonant Perception over Time

Description of the Hypothetical Study and Simulated Data

For this example, our participants are 30 English speakers who are classroom learners of L2 Spanish. We'll assume that we collected data from them once per semester over four semesters of intensive language instruction, for a total of five data points: two in the first semester (one at the beginning and another at the end) and one at the end of each semester thereafter. We're interested in gauging how participants' ability to perceive voiced and voiceless stops changes over the course of language instruction. At each session, participants complete a two-alternative forced choice identification task on which they hear Spanish minimal pairs beginning with /b/ or /p/ and must identify them. There are 10 words beginning with /b/ and 10 beginning with /p/ for a total of 20 trials. In total, there are 3,000 observations: 30 participants × 5 sessions × 2 sounds × 10 trials. For this example, I simulated a perfectly balanced and complete data set in which there is no participant attrition and no data loss. We'll deal with missing data in subsequent chapters.

48 Researching Speech Perception

Our independent, or predictor, variables are:

- Session, which we will treat as a continuous variable
- Target Sound, a categorical variable with two levels: /b/ or /p/ (in the data, we can call this variable "sound" to make it shorter and easier to use in the analysis code, but in the text, when describing results, we'll refer to it as "Target Sound" to be as clear as possible)
- Session × Sound, an interaction term that will allow us to test whether the rate of change in identification accuracy varies as a function of sound

Our dependent variable in the original data set is a binary measure that indicates whether the participant responded correctly (1) or incorrectly (0) on each trial.

Preliminary Steps

An important first step in longitudinal data analysis and, indeed, any data analysis, is data visualization, which means generating a plot of the data. Generally, it's a good idea to plot the group data as well as a subset of individuals to examine the group trend and individual variability in change over time. We can plot the binary outcome variable, but that plot won't be very informative, so first we need to do some data wrangling to get a mean accuracy score for each participant at each session for each sound (remember that we can use mean scores, pooling over items, for descriptive analysis and inspection, but we shouldn't use mean scores in our inferential analyses). I won't go into too much detail about data wrangling, but getting a summary data set is easy using the group_by() and summarize() functions, as shown in the following chunk of code:

```
data.stopid.summary <- data.stopid %>%
    group_by(participant, session, sound) %>%
    summarize(accuracy = mean(correct))
```

This chunk of code "tells" R to create a new variable, "Accuracy," by averaging over trials for each combination of session and target sound. Thus, each participant should end up with 10 means (5 sessions × 2 sounds). Figure 2.1 shows the group trend, revealing several interesting patterns: (1) accuracy for Spanish /b/ was near ceiling for the entire study; (2) accuracy for Spanish /p/ was much lower at the outset of the study but improved significantly over time; (3) trajectories look mostly linear; (4) the 95% CI around the point estimates for session means suggests much more variability in the identification of /p/ than in the identification of /b/ because the confidence interval for /p/ is much wider at each session than the confidence interval for /b/.

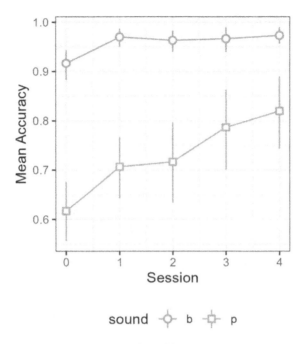

FIGURE 2.1 Mean Stop Consonant Identification Accuracy Over Time.

Having done a preliminary inspection of the data to get a sense of how participants' identification accuracy changed over time, we're now ready to move to the analysis. First, we do some preliminary checking of the assumptions of ANOVA, notably normality and homogeneity of variance. To check for normality, we can create a histogram of mean accuracy scores, and to get a sense of homogeneity of variance, we can create a boxplot or violin plot. We will also formally check these assumptions after we run the ANOVA, but it's worth doing a preliminary check in advance, if only for the sake of anticipating potential issues. Creating a histogram of accuracy scores for each sound at each session shows that /p/ accuracy is reasonably normally distributed but /b/ accuracy is highly negatively skewed (the long tail is to the left). This is expected because we saw that on average participants showed near-perfect accuracy for /b/ identification over time (i.e., mean scores >90%). Creating a boxplot suggests far more variability in scores for /p/ than for /b/, which is also in line with our expectations based on the 95% CIs shown in Figure 2.1. Table 2.9 gives descriptive statistics for mean identification accuracy by phone over time. Again, the means and standard deviations point to high overall accuracy for /b/, lower but improving accuracy for /p/, and more variability in the identification of /p/ than in the identification of /b/.

50 Researching Speech Perception

TABLE 2.9 Descriptive Statistics for Mean Accuracy Over Time by Target Sound

Session	/b/	/p/
	M (SD)	M (SD)
0	0.92 (0.28)	0.62 (0.49)
1	0.97 (0.17)	0.71 (0.46)
2	0.96 (0.19)	0.72 (0.45)
3	0.97 (0.18)	0.79 (0.41)
4	0.97 (0.16)	0.82 (0.38)

Before we move forward with the ANOVA, we need to talk about violating statistical assumptions. It's clear from our preliminary diagnostics that homogeneity of variance is not upheld, nor is normality, considering the fact that the identification scores for /b/ are extremely skewed. Once we run the analysis, we may find that sphericity is violated as well. We have a few options. We can move forward with the ANOVA, reporting when assumptions are violated. In this case, we would warn readers to interpret results with caution because estimates may not generalize to the population. Another option would be to reduce the data set to the /p/ identification data because based on our initial inspection of the data, participants did not have any difficulty identifying /b/ targets. In fact, this would fit with what we know about English speakers' perception of Spanish stops, so the decision to focus on /p/ would be a principled one, based on our understanding of the English and Spanish sound systems. However, if we make the decision to reduce the data set to /p/, then we must recognize that we are no longer analyzing and estimating participants' ability to identify Spanish stops accurately, but rather their ability to identify voiceless stops. This distinction is not trivial because if we analyze the /p/ data without considering the /b/ data we miss the fact that identifying /p/ accurately depends, at least in part, on identifying /b/ accurately. Put another way, the two are related, and once we build the mixed-effects model, we can take this interrelatedness into account by creating a model in which the intercept represents the mean likelihood of identifying a stop, both /b/ and /p/, correctly. I mention these options because data analysis involves extensive decision-making that may not be reported in the manuscript. Most decisions involve trade-offs, which means it's especially important to report, whenever possible, the rationale behind the analytical approach. For this example, we'll analyze the complete data set, including both /b/ and /p/ data, acknowledging violations as needed.

Analysis 1: ANOVA

There are several R packages that can be used for ANOVA. Here I will show two functions for running ANOVA, aov_ez() and aov_car(), both from the *afex* package (Singmann et al., 2023). As its name suggests, the syntax for aov_ez() is very straightforward: you specify the id, or grouping variable, the dependent variable (dv), between- and within-subjects contrasts, and the dataframe, as illustrated in the following chunk of code.

```
aov_ez(
    id = "participant",
    dv = "accuracy",
    within = c("session", "sound"),
    data = data.stopid.summary)
```

I have omitted the line for between-subjects effects because in this example there are none, but between-subjects factors are specified in the same way as within-subjects factors. I don't need to specify an interaction term in this model because including Session and Sound as within-subjects factors will automatically generate a Session × Sound interaction.

Although the aov_ez() is intuitive to use, I prefer to use the aov_car() function first because it makes what the analysis is doing more explicit and second because its syntax mirrors the syntax of the mixed-effects model.

```
aov_car(accuracy ~ session * sound + Error(participant/(session * sound)),
    data = data.stopid.summary)
```

We can read this code as "Accuracy is predicted by the interaction of Session and Sound with by-participant error terms or residuals." Note that with aov_car we have to specify the error term, which includes indicating within-subjects effects after a forward slash. In fact, within-subjects effects only need to be specified in the error term, so we could drop them from the first part of the model.

```
aov_car(accuracy ~ Error(participant/(session * sound)),
    data = data.stopid.summary)
```

Both aov_ez and aov_car will produce the exact same result. Once we run the analysis and save it to an object, we can call the object itself, which will return the ANOVA table with a default Greenhouse-Geisser correction for sphericity. We can also request a comprehensive summary of the model object using the summary() function, which will provide detailed

52 Researching Speech Perception

information on sphericity. The outcome of this analysis shows that Session, Target Sound, and the interaction are all statistically significant ($p < 0.001$ for each term). Mauchly's test for sphericity shows that sphericity has been violated for both the session and session * sound terms. Even if sphericity were not violated, I agree with Larson-Hall's (2016) recommendation to apply the correction regardless.

We can inspect the residuals of the model to check that they are normally distributed by using the residuals() function and the hist() function to plot them, as shown in the following code.

```
residuals(stopid.anova) %>%
    hist()
```

The plot suggests both skew (long left tail, indicative of negative skew) and kurtosis (a peaked distribution). The fact that the residuals are not normally distributed is not surprising given what we know about the normality and homogeneity of the data set.

Generalized eta-squared, which is given as "ges" in R, is an effect size that indicates the amount of variance that the term in the model explains. According to our ANOVA results, Session explains about 5.10% of the variance in identification accuracy, Target Sound 33.90%, and Session × Target Sound 1.90%. All these effects are statistically significant, and if we were to report this analysis, we might say something like: "We found a main effect for Session (Greenhouse-Geisser corrected $F(3, 73) = 9.87$, $p < 0.001$, $\eta^2_G = 0.051$), a main effect for Target Sound ($F(1, 29) = 83.17$, $p < 0.001$, $\eta^2_G = 0.339$), and a Session × Target Sound interaction (Greenhouse-Geisser corrected $F(3, 92) = 4.77$, $p = 0.003$, $\eta^2_G = 0.019$). All these effects were statistically significant, but effect size estimates suggest that Target Sound predicted most of the variance in performance, followed by Session, and then the interaction term."

The model showed that Session and the Session × Target Sound interaction are significant predictors, so we know that participants improved over time and that identification accuracy for /b/ and /p/ showed different rates of change. In this analysis, we can think of Session in two ways. If we conceptualize Session as a continuous predictor, then we are interested in obtaining an estimate for the mean rate of change over time. If, on the other hand, we conceptualize Session as a categorical predictor, then we are interested in comparing different levels of Session to one another. For instance, we might want to compare adjacent data points (Session 1 vs. 2, 2 vs. 3, etc.) to determine if there is a statistically significant change in mean identification accuracy between sessions. Another comparison we could make is between the first and last data points (Session 1 vs. 5) to get a sense of the overall amount of change that occurred. In ANOVA, we must treat Session as a factor (in fact, the `aov_car` function factorizes within-subjects variables by default), which means that we need to do some work to get our pairwise estimates. Put another way, the ANOVA tells us that there are significant differences in identification accuracy by Session, but it doesn't tell us where those differences lie. We can get pairwise contrasts, grouped by Target Sound, using the *emmeans* package (Lenth, 2023). The default of the emmeans() function is to compare all levels to one another. In our data set, this would mean 10 comparisons for /b/ and 10 for /p/ (e.g., for /b/, 1–2, 1–3, 1–4, 1–5, 2–3, 2–4, 2–5, 3–4, 3–5, and 4–5). We can generate the full matrix, grouped by Target Sound, using the following code:

```
emmeans(stopid.anova, pairwise ~ session | sound)
```

In this code, we enter the model object (stopid.anova) and request pairwise comparisons by (~) session, grouped by target sound, where the vertical bar indicates a grouping variable. This is not a very good approach for two reasons. First, we may not be interested in all these comparisons (e.g., (Why) should we compare performance at sessions 1 and 3?). Second and related, carrying out so many comparisons results in a loss of power for detecting the differences we actually care about. If we want to get a specific set of comparisons, we need to set them ourselves. We can create a priori comparisons by generating a reference grid object and then specifying comparisons based on that grid. First, we generate a reference grid:

```
rgrid <- emmeans(stopid.anova, ~ session * target_sound)
```

Then, we specify what we want. In this case, we will compare all adjacent data points and the first and last data points for each sound. We can do that by making a list of contrasts, where we assign a value of −1 to our baseline data point, a value of 1 to our comparison data point, and a value of 0 to all other data points:

```
contrasts <- list(
b_1v2 = c(-1, 1, 0, 0, 0, 0, 0, 0, 0, 0), # b session 1 vs. session 2
b_2v3 = c(0, -1, 1, 0, 0, 0, 0, 0, 0, 0), # b session 2 vs. session 3
b_3v4 = c(0, 0, -1, 1, 0, 0, 0, 0, 0, 0), # b session 3 vs. session 4
b_4v5 = c(0, 0, 0, -1, 1, 0, 0, 0, 0, 0), # b session 4 vs. session 5
b_1v5 = c(-1, 0, 0, 0, 1, 0, 0, 0, 0, 0), # b session 1 vs. session 5
p_1v2 = c(0, 0, 0, 0, 0, -1, 1, 0, 0, 0), # p session 1 vs. session 2
p_2v3 = c(0, 0, 0, 0, 0, 0, -1, 1, 0, 0), # p session 2 vs. session 3
p_3v4 = c(0, 0, 0, 0, 0, 0, 0, -1, 1, 0), # p session 3 vs. session 4
```

54 Researching Speech Perception

```
p_4v5 = c(0, 0, 0, 0, 0, 0, 0, 0, -1, 1), # p session 4 vs. session 5
p_1v5 = c(0, 0, 0, 0, 0, -1, 0, 0, 0, 1)) # p session 1 vs. session 5
```

Remember that the location of the values in the list of contrasts we create is based on the reference grid, so now we combine these contrasts with the grid using the contrast() function to get estimated mean differences between the data points we have specified:

```
contrast(rgrid, contrasts)
```

This code returns a table, which I have minimally edited for the sake of presentation (Table 2.10). To get the 95% confidence intervals for the pairwise comparisons, we can pipe (%>%) into the confint() function:

```
contrast(rgrid, contrasts) %>%
confint()
```

As shown in Table 2.10, there was significant improvement from the first to the last session for both /b/ and /p/, but the magnitude of the coefficient for /p/ is nearly four times as large as it is for /b/. Furthermore, whereas the confidence interval for /b/ ranges from a negligible improvement of 0.02 units to a modest improvement of up to 0.09 units, the interval for /p/ suggests values indicative of much larger gains even at its lower end (0.11). In short, participants' identification of /p/ improved far more than their identification of /b/. The pairwise contrasts for adjacent data points provide insight into where development was observed: from the first to the second session for /b/ and /p/, and from the third to the fourth session for /p/.

TABLE 2.10 Pairwise Session Contrasts for Identification Accuracy by Target Sound

Contrast	Estimate	SE	df	t	p	95% CI
b_1v2	0.053	0.016	29	30.247	0.003	[0.020, 0.087]
b_2v3	−0.007	0.011	29	−00.626	0.536	[−0.028, 0.015]
b_3v4	0.003	0.015	29	00.226	0.823	[−0.027, 0.034]
b_4v5	0.007	0.014	29	00.494	0.625	[−0.021, 0.034]
b_1v5	0.057	0.018	29	30.195	0.003	[0.020, 0.093]
p_1v2	0.090	0.044	29	20.056	0.049	[0.000, 0.180]
p_2v3	0.010	0.046	29	00.216	0.831	[−0.085, 0.105]
p_3v4	0.070	0.032	29	20.197	0.036	[0.005, 0.135]
p_4v5	0.033	0.022	29	10.505	0.143	[−0.012, 0.079]
p_1v5	0.203	0.047	29	40.317	<0.001	[0.107, 0.230]

Setting a priori contrasts is beneficial from a conceptual standpoint because it forces you to be clear about what you want to compare and why. It's also beneficial from a statistical standpoint because running fewer contrasts increases statistical power (i.e., power is not subdivided among irrelevant comparisons). The estimated differences will not change from one analysis to the other, but p values and the width of the 95% CIs will. For instance, for /b/ identification at session 1 versus session 2 in the full grid, the 95% CI is [0.006, 0.101], a width of 0.095 units, compared to a width of 0.067 units for the 95% CI for the a priori contrast. And for the first /p/ comparison, the 95% CI in the full grid is [−0.037, 0.217], a width of 0.254 units, versus a width of 0.180 units for the a priori 95% CI.

From the ANOVA, we know that participants identified /b/ targets significantly more accurately than /p/ targets, identification accuracy improved significantly over time, and this improvement was greater for /p/ than for /b/. Specifically, the magnitude of the gain from the first to the last session was four times greater for /p/ than it was for /b/, and the limits of the confidence intervals indicate that the gain for /p/ was likely to be substantial even at its lower end.

Analysis 2: Mixed-Effects Model

When we fit a mixed-effects model, we work with the trial-level data. In the trial-level data set, we have a variable (a column) called "correct," which indexes whether the participant responded correctly to each trial: 0 = incorrect response, 1 = correct response. Thus, we have a different type of outcome variable altogether, and so our analysis will also be different. Whereas with the ANOVA, we estimated differences in mean accuracy over time as a function of the target sound, with the mixed-effects model we estimate differences in the probability of responding correctly, considering both participant and trial characteristics. We use a logistic mixed-effects regression model (or more precisely, a binomial model) to estimate the likelihood of responding correctly. The syntax for the mixed-effects model is remarkably similar to the syntax we used to create the ANOVA with aov_car(), except we include syntax to generate by-participant and by-trial random effects.

```
stopid_mem <- glmer(correct ~ session * sound +
                    (1 | participant) +
                    (1 | trial),
                data = data_stopid, family = "binomial")
```

Here, we call the glmer() function to fit the generalized linear mixed-effects regression. As with aov_car(), the outcome variable goes to the left of the tilde and the predictors go to the right. Random effects are specified in

56 Researching Speech Perception

parentheses. The random effect grouping variable goes to the right of the vertical bar, and the random effects go to the left. The number 1 represents the intercept, so in the model given above, we ask the model to fit by-participant and by-trial random intercepts. We could omit the "1" because when a random effect grouping is specified the intercept is automatically fit (and I did omit the "1" from the fixed effects where it would refer to the fixed intercept; this is simply a habit I've developed). The intercept is the only effect that can be specified using a number, and this convention is arbitrary. Finally, we identify the data set and specify that we are fitting a binomial model (family = "binomial") because our outcome variable is binary (0/1). Once we fit the model, we can get a summary by using the summary() function on the model object. This will return estimates of the log odds, *SE*, and so on. Log odds are not easy to interpret, so I prefer to use the tab_model() function of the *sjPlot* package (Lüdecke, 2022) to convert the log odds to odds ratios (*OR*), which also double as an effect size. The tab_model() function accepts many optional arguments. In the code given below, I have included two, show.stat = T and show.se = T, to indicate that the test statistic (*z*) and the *SE* should be given in the model output.

```
tab_model(stopid.mem, show. stat = T, show.se = T)
```

An *OR* below 1 indicates that the predictor disfavors the outcome, and an *OR* above 1 indicates that the predictor favors it. If the 95% CI for the *OR* crosses 1, that is the same as crossing 0 on a linear scale; in other words, crossing 1 indicates that a null effect is plausible for the data set. The *OR* is multiplicative, such that an *OR* of 2 would indicate that for a 1-unit change in the predictor, the outcome would be twice as likely. One important note is that the *OR* operates in relation to the base likelihood, given by the intercept. Thus, even if a predictor has an *OR* of 3, the overall likelihood of the outcome may be relatively low if the baseline likelihood is low (commercials and news outlets often get this wrong or fail to acknowledge this point altogether; if a certain behavior increases the likelihood of developing an illness by 50%, *OR* = 1.5, this does not mean that a person who engages in that behavior now has a 50% chance of developing the illness, but rather the baseline rate of illness is increased by 50%, such as from 1% to 1.50%).

Table 2.11 shows the model. Before we review the model, I want to point out two details about the functionality of the tab_model() function. First, because *p* values for mixed-effects models are approximated, different functions (e.g., summary() vs. tab_model()) may return different values if they use different approximations. Second, tab_model() returns variances for random effects, but *SD*s should be reported. To my knowledge, there

TABLE 2.11 Summary of Logistic Mixed-Effects Model Fit to the Stop Identification Data

Fixed effects	OR	SE	z	95% CI	p
Intercept	18.27	4.71	11.26	[11.02, 30.28]	<0.001
Session	1.34	0.13	3.05	[1.11, 1.62]	0.002
Target Sound: /p/	0.10	0.03	–8.98	[0.06, 0.16]	<0.001
Session × Target Sound: /p/	0.99	0.10	–0.10	[0.80, 1.22]	0.923

Random effects	SD				
Speakers Intercepts	0.73				
Trials Intercepts	0.30				

is no optional argument to convert the variances to *SD*s, but this conversion can be done manually by taking the square root of the values given by tab_model() or by generating a summary of the model using summary().

This model has taken Target Sound = /b/ as the baseline, which means that (1) the intercept refers to the likelihood of responding correctly on a /b/ trial, (2) Session refers to the linear rate of change in the likelihood of identifying /b/ accurately, (3) Target Sound: /p/ refers to the adjustment to the intercept—the adjustment to the likelihood of responding correctly— on a /p/ trial, and (4) Session × Target Sound: /p/ refers to the adjustment to the linear rate of change of /p/ trials. Put another way, because /b/ has been set as the reference level, all estimates must be interpreted with respect to that reference. Unlike ANOVA, where Session is factorized, in the mixed-effects model, Session is treated as a continuous variable, and, as a result, the estimate represents the linear rate of change over time. Overall, participants were very likely to respond correctly on a /b/ trial (*OR* for the intercept > 1), but far less likely to respond correctly on a /p/ trial (*OR* for Target Sound: /p/ < 1). The *OR* for Session, which is greater than 1, shows that over time, participants were more likely to identify the stop consonant correctly, and the *OR* for the interaction term, which is essentially 1, demonstrates that the rates of change for /b/ and /p/ trials were not significantly different. The *SD*s for the random effects suggest that there was more variability across participants than across trials.

This model is useful, but what if we wanted to estimate the overall likelihood of responding correctly, considering both /b/ and /p/ trials? We can do that by contrast-coding the Target Sound variable. Contrast-coding means assigning numeric values whose sum is 0 to the levels of the factor. In

58 Researching Speech Perception

this case, we can assign a value of –0.50 to /b/ and a value of 0.50 to /p/ (Linck & Cunnings, 2015). We can do this by creating a new variable in our dataframe using the ifelse() function.

```
data.stopid <- data.stopid %>%
mutate(sound.c = ifelse(sound == "b", -0.50, 0.50))
```

Briefly stated, this code takes the dataframe and adds a new variable, "sound.c," by referencing the original variable. If that variable is "b," it assigns a value of –0.50, and if it is anything else (i.e., "p" in this case), it assigns a value of 0.50. Now we can refit the model. The estimates for the intercept and effect of Session will change because we have changed the coding of Target Sound, but the other estimates will not change. In the updated model, given in Table 2.12, we can see that the *OR* for the intercept has decreased substantially. The intercept now represents the average likelihood of responding correctly at the outset of the study, considering both /b/ and /p/ trials. The estimate for Session has not changed much at all because in the original model there was virtually no difference in the rate of change for /b/ and /p/.

Lastly, we should report marginal and conditional R^2. Marginal R^2 represents the amount of variance explained by the fixed effects. For our model, marginal $R^2 = 0.282$, which means that the fixed effects explain approximately 28% of the variance in identification accuracy. Conditional R^2 represents the variance explained by the complete model, including both fixed and random effects. In our model, conditional $R^2 = 0.396$. Both should be reported, but most of the time, we're more interested in marginal R^2. At this point, we could integrate and test additional random effects, such as

TABLE 2.12 Summary of Logistic Mixed-Effects Model Fit to the Stop Identification Data: Contrast-Coded Target Sound

Fixed effects	OR	SE	z	95% CI	p
Intercept	5.72	1.07	9.32	[3.96, 8.25]	<0.001
Session	1.33	0.07	5.42	[1.20, 1.48]	0.002
Target Sound	0.10	0.03	–8.98	[0.06, 0.16]	<0.001
Session × Target Sound	0.99	0.10	–0.10	[0.80, 1.22]	0.923

Random effects	SD				
Speakers					
Intercepts	0.73				
Trials					
Intercepts	0.30				

Note. Target Sound has been contrast-coded: /b/ = –0.50 and /p/ = 0.50.

by-participant random slopes for Session and Target Sound. To avoid overwhelming you with details at this stage, I will save this information for the next chapter, but interested readers can refer to the R code for an example of fitting random slopes to these data.

Example 2: Vowel Perception over Time

Description of the Hypothetical Study and Simulated Data

For this example, we're going to assume that we assessed 30 L2 English speakers' vowel identification accuracy over their first year of immersion in an L2 environment. This example is based on Munro and Derwing (2008), who examined L2 English speakers' production accuracy over a yearlong window. Following their study, we'll assume that we have six data points, equally spaced at two month intervals. We're interested in participants' perception of two especially challenging L2 English vowel contrasts: /i/-/ɪ/ and /æ/-/ɛ/ (which I'll refer to as "beat-bit" and "bat-bet"). We'll assume that we included 10 items for each target vowel for a total of 40 items, which participants identified at each session. For now, we'll assume we have no missing data (I cover missing data in the next chapter), which means that we have a data set consisting of 7,200 observations: 30 participants × 6 sessions × 4 vowel targets × 10 items (or trials) per vowel.

We have two analytical options for our vowel targets: (1) analyze the identification accuracy of individual vowels, in which case, we do not need to manipulate the data structure at all or (2) analyze identification accuracy by vowel contrast, in which case, we need to generate a new variable that indexes the contrast to which each vowel belongs. In option (1) Vowel would be a factor with four levels, whereas in option (2) Contrast would be a factor with two levels. Neither choice is objectively right or wrong. Rather, the use of one approach or the other depends on our research objectives. For this analysis, we're interested in comparing identification accuracy by contrast. Put another way, we want to examine how participants' identification of /i/-/ɪ/ changes compared to their identification of /æ/-/ɛ/, perhaps because we have a hypothesis that one of those contrasts might develop more rapidly than the other. Following this conceptualization, we can summarize the data structure as: 30 participants × 6 sessions × 2 contrasts × 2 vowels × 10 trials.

Our independent, or predictor, variables in this data set are:

- Session, which we can treat as a continuous variable because the intervals are equally spaced at two-month intervals. This variable tests whether there is a relationship between Session and identification accuracy, that is, if participants' identification accuracy improved over time.

60 Researching Speech Perception

- Contrast, a categorical variable with two levels that indexes the two contrasts we are interested in examining: /i/-/ɪ/ and /æ/-/ɛ/. In the data set, we will refer to these contrasts as "beat-bit" and "bat-bet" to avoid using phonetic symbols and special characters.
- Session × Contrast, an interaction term. This variable tests if the rate of change in identification accuracy differs as a function of target contrast.

Our dependent, or outcome, variable is identification accuracy, which is a binary measure (0/1) referring to whether the participant selected the correct response on the identification task.

Preliminary Steps

As before, we begin by generating descriptive statistics and preliminary descriptive plots to examine how identification accuracy changes over time. Here I focus on analyzing by contrast, but interested readers can also follow a similar procedure to analyze by vowel. As shown in both Table 2.13 and Figure 2.2, participants were far more accurate in their identification of the beat-bit contrast than they were in their identification of bat-bet. Identification of both contrasts improved over time, but bat-bet seems to have improved more, likely because there was more room for improvement in the first place.

The density plot and boxplot, both of which can be accessed in the R code, suggest that the variance in scores increased as session increased, especially for the bat-bet contrast. This means that homogeneity of variance may be a problem for the ANOVA.

Analyses: ANOVA and Mixed-Effects Model

For this example, for the sake of space, I present an abbreviated overview of the analysis. As expected, the ANOVA showed that the assumption of

TABLE 2.13 Descriptive Statistics for Mean Identification Accuracy Over Time by Contrast

	beat-bit	*bat-bet*
Session	*M (SD)*	*M (SD)*
0	0.71 (0.45)	0.55 (0.50)
1	0.76 (0.42)	0.61 (0.49)
2	0.80 (0.40)	0.63 (0.48)
3	0.81 (0.39)	0.68 (0.47)
4	0.82 (0.38)	0.71 (0.45)
5	0.84 (0.37)	0.73 (0.44)

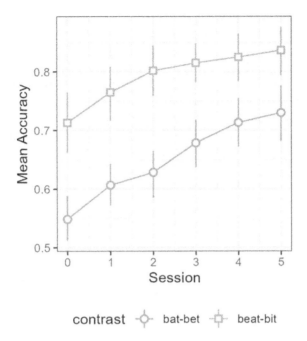

FIGURE 2.2 Mean Vowel Identification Accuracy Over Time.

sphericity was violated for Session ($p < 0.001$). The default in R is to apply a Greenhouse-Geisser correction, and as I mentioned before I agree with Larson-Hall that it's probably appropriate to apply that correction regardless of the outcome of the sphericity test. After applying the correction, the main effects of Session ($F(3, 96) = 16.69$, $p < 0.001$, $\eta^2_G = 0.122$) and Contrast ($F(1, 29) = 280.79$, $p < 0.001$, $\eta^2_G = 0.228$) are statistically significant and explain approximately 12% and 23% of the variance in accuracy, respectively. The interaction term, however, is not: $F(4, 120) = 1.43$, $p = 0.228$, $\eta^2_G = 0.007$. At this point, we could use the *emmeans* package (Lenth, 2023) to generate pairwise comparisons for Session, which would help us determine whether participants improved from one session to the next and how much they improved from the start of the study to the end. For the sake of space, I only report on the difference in performance between the first and last sessions for each contrast. To report on this procedure, we might say something like the following: "We used the *emmeans* package to generate a reference grid. Using this reference grid, we then specified two a priori comparisons to estimate the difference in performance on each contrast between the first and last data points. Both comparisons were statistically significant: for bat-bet, *estimate* = 0.182 (95% CI = [0.114, 0.249]), $SE = 0.033$,

$t = 5.52$, $p < 0.001$; for beat-bit, *estimate* $= 0.123$ (95% CI $= [0.066, 0.180]$), $SE = 0.030$, $t = 4.42$, $p < 0.001$. Participants made statistically significant gains in mean identification accuracy over the course of the study, and as the estimates demonstrate, gains were greater for bat-bet than for beat-bit."

The mixed-effects model looks remarkably similar to the model we fit for the stop identification data. We begin by fitting a model with fixed effects for Session, Contrast, and their interaction, and by-participant and by-trial random intercepts. In the code given below, the contrast.c fixed effect refers to a contrast-coded variable for Contrast (beat-bit $= -0.50$, bat-bet $= 0.50$).

```
vowelid.mem <- glmer(correct ~ session * contrast.c +
                        (1 | participant) +
                        (1 | trial),
                    data = data.vowelid, family = "binomial")
```

At this point, we could try fitting by-participant random slopes for Session and Contrast, and we could also try modeling by-trial random slopes. I tried fitting the by-participant random slopes in separate models (e.g., a model with by-participant random slopes for Session and another model with by-participant random slopes for Contrast), but neither model converged. This is somewhat surprising for the by-participant random slopes for Session because I simulated those, but it's not surprising for the random slopes for Contrast, which I didn't simulate. In short, then, the baseline model with random intercepts is the most appropriate model for this data set, or at least the best model that we can fit at this stage (we'll talk about how to deal with model convergence issues in a subsequent chapter). This model is reported in Table 2.14.

TABLE 2.14 Summary of Logistic Mixed-Effects Model Fit to the Vowel Identification Data

Fixed effects	OR	SE	z	95% CI	p
Intercept	2.13	0.33	4.89	$[1.57, 2.89]$	<0.001
Session	1.19	0.02	10.01	$[1.15, 1.23]$	<0.001
Contrast	0.36	0.10	-3.77	$[0.21, 0.61]$	<0.001
Session × Contrast	1.10	0.03	0.17	$[0.94, 1.08]$	0.867

Random effects	SD				
Speakers					
Intercepts	0.41				
Trials					
Intercepts	0.79				

Note. Contrast has been contrast-coded: beat-bit = −0.50 and bat-bet = 0.50.

This model largely aligns with the results of the ANOVA. Overall, the fact that the *OR* for the intercept is significant and above 1 shows that participants were more likely to respond correctly than incorrectly, considering both beat-bit and bat-bet trials. Likewise, the estimate for Session shows that they were more likely to respond correctly over time. And the contrast-coded Contrast variable demonstrates that participants were more likely to respond correctly on beat-bit trials than on bat-bet trials. Interpreting contrast-coded effects with logistic models that return ORs can be challenging, so I recommend recovering the estimates using *emmeans*. The interaction term was not significant, which suggests similar rates of change on each contrast.

Summary and Recommendations

In this chapter, we have examined approaches to studying baseline speech perception. We have discussed the two broad types of perception tasks that researchers typically use: discrimination and identification (as well as labeling, which I conceptualize as a variant of an identification task). We have also discussed the decisions researchers must make when designing the task, including the type of stimuli, number of talkers that produce them, and counterbalancing and randomization. Perception data always yield binary trial-level responses, which means that the distribution of perception data is binomial. To analyze these data using ANOVA, data must be pooled over trials to create participant-level averages, ignoring variance in items/trials. For this reason, the mixed-effects modeling approach is advantageous insofar as a binomial mixed-effects regression model can be fit to the trial-level data. Below is a summary of recommendations for conducting research in this area.

- Include both discrimination and identification tasks to tap into different aspects of speech perception learning and consider collecting both accuracy and reaction time data to provide complementary insights into processing ability and processing efficiency.
- Include multiple stimuli (at least 10) per target item or contrast or have participants respond to the same stimuli multiple times to ensure sufficient statistical power for estimating by-participant and by-item effects.
- Include multiple talkers and ensure that the anchor and target stimuli presented on discrimination task trials are produced by different talkers (e.g., A and X are produced by different talkers, A and B are produced by the same talker and X by a different talker).
- Carefully consider the characteristics of the target stimuli with respect to their generalizability.

64 Researching Speech Perception

- Use mixed-effects models to simultaneously estimate participant and item-/trial-level effects. Mixed-effects models also allow for the quantification of individual differences in baseline performance and learning (rate of change) via random effects.
- Aim for transparency: Explain all design decisions and acknowledge limitations. Make materials, data, and analysis code publicly available whenever possible.

Chapter Questions

1. How does L1 perceptual attunement create challenges for L2 perception?
2. Why are crosslinguistic assimilation patterns important? What do theoretical models say about them?
3. Think of a language pair that you're familiar with (e.g., English-Spanish, English-Korean, Spanish-Korean). Come up with a target contrast in that language that is likely to be difficult for nonnative listeners, and explain why it is likely to be difficult. Then, come up with a research question based on that contrast and describe the methods you could use to answer that question.
4. Based on your response to 3, come up with a perception task and a stimulus creation grid that you could use to generate stimuli for the task. You may want to use the perception task design worksheet given in Table 2.6.
5. Re-analyze the vowel identification data by vowel, that is, treating vowel as a factor with four levels. Compare the results of the analysis to the results of the analysis by contrast.

References

Baayen, H. R., & Milin, P. (2010). Analyzing reaction times. *International Journal of Psychological Research*, *3*(2), 12–28. https://doi.org/10.21500/20112084.807

Best, C. T., & Tyler, M. D. (2007). Nonnative and second-language speech perception: Commonalities and complementarities. In M. J. Munro & O.-S. Bohn (Eds.), *Second language speech learning: The role of language experience in speech perception and production* (pp. 13–24). John Benjamins.

Chang, C. B. (2019). The phonetics of second language learning and bilingualism. In W. E. Katz & P. F. Assmann (Eds.), *The Routledge handbook of phonetics* (pp. 427–447). Routledge.

Chládková, K., & Paillereau, N. (2020). The what and when of universal perception: A review of early speech sound acquisition. *Language Learning*, *70*(4), 1136–1182. https://doi.org/10.1111/lang.12422

Darcy, I., Dekydtspotter, L., Sprouse, R. A., Glover, J., Kaden, C., McGuire, M., & Scott, J. H. (2012). Direct mapping of acoustics to phonology: On the lexical encoding of front rounded vowels in L1 English– L2 French acquisition. *Second Language Research, 28*(1), 5–40. https://doi.org/10.1177/0267658311423455

Darcy, I., & Krüger, F. (2012). Vowel perception and production in Turkish children acquiring L2 German. *Journal of Phonetics, 40*(4), 568–581. https://doi.org/10.1016/j.wocn.2012.05.001

Dmitrieva, O., Chiara, C., de Leeuw, E., & Kartushina, N. (2022). Native speech perception in the context of multilingualism and language learning [Special issue]. *Languages.* https://www.mdpi.com/journal/languages/special_issues/native_speech_perception

Duñabeitia, J. A., Baciero, A., Antoniou, K., Antoniou, M., Ataman, E., Baus, C., Ben-Shachar, M., Çağlar, O. C., Chromý, J., Comesaña, M., Filip, M., Đurđević, D. F., Dowens, M. G., Hatzidaki, A., Januška, J., Jusoh, Z., Kanj, R., Kim, S. Y., Kırkıcı, B., ... Pliatsikas, C. (2022). The multilingual picture database. *Scientific Data, 9*(1), 431. https://doi.org/10.1038/s41597-022-01552-7

Escudero, P., & Boersma, P. (2004). Bridging the gap between L2 speech perception research and phonological theory. *Studies in Second Language Acquisition, 26*(4), 551–585. https://doi.org/10.1017/s0272263104040021

Flege, J. E. (1995). Second language speech learning: Theory, findings, problems. In W. Strange (Ed.), *Speech perception and linguistic experience: Issues in cross-language research* (pp. 233–277). York Press.

Flege, J. E. (2003). A method for assessing the perception of vowels in a second language. In E. Fava & A. Mioni (Eds.), *Issues in clinical linguistics* (pp. 19–42). Unipress.

Flege, J. E., & Bohn, O.-S. (2021). The revised speech learning model. In R. Wayland (Ed.), *Second language speech learning: Theoretical and empirical progress* (pp. 3–83). Cambridge University Press.

Flege, J. E., & Eefting, W. (1987). Production and perception of English stops by native Spanish speakers. *Journal of Phonetics, 15*, 67–83. https://doi.org/10.1016/S0095-4470(19)30538-8

Holliday, J. J. (2019). The perception and production of word-initial Korean stops by native speakers of Japanese. *Language and Speech, 62*(3), 494–508. https://doi.org/10.1177/0023830918785649

Judd, C. M., Westfall, J., & Kenny, D. A. (2012). Treating stimuli as a random factor in social psychology: a new and comprehensive solution to a pervasive but largely ignored problem. *Journal of Personality and Social Psychology, 103*(1), 54–69. https://doi.org/10.1037/a0028347

Kim, D., Clayards, M., & Goad, H. (2018). A longitudinal study of individual differences in the acquisition of new vowel contrasts. *Journal of Phonetics, 67*, 1–20. https://doi.org/10.1016/j.wocn.2017.11.003

Krautz, A. E., & Keuleers, E. (2022). LinguaPix database: A megastudy of picture-naming norms. *Behavioral Research Methods, 54*(2), 941–954. https://doi.org/10.3758/s13428-021-01651-0

Kuhl, P. K. (1991). Human adults and human infants show a "perceptual magnet effect" for the prototypes of speech categories, monkeys do not. *Attention, Perception, & Psychophysics, 50*(2), 93–107. https://doi.org/10.3758/bf03212211

Kuhl, P. K., Conboy, B. T., Coffey-Corina, S., Padden, D., Rivera-Gaxiola, M., & Nelson, T. (2008). Phonetic learning as a pathway to language: new data and native language magnet theory expanded (NLM-e). *Philosophical Transactions of the Royal Society B Biological Sciences*, *363*(1493), 979–1000. https://doi. org/10.1098/rstb.2007.2154

Larson-Hall, J. (2016). *A guide to doing statistics in second language research using SPSS and R*. Routledge.

Lenth, R. (2023). _emmeans: Estimated Marginal Means, aka Least-Squares Means_. R package version 1.8.4-1, <https://CRAN.R-project.org/package=emmeans>.

Linck, J. A., & Cunnings, I. (2015). The utility and application of mixed-effects models in second language research. *Language Learning*, *65*(S1), 185–207. https://doi.org/10.1111/lang.12117

Lisker, L., & Abramson, A. S. (1964). A cross-language study of voicing in initial stops: Acoustical measurements. *Word*, *20*(3), 384–422. https://doi.org/10.10 80/00437956.1964.11659830

Lüdecke, D. (2022). _sjPlot: Data Visualization for Statistics in Social Science_. R package version 2.8.11, <https://CRAN.R-project.org/package=sjPlot>.

Luke, S. G. (2017). Evaluating significance in linear mixed-effects models in R. *Behavioral Research Methods*, *49*(4), 1494–1502. https://doi.org/10.3758/ s13428-016-0809-y

MacKay, I. R., Meador, D., & Flege, J. E. (2001). The identification of English consonants by native speakers of Italian. *Phonetica*, *58*(1–2), 103–125. https:// doi.org/10.1159/000028490

MacKay, I. R. A., Meador, D., & Flege, J. E. (1997). Nonnatives' identification of English consonants in noise. *Journal of the Acoustical Society of America*, *101*(5). https://doi.org/10.1121/1.418944

Macmillan, N. A., & Creelman, C. D. (2005). *Detection Theory: A User's Guide* (2nd ed.). Lawrence Erlbaum Associates.

Munro, M. J., & Derwing, T. M. (2008). Segmental acquisition in adult ESL learners: A longitudinal study of vowel production. *Language Learning*, *58*(3), 479–502. https://doi.org/10.1111/j.1467-9922.2008.00448.x

Nagle, C. L., & Baese-Berk, M. M. (2022). Advancing the state of the art in L2 speech perception-production research: Revisiting theoretical assumptions and methodological practices. *Studies in Second Language Acquisition*, *44*(2), 580–605. https://doi.org/10.1017/s0272263121000371

Saito, K., Cui, H., Suzukida, Y., Dardon, D. E., Suzuki, Y., Jeong, H., Révész, A., Sugiura, M., & Tierney, A. (2022). Does domain-general auditory processing uniquely explain the outcomes of second language speech acquisition, even once cognitive and demographic variables are accounted for? *Bilingualism: Language and Cognition*, *25*(5), 856–868. https://doi.org/10.1017/ s1366728922000153

Schertz, J., Cho, T., Lotto, A., & Warner, N. (2015). Individual differences in phonetic cue use in production and perception of a nonnative sound contrast. *Journal of Phonetics*, *52*, 183–204. https://doi.org/10.1016/j.wocn.2015.07.003

Singmann, H., Bolker, B., Westfall, J., Aust, F., & Ben-Shachar, M. (2023). _afex: Analysis of Factorial Experiments. R package version 1.2-1, <https://CRAN.R-project.org/package=afex>.

Strange, W. (2011). Automatic selective perception (ASP) of first and second language speech: A working model. *Journal of Phonetics*, *39*(4), 456–466. https:// doi.org/10.1016/j.wocn.2010.09.001

Sun, H., Saito, K., & Tierney, A. (2021). A longitudinal investigation of explicit and implicit auditory processing in 12 segmental and suprasegmental acquisition. *Studies in Second Language Acquisition*, *43*(3), 551–573. https://doi.org/10.1017/s0272263120000649

Székely, A., D'Amico, S., Devescovi, A., Federmeier, K., Herron, D., Iyer, G., Jacobsen, T., & Bates, E. (2003). Timed picture naming: Extended norms and validation against previous studies. *Behavior Research Methods, Instruments, & Computers*, *35*(4), 621–633. https://doi.org/10.3758/BF03195542

Trubetzkoy, N. S. (1969). *Principles of Phonology* (C. Baltaxe, Trans.). University of California Press. (Original work published 1939).

Werker, J. F., & Tees, R. C. (1984). Phonemic and phonetic factors in adult cross-language speech perception. *Journal of the Acoustical Society of America*, *75*(6), 1866–1878. https://doi.org/10.1121/1.390988

3

RESEARCHING THE PRODUCTION OF SPECIFIC FEATURES

Introduction

Unlike other aspects of linguistic competence, pronunciation has a physical, or motor, component. Once the speaker can successfully distinguish between L2 sounds, they need to learn how to produce those sounds. Production can be conceptualized and measured in a variety of ways, from the production of specific segmental and suprasegmental features, such as individual vowels and consonants, word stress, and intonation, to global, listener-based dimensions of speech, such as comprehensibility and accentedness (Saito & Plonsky, 2019). In this chapter, I address the production of specific features. I discuss the production of global features in Chapter 5.

L2 speech production research has been shaped by two strands of work, one more theoretical and another more applied. Early theoretical research had a strong focus on examining the variables that were associated with phonetic nativelikeness. Studies carried out during the 1980s and 1990s sampled speech from individuals who had begun learning the L2 at a range of ages, from very early childhood to late adolescence and beyond, often using highly controlled production tasks such as reading to determine at what age nativelike pronunciation was no longer possible (e.g., Flege et al., 1999). At the time, there was intense interest in age effects in language learning, particularly the notion that a neurobiological critical period might exist for language acquisition (Lenneberg, 1967). To be clear, there was no question about the importance of age. What was at issue was whether nativelike behavior, defined in relation to monolingual comparison groups, was possible after a certain age and whether the relationship between age and attainment

DOI: 10.4324/9781003279266-3

showed an abrupt cut-off or a gradual decline (see, e.g., Long, 1990; for a more recent overview, see Birdsong, 2018). It's worth mentioning that in the most comprehensive and methodologically rigorous study to date, Abrahamsson and Hyltenstam (2009) showed that virtually no L2 Swedish learners, including early learners, performed like Swedish monolinguals (see also Stölten et al., 2015). In the intervening years, researchers have called into question the usefulness of monolingual comparison groups (Andringa, 2014), and pronunciation researchers have advocated for a shift away from such groups (Sakai, 2018).

In conjunction with the age of onset research that was popular at the time, studies also set out to understand how experiential variables such as quantity and quality of L1 and L2 use affected nativelikeness. Nearly all work had a cross-sectional design, where individuals representing a continuum of age of acquisition and amount of L2 use were recruited. Correlation and regression were used to quantify the strength of association between these variables, listener-assessed foreign accent, and acoustic-phonetic outcome measures. Between-group comparisons were also carried out by sorting individuals into age of acquisition (e.g., 0–3, 3–6, 6–9) and language use (low and high) bins. Results showed that individuals with an earlier age of onset, higher amount of L2 use, and lower amount of L1 use tended to have more nativelike pronunciation in the L2, but these general patterns masked considerable individual variability in outcomes. Notably, some learners with a very young age of onset produced L2 sounds whose phonetic properties deviated from monolingual norms, and some later learners produced sounds that were comparable to those produced by monolingual L1 speakers. On the whole, this body of work has provided rich insight into how the L1 and L2 interact, underscoring the interconnectivity of bilingual phonological systems. It also laid the basis for the Speech Learning Model (Flege, 1995; Flege & Bohn, 2021), which has been one of the most influential models of L2 sound learning. At the same time, L2 speakers often produce accented speech that is perfectly intelligible and highly comprehensible (Munro & Derwing, 1995), which means that the nonnativelike realization of specific sounds does not always cause communication problems.

A second strand of applied research has therefore taken an intelligibility-based approach to the production of the sounds and prosody of the L2. The basic goal of research in this area is to understand what types of pronunciation issues are likely to affect the intelligibility and comprehensibility of L2 speech. While few learners will produce phonetically nativelike speech, all learners can achieve intelligibility and comprehensibility, and in some cases, they may come to produce intelligible L2 sounds automatically, without the need for targeted pronunciation instruction. In other words, some pronunciation structures may develop on their own, as learners gain experience and have opportunities to interact in the L2. In that case, instructional time can be allocated to the features that either do not improve on their own much at all or do not improve to such an extent that production is intelligible. As Derwing stated in her discussion of goals for pronunciation teaching, "Wouldn't it be helpful to have some longitudinal studies to know which aspects of pronunciation will likely take care of themselves over time? Such information would allow teachers to focus on intransigent problems" (2010, p. 27). It should come as no surprise, then, that a growing body of longitudinal pronunciation research has attempted to shed light on this topic (for a synthesis of longitudinal studies, see Nagle, 2021a).

Derwing, Munro, and colleagues studied native Mandarin and Slavic language speakers who had immigrated to Canada, measuring various aspects of their production over a seven-year period and reporting their findings in several publications. In terms of vowel production, learners' vowel intelligibility improved approximately 10% over the first year, with most gains concentrated during the first six months of immersion (Munro & Derwing, 2008). Crucially, speaking to Derwing's point about certain pronunciation features "taking care of themselves," some vowels were very intelligible from the outset of the study (/i/ and /oʊ/), and others improved significantly, reaching a relatively high level of intelligibility by the end of the first year (/eɪ/ and /ʌ/). However, some vowels that improved significantly did not reach a comparably high level of intelligibility (/ɪ/ did not pass 50% identification accuracy for either group), and others that were intermediate in terms of their initial intelligibility did not improve at all (/ɛ/, /ʊ/, and /ɑ/). In another study, Munro, Derwing, and Thomson (2015) examined learners' consonantal production over a two-year period. In addition to tracing trajectories for word-initial and word-final singleton consonants and consonant clusters over time, the authors also evaluated the specific sounds and clusters that surpassed a 90% intelligibility threshold. Results were highly variable, leading the authors to question whether it would be advisable (or even possible) to create a common pronunciation syllabus for the two groups (Munro, 2021). Despite the clear need for individualization, findings suggested a few common problem areas: word-final /ld/ and /nd/ and word-initial /θ/ and /ð/. From these studies, it's easy to see why longitudinal research is so valuable. First, it reveals which structures would be ideal candidates for intervention (e.g., because they don't improve or improve relatively little). Longitudinal research also sheds light on issues of timing. For instance, certain structures could be trained from the start, whereas others that develop naturally, as a result of L2 exposure and use, could be trained later, once their development stabilizes and assuming the production of those features continues to show a low level of intelligibility.

Target Structures

One of the first issues that researchers face is selecting a good target structure. There are a few criteria that we can use. First, it is important to have a solid understanding of the problems that L2 learners face when producing the target feature. As discussed in the previous chapter, in some cases, learners might not notice a difference between the way the feature is produced in the L1 and the way it is produced in the L2. In that case, they may produce the L2 structure following the phonetic grammar, or rules, of their L1, which minimally will result in accented speech but could also lead to intelligibility and comprehensibility problems. This is a perception problem. The speaker does not perceive a difference between the L1 and L2 sounds, and, as a result, they do not produce a difference. In some cases, the L1 and L2 have the same number of phonological categories, but the phonetic implementation of those categories differs. English and Spanish stop consonants are a good example. Both languages contain phonologically voiced and voiceless stops (e.g., /b/ and /p/), but their phonetic implementation is different. In English, /b/ is typically realized as a voiceless unaspirated stop and /p/ is realized as a voiceless aspirated stop. In Spanish, on the other hand, /b/ is voiced and /p/ is a voiceless unaspirated stop. English and Spanish speakers are certainly aware of the fact that both languages contain voiced and voiceless stops, but they may not realize that the phonetic realization of those stops is different. That is, they may equate the phonological categories across both languages, leading Spanish speakers to produce English /p/ according to Spanish norms ([p]) and English speakers to produce Spanish /p/ according to English norms ([pʰ]). The same is true of the voiced stops: English speakers might produce Spanish /b/ as [p] and Spanish speakers English /b/ as [b]. Listeners are sensitive to the phonetic properties of stops when evaluating foreign accent (Major, 1987; Schoonmaker-Gates, 2015), but whether nonnativelike production affects intelligibility remains an open question. At least for English-speaking learners of Spanish, the answer seems to be no (Nagle et al., 2023). At issue is the fact that some phonetic deviations would certainly lead to intelligibility problems, whereas others might not. This highlights one of the core objectives that contemporary research on the production of specific features must achieve: understanding the relationship between acoustic/phonetic accuracy and intelligibility and comprehensibility (Nagle et al., 2023).

Stop consonants are a good target structure for another reason. Because they have been extensively researched, their acoustic properties are very well understood (Abramson & Whalen, 2017). Across many languages, voice onset time (VOT) is the primary phonetic cue to stop consonant voicing. VOT is a temporal measure that refers to the time that elapses between the onset of voicing and stop release (Lisker & Abramson, 1964). VOT is a continuous phonetic measure that is generally divided into three ranges: prevoiced stops, in which voicing begins prior to stop release and VOT is coded as a negative value, and short- and long-lag stops, in which voicing begins after stop release. Short-lag stops have VOT values between 0 and 30 ms, and long-lag stops have values above 30 ms, but these cut-off values are somewhat arbitrary. Acoustically, then, Spanish and English show the phonological-phonetic configuration displayed in Figure 3.1. In the figure, approximate crossover boundaries are indicated using a vertical black bar. As shown, the voicing boundary in English (i.e., when an English listener stops hearing /b/ and starts hearing /p/) occurs at approximately 30 ms VOT, whereas the boundary in Spanish occurs around 0 ms VOT. Thus, to produce phonologically accurate second language stops, Spanish speakers need to produce English /p/ with more aspiration than in Spanish, that is, with VOT values that exceed 30 ms, and English speakers need to produce Spanish /b/ with prevoicing, with VOT values below 0 ms. To produce phonetically accurate stops, English and Spanish speakers would need to align their VOT with the phonetic norms of the target language. English speakers who produce prevoiced stops in English could transfer their production into Spanish to produce phonologically accurate stops, but the precise phonetic characteristics of those stops may not match the phonetic norms of Spanish voicing, where voiced stops are produced with more prevoicing than in English. These types of configurations allow researchers to test the acquisition of phonological and phonetic detail in the target language, testing both the phonetic and phonological accuracy (i.e., intelligibility) with which L2 sounds are produced.

Sometimes, the L1 and L2 involve the same phonological and phonetic categories, but the precise phonetic characteristics of L2 segments differ. This is especially true of stop consonant VOT, where languages tend to select specific ranges within the modal categories given above (Cho et al., 2019). Language-specific VOT allows researchers to examine how the

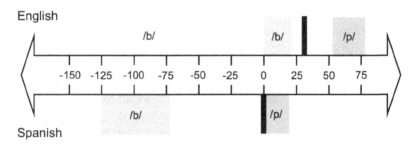

FIGURE 3.1 Schematic Representation of Stop Consonant Voicing Contrasts in English and Spanish.

degree of crosslinguistic similarity affects the acquisition of L2 sounds. A good example of this scenario is Japanese voiceless stops, which are phonetically aspirated but show a different amount of aspiration (i.e., VOT) than their English counterparts. English voiceless stops tend to have a slightly longer VOT than Japanese voiceless stops, which could make it especially difficult for learners to detect and produce those differences (Riney & Takagi, 1999).

L2 vowels are another frequently researched L2 segment. Like stops, the acoustic properties of vowels are well understood. Vowels can be defined in terms of spectral differences in the first formant (F1), which indexes height, or the position of the tongue in the vertical plane, and the second formant (F2), which indexes frontness, or the position of the tongue in the horizontal plane. Additional measures may be needed depending on the vowel contrast. For instance, the third formant (F3) is associated with rounding and can be measured for rounded versus unrounded vowels (e.g., French /y/). Researchers also take duration into account because speakers often use duration to mark phonological contrasts before they begin to make full use of spectral cues (F1 and F2). Vowels are an important target measure because they tend to have a high functional load. If speakers do not reliably distinguish between L2 vowel contrasts, such as the English /i/-/ɪ/ contrast in "beat" versus "bit," then they might experience significant intelligibility and comprehensibility issues.

Until now, we have discussed potential perceptual problems and the impact they might have on production. However, sometimes the problem is not perceptual at all, but rather articulatory. English-speaking learners of French perceive a difference between the French uvular fricative /ʁ/ or trill /ʀ/ and the English retroflex /ɹ/ articulation. Likewise, English-speaking learners of Spanish tend to hear a clear difference between the Spanish tap /ɾ/ and trill /r/ and the English /ɹ/. In other words, learners may equate the rhotic sounds at a phonological level, recognizing that the sounds have a similar function in each language, but they do not equate them at a phonetic level (Best & Tyler, 2007). However, learners may have trouble producing those sounds because of their complex articulation. Unlike stop consonants, which have a well-defined and, in many languages, unitary phonetic cue (VOT), liquid consonants such as rhotics are notoriously difficult to define in unambiguous acoustic terms. That is, in languages like Spanish, English, French and so on, where VOT is the phonetic cue to phonological stop consonant distinctions, researchers can quantify production on a continuous temporal scale, but for rhotics, like the Spanish tap and trill, there is no single, continuous acoustic measure along which English speakers' progression from retroflex /ɹ/ to Spanish /ɾ/ and /r/ can be quantified. Instead, researchers generally use categorical coding schemes that are based on the range of realizations evident in the data and the types of realizations that occur in native speech. Face (2006) used nine categories, Rose (2010) used seven, and Bongiovanni et al. (2015) used 12. Moreover, in all three studies, the authors studied tap and trill production in the intervocalic context, where categories can be most easily viewed and categorized, even though the tap and trill can occur word-initially, word-finally, and in a range of consonant clusters. This is not a criticism of the authors' research, but rather should be taken as evidence that the range of realizations would be different and possibly even more complex if production in different phonetic environments were taken into consideration. Once learners begin producing taps and trills, the duration of each segment and the number of occlusions for the trill can be quantified in a relatively straightforward manner, but until then, a combination of acoustic variables and categorical coding schemes may be necessary to capture all relevant aspects of production. For example, in their study on English speakers' production of French /ʁ/ in a range of environments, Colantoni and Steele (2007) took two phonetic measures—percentage of the token that was voiced and length—and sorted tokens into six categories. Ultrasound imaging studies that allow the researcher to track tongue position in real time could be particularly helpful for understanding how learners come to produce perceptually distinguishable yet articulatorily complex L2 sounds.

To this point, I have reviewed individual segments and contrasts that are difficult to produce due to perceptual assimilation and articulatory complexity. Researchers also investigate the acquisition of phonotactic constraints and phonological processes. Phonotactic constraints operate at the level of syllable structure and often involve a scenario where the L2 allows a wider range of syllable structures than the L1, especially with respect to consonant clusters. In Spanish, /s/-initial clusters are disallowed, whereas in English, many words begin with /sC/ (e.g., *school*, *spring*). One repair strategy that Spanish speakers adopt is /e/ epenthesis, whereby they produce /sC/ words with an initial /e/, which brings the word in line with Spanish syllable structure: *school* is realized as [es.kul], allowing the /sC/ cluster to be syllabified into two syllables rather than one. In one notable study, Abrahamsson (1999) tracked this process longitudinally in a Spanish-speaking learner of Swedish (Swedish, like English, allows /sC/ onsets). In this case, Abrahamsson's focus was not on analyzing the phonetic features of epenthetic /e/, but rather on documenting patterns of epenthesis in relation to the segments that made up the cluster.

Researchers are also interested in examining the acquisition of phonological patterns and alternations, which can provide insight into the environments in which variants are likely to emerge as well as whether this type of learning is categorical or gradient. Spanish voiced stops are a good

Researching the Production of Specific Features **75**

example of a complex phonological alternation that proves challenging for learners. In Spanish, phonologically voiced stops have stop and fricative or approximant allophones. According to traditional accounts, the stop allophone occurs after a pause or nasal (and for /d/, after /l/), whereas the fricative or approximant occurs in all other contexts. This description is, in fact, overly simplistic, given that empirical data show that speakers sometimes produce reduced variants after nasals and full stops in contexts where a fricative or approximant would be favored (Eddington, 2011). Researchers have examined English-speaking learners of Spanish to determine if they acquire this alternation and, if so, what factors condition the degree of weakening they produce. That is, researchers have used this feature to investigate whether learners acquire this pattern in a categorical fashion, treating all contexts as similar, or if they produce varying levels of lenition, which would suggest attunement to the characteristics of the input they receive (Shea & Curtin, 2011).

In summary, there are several concepts that underpin target structure selection. On the one hand, researchers may select a particular target structure because they are interested in understanding how L2 speakers produce it over time and if their production reaches an acceptable level of intelligibility in the absence of targeted instruction (Derwing, 2010). In this case, the target structure is known or hypothesized to have an important impact on the intelligibility and comprehensibility of L2 speech (e.g., L2 vowels). In other cases, the target structure is selected because of what it represents: a complex crosslinguistic mapping between the L2 sound and its L1 counterpart. Sometimes, researchers are interested in studying the production of individual sounds, whereas in others, they may be concerned with syllables or phonological processes. Thus, in thinking about target structures, it's important to consider what type of problem(s) L2 learners might face as well as the potential communicative outcome of inaccurate production (e.g., foreign accent vs. reduced intelligibility). Often this involves thinking about the number of phonological categories in the L1 and L2, their patterning, and their phonetic properties.

I have tried to synthesize this information in a flowchart with examples. The flowchart is not exhaustive, but it's illustrative of how you can think about some of the issues involved in selecting structures for production research. You should read Figure 3.2 from left to right, answering each question as you go. At the terminal ends on the right, I have given an example of an L1-L2 pairing and target structure that would be representative of each category. Again, these are but a few examples among many and represent some of the most frequently studied structures in production research. Further, although these examples pose challenges for L2 learners, there is tremendous variability even within highly similar learner groups,

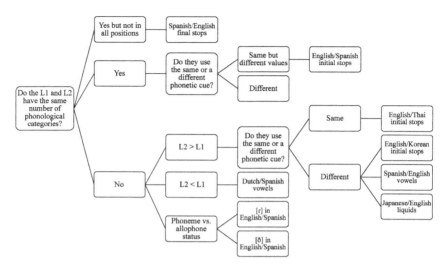

FIGURE 3.2 Flowchart of Crosslinguistic Considerations in Production Research with Examples.

which means that for some individuals these sounds may be especially challenging, whereas others may have no problem producing them whatsoever.

It's worth repeating that target structures are used to test something. They are rarely the object of study in and of themselves. Stop consonant contrasts have been frequently studied because they are typologically common (stops occur in all languages; Maddieson, 1984) and their acoustic properties are well understood. They have been used to test questions related to the timing and scope of crosslinguistic interaction in bilingual speech production (Amengual, 2012), the effect of visual feedback training for L2 pronunciation (Olson & Offerman, 2021), and the relationship between speech perception and speech production during second language learning (Casillas, 2020; Nagle, 2018, 2021b). Likewise, vowels have been used to test hypotheses concerning the role of L1 vowel category precision in L2 production (Kartushina & Frauenfelder, 2014), naturalistic/automatic pronunciation learning (Munro & Derwing, 2008), and the role of visual feedback training (Rehman, 2021). Certainly, there is a need to diversify target structures in pronunciation research—the research topics listed above can and should be tested with other structures to understand if there are any segment-specific findings versus findings that apply generally across most, if not all, target structures—but researchers should be clear about the goals of their work and select target structures based on those goals. To that point, it is often helpful to consider the novelty of the target structure, methods, and research questions. Stop consonants are not novel, but because they are well understood, novel methods can be applied to study them, and new research questions can be asked. The same is not necessarily true of a less frequently researched target structure. In that case, researching a novel structure that is not necessarily well understood in terms of its phonetic properties, the difficulties that learners tend to have, etc. with novel methods and/or new research questions could prove problematic. After all, innovation in one or two areas is genius, but innovation in all areas is madness. The research world tends to respond well to incremental change. A good example of this principle is Earle and Myers' (2014, 2015a, 2015b) research on the role sleep plays in helping individuals build new phonetic categories. Combining the science of sleep with second language sound training was novel, but they tested their hypotheses using standard methods with well-researched target structures.

Speech Production Tasks and Stimuli

Speech can be elicited using a variety of tasks, ranging from controlled production tasks such as word, sentence, and paragraph reading to spontaneous tasks such as picture narration. Speech can also be elicited in monologic and dialogic (i.e., interactive) contexts. The type of task used depends on the research questions and the type of analysis envisioned. One central concern in research on specific features is collecting enough tokens of the target feature for reliable analysis. Flege (1987) suggested a minimum of 5–10 tokens per target feature. It's important to remember that pronunciation research involves multiple, nested levels of structure: speakers complete tasks and, within these tasks, they produce tokens embedded in different utterances, words, and linguistic environments. Oftentimes, researchers are interested in examining variables at each level of structure. For instance, at the highest level, researchers want to characterize speaker behavior, describing the ways in which speakers, both individually and as a group, produce the target feature. Moving down the nesting hierarchy, they may also be interested in variation in production depending on the task. And at the lower levels of structure, they might be concerned with production in certain types of words (e.g., high vs. low frequency, familiar vs. unfamiliar, real vs. nonsense) or in particular linguistic environments (e.g., vowels produced after a stop vs. after a fricative, stops produced in word-initial vs. word-medial position). Considering these levels of structure/analysis, it's important to obtain a sufficiently representative speech sample. Indeed, this issue strikes at the very heart of the validity and generalizability of speech production research. If researchers do not collect enough tokens in the contexts of interest, then results may not be representative and generalizable. On the other hand, collecting too much data can lead to an excessively large data set that is costly to analyze in terms of both time and effort. I mention this point up front

78 Researching the Production of Specific Features

because thinking about how much data a study will generate for coding and analysis is useful for rightsizing your research.

Three types of tasks have been used in the specific feature literature: reading tasks, imitation tasks, and picture tasks. On reading tasks, the speaker is asked to read a word, sentence, or paragraph aloud. Such tasks are advantageous because they give the researcher complete control over the environments, both word-level and prosodic, in which the target feature occurs, and there is no ambiguity in what the speaker is being asked to produce. However, because reading tasks have an orthographic basis, they do not tap exclusively into pronunciation but rather test other related skills, such as knowledge of grapheme-to-phoneme mappings. This can be especially problematic in languages that have an opaque orthography, such as English or French. If participants don't produce the target feature accurately, it may not be due to pronunciation at all, but rather to an incomplete knowledge of sound-spelling relationships. If participants are high-proficiency, literate L2 users, then such issues may not present much of a confound, but care must be taken when using reading tasks with low-proficiency speakers. For such learner samples, reading tasks should be avoided unless the researcher can select high-frequency words that are likely to be familiar to participants, and, even then, the researcher should check to make sure that participants actually know the words they are being asked to produce.

Repetition, or imitation, tasks are commonly used in research on the initial stages of L2 pronunciation learning. On a repetition task, the participant hears a pronunciation model and is asked to repeat after that person, often after a short delay, which is introduced to ensure that the participant processes the auditory stimulus the model provided. In other words, introducing an interstimulus interval between presentation and repetition forces the participant to engage in phonological processing rather than relying on immediate repetition from auditory memory (for commentary, see Chapter 1), which could potentially bypass the phonological system altogether. As this description suggests, repetition tasks are hybrid, insofar as they engage both perception and production. As a result, it becomes difficult to isolate the source of production difficulties, which could be perceptual—the participant does not process the auditory stimulus accurately, leading to production problems—or articulatory, the participant processes the stimulus accurately but does not produce it accurately.

Picture naming and description tasks have the potential to avoid both orthographic and auditory confounds, providing unbiased information on participants' production of specific features. On a picture naming task, the participant sees an image and is asked to name the word it represents aloud. Although the participant is not exposed to orthography, some of the same issues with word frequency, familiarity, and, in this case, imageability apply.

Even if words are frequent, familiar, and imageable, researchers should not expect participants to name every word. Picture naming, when implemented using images representing a single word, is a controlled task, but picture description can also be used to elicit the production of specific features under more spontaneous conditions. Saito and colleagues (e.g., Saito & van Poeteren, 2017) have used a timed picture description task across a series of studies for that purpose. On their version of the task, the participant receives a set of target words first and then an image and is asked to describe the image using the target words, which are no longer available and are not printed on the image itself. The task is time-controlled, so participants have a limited window to produce a response. This task is advantageous because it taps into a more spontaneous production mode, where the L2 speaker must simultaneously manage pronunciation, grammar, and vocabulary when describing each image. Thus, such a task elicits production under more realistic speaking conditions. At the same time, the inclusion of orthography, which in this case is necessary to ensure that participants produce the target feature, may muddy the water. Yet, no task is without limitations, which is why researchers often include multiple production tasks to get a comprehensive and accurate picture of L2 speakers' production. As Saito and Plonsky (2019) suggested, one of the key questions in contemporary L2 pronunciation research is understanding how L2 speakers move from declarative pronunciation knowledge to the automatized use of L2 features in spontaneous speech. As a result, including several tasks along the controlled-spontaneous continuum can enhance that line of work.

Collecting, Coding, and Analyzing Production Data

Collecting the Data

Once you design the task, you need to collect and code the data. To get good production data, it's important to keep a few things in mind. First, participants should be recorded in a quiet, sound-attenuated space using a high-quality microphone (e.g., Shure). For acoustic analysis, it's particularly important that there is little ambient noise. Vents, power systems, and even devices such as computers can produce a surprising amount of noise, noise that we no longer notice because we have grown accustomed to it but that appears nonetheless in the acoustic signal. Before you pick a space for data collection, make a few test recordings, including recording at different times of the day if the space is in a moderate-to-high traffic area where people may be talking, doors may be closing, etc. You should also expect to calibrate the microphone with most, if not all speakers. Participants naturally vary in terms of how loudly they speak, so taking a minute to adjust the

80 Researching the Production of Specific Features

microphone input, test the microphone with the participant, and inspect the quality of the recording is beneficial.

There are many ways to collect production data, ranging from the presentation of stimuli in PowerPoint slides to experiment management software such as PsychoPy or Gorilla. In the past, it was common to record entire tasks by starting the recording at the beginning of the task and ending the recording at the end of the task. This would still be the case for data collection using PowerPoint. However, experiment management software has advanced and will continue to do so, and with some platforms and software, it's possible to create a workflow where individual audio files are captured and saved. This is advantageous because it drastically reduces processing time if each target is saved to a separate file. Another important point about production tasks is pacing. Sometimes, a self-paced task is sensible, but in many cases, if participants control the pace of the task, they may click to advance while they are producing the target word or otherwise move around the recording space, generating clicks and other forms of noise that can compromise recording quality. As a result, I recommend creating a task that automatically advances on a timer, such as four seconds after the presentation of the target word or image. The length of the timer depends on what the participant is asked to do and should also be piloted to ensure a comfortable pace. Finally, don't discount paper-and-pencil style data collection. For instance, if you have to travel to participants, you may be able to take a laptop and microphone, but that may not always be possible. Notecards and handheld recorders can also be used for data collection, and in that case, the researcher would manage the notecards for participants, displaying them one at a time to control the pace of the task.

Coding and Analyzing the Data

Production data for specific features can be coded and analyzed in several ways depending on the goals of the research. On the applied side, researchers are interested in issues of intelligibility, that is, whether the listener perceives what the speaker intended to produce, irrespective of phonetic accuracy. There is not a straightforward, linear relationship between phonetic/acoustic accuracy and intelligibility. L2 speakers may produce intelligible L2 contrasts using different cues than native speakers (e.g., duration to distinguish between English short-lax vowels when native English speakers produce robust spectral differences). Thus, nonnativelike production does not necessarily equate to a lack of intelligibility, which is why researchers have advocated for using listener-based measures and combining them with other scoring/evaluation schemes (Saito & Plonsky, 2019). Intelligibility has been measured using transcription and alternative forced-choice tasks.

On a transcription task, the word is played for the listener, and the listener is asked to transcribe exactly what they hear. Typically, researchers want to elicit listeners' first impression of the speech they are evaluating, that is, what listeners initially perceive without allocating additional processing effort, so on a transcription task involving words or short utterances, only one play-back of the target stimulus is allowed. On an alternative forced-choice task, the word is played, and the listener is asked to select what they hear from two or more options. These options may be minimal pairs, words illustrating different categories (e.g., the vowels in *heed*, *hid*), or International Phonetic Alphabet (IPA) symbols, depending on the expertise of the listener. These options are usually presented orthographically. In some cases, an "unsure" option may be included. L2 tokens may be ambiguous, falling between two categories, so including an "unsure" response option prevents guessing and affords the researcher the opportunity to analyze those responses as a sepa-rate category or to treat them as instances of unintelligibility.

On the other end of the spectrum, acoustic analysis can reveal informa-tion about the precise phonetic characteristics of specific features. Acous-tic analysis provides insight into phonetic accuracy and issues of (foreign) accent. Acoustic analysis is also useful because L2 speakers may produce a distinction that listeners do not (yet) perceive, a distinction that would therefore not be captured using listener-based judgments alone. Acoustic analyses are carried out using software such as Praat. A full discussion of such techniques is beyond the scope of this volume, but there are several excellent resources on the topic that readers can consult (Baart, 2009; Col-antoni et al., 2015; Johnson, 2011; see Baart for a concise introduction to acoustic analysis, Johnson for a more advanced and in-depth treatment, and Colantoni et al. for application to L2 topics). Nevertheless, a few aspects of acoustic analysis deserve commentary here. First, such analyses are generally considered objective, but even with acoustic analysis, the researcher must make decisions about what to analyze and how it should be quantified (i.e., where to place the cursor, create boundaries), and these decisions affect results. Therefore, for the sake of replication and transparency, whenever acoustic measures are used, researchers should provide a detailed descrip-tion of how they annotated the speech file, including the visual and auditory cues they used to segment speech. That description should include several figures—which can be included as appendices if space and formatting are an issue—of the waveform, spectrogram, and accompanying TextGrid. Speech files, TextGrids, and segmentation notes should be made publicly available to other researchers. If forced alignment, automatic measurement software, and Praat scripts are used during the annotation and extraction process, that information should also be comprehensively described. Researchers should also provide insight into how they dealt with ambiguous and/or anomalous

82 Researching the Production of Specific Features

stimuli, as well as a summary of the proportion of tokens that were produced in an unanticipated way. In short, researchers should be able to replicate the acoustic analysis procedures described in published research reports.

Until this point, researchers have typically focused on defining accuracy either through listener-based intelligibility judgments or acoustic analysis. Yet, these two analyses can provide complementary perspectives on production accuracy and should be combined when feasible and relevant to the research questions. Even if there is little reason to believe speakers have any intelligibility problems, as may be the case for many highly proficient L2 users, collecting intelligibility data can still provide an important baseline against which phonetic accuracy measures can be interpreted. Those measures can also be coordinated to understand the relationship between phonetic cues and intelligibility. For example, Saito and van Poeteren (2017) found that F2 and duration explained approximately 50% of the variance in Japanese speakers' production of intelligible English /ɹ/. In contrast, F3, the primary cue to the /l/-/ɹ/ contrast in native English speech, was predominantly associated with phonetic accuracy, not intelligibility. These findings reinforce the view that speakers can make themselves intelligible using a range of phonetic cues, including cues that may not be the most robust or reliable predictors of contrast in native speech.

Acoustic measurements also prove especially useful for examining subtle degrees of crosslinguistic phonetic influence and attainment in very advanced L2 users. These subtle differences in production are often imperceptible to listeners yet easily detectable at an acoustic level. Stölten et al. (2014) used VOT measurements to examine ultimate attainment in Spanish-Swedish bilinguals, all of whom passed as native speakers of Swedish. Despite passing as native speakers, nearly 30% of early L2 learners and 50% of late L2 learners did not produce Swedish voiceless stops with nativelike VOT, which points to persistent age effects even in early-onset L2 learning.

Statistical Analysis

Like perception research, production research generates complex data sets that are not easily, appropriately, and comprehensively analyzed using traditional techniques such as analysis of variance (ANOVA). For instance, Munro and Derwing (2008) examined Mandarin and Slavic language speakers' vowel production over a yearlong period. In their study, speakers produced English vowel categories in /p_t/ and /b_t/ contexts, and vowel intelligibility was evaluated by groups of trained and untrained listeners. Their study included 24 Mandarin speakers and 20 Slavic language speakers, ten English vowels, and two phonological environments (i.e., vowels produced after voiced and voiceless stops). Productions were evaluated by four trained listeners and 13 untrained listeners. If we map their data onto a visualization, we end up with something similar to Figure 3.3. In this visualization, I have shown all levels of data structure. For the sake of space, I haven't shown all levels of all variables (e.g., I only included the trained listener group; to represent the data structure completely, we would need to duplicate the entire figure for untrained listeners). Predictor variables (fixed effects) are shown in boldface, and sampling units (random effects) are shown in italics. In the original study, speakers produced one token per vowel per target context. However, the Tokens tier is shown here to illustrate the fact that in many designs multiple tokens are elicited per vowel and target context.

The best way to handle this type of hierarchical data with multiple sampling units such as listeners and speakers is with mixed-effects models. A mixed-effects model is a powerful form of regression that allows the researcher to assess relationships between fixed effects (independent variables) and an outcome measure (dependent variable) while accounting for random effects. As a reminder, fixed effects are "fixed" because their levels are known or fixed and their interpretation or meaning does not change from one study to the next. "L1 Slavic language speakers" in Munro and Derwing (2008) means the same thing as "L1 Slavic language speakers" in another

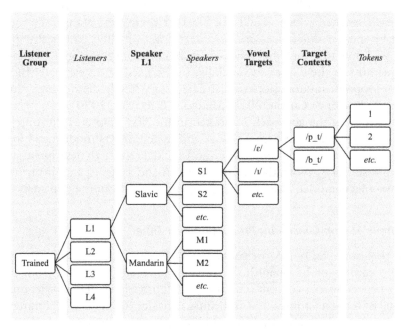

FIGURE 3.3 Visualization of the Data Structure and Variables in Munro and Derwing (2008).

84 Researching the Production of Specific Features

study. Random effects are random because they are randomly sampled from a larger population of potential units and because the meaning of the levels changes. The speakers and listeners included in Munro and Derwing (2008) are a sample drawn from the population of all potential speakers and listeners meeting study criteria (e.g., L1 Slavic language speakers). And, Speaker 1 and Listener 1 in Munro and Derwing (2008) are not the same as Speaker 1 and Listener 1 in another study (for a recap with helpful references, please see the introductory chapter on data analysis).

The most common random effect is a random intercept, which adjusts the value of the fixed effect for all levels of the random effect. That is, a random intercept computes a unique value for each level of the random effect. For instance, in Munro and Derwing's (2008) study, some speakers undoubtedly produced vowels that were more intelligible on average, whereas others produced vowels that were less intelligible. The fixed intercept represents the average intelligibility of the group as a whole, whereas the random intercepts represent the estimated intelligibility of each individual speaker, scattered around the fixed effect. However, the most powerful aspect of a mixed-effects model is the ability to estimate random slopes. In Munro and Derwing (2008), the fixed effect of Time would represent the average rate of change in vowel intelligibility for the group over the yearlong period. Random slopes for Time would adjust the Time-Intelligibility relationship for each speaker, which would test whether there were statistically significant by-speaker differences in rate of learning over time. Practically speaking, we know that such differences exist, but random slopes give us a means of quantifying the degree of variability in the fixed-effect estimate. Including appropriate random slopes is also a necessary step in developing accurate models (Brauer & Curtin, 2018; Meteyard & Davies, 2020).

Continuing the approach I adopted in the first chapter, I illustrate two analyses: repeated measures ANOVA and mixed-effects modeling. I follow the same general procedure: first, inspect the data through descriptive statistics and summary plots, then fit the ANOVA and assess it, and finally fit the mixed-effects model, assess it, and compare results from the two analyses.

Example 1: Stop Consonant Production over Time

For this example, our participants are 30 English speakers who are classroom learners of L2 Spanish. We'll assume we collected data from them once per semester over four semesters of intensive language instruction, for a total of five data points: two in the first semester (one at the beginning and another at the end) and one at the end of each semester thereafter. We're interested in gauging how participants' production of voiceless stops changes over the course of language instruction, that is, as a result of communicative

Researching the Production of Specific Features **85**

language instruction without a specific focus on pronunciation. At each session, participants complete a picture-naming task as a measure of their controlled production ability and a timed picture description task as a measure of their semi-spontaneous production ability. On each task, they produce ten target items with word-initial /p/. Thus, in this simulated data set, we have 3,000 observations: 30 participants × 5 sessions × 2 tasks × 10 items. We'll continue to assume that the data set is perfectly balanced with no participant attrition and no data loss. We'll also assume that we have already prepared the data for analysis by annotating and extracting the VOT of each target item.

Our independent, or predictor, variables in this data set are:

- Time, which we can treat as a continuous variable because the intervals are equally spaced, each occurring after one semester of instruction. This variable tests whether there is a relationship between time and VOT, or if there is significant change in VOT production over time.
- Task, a categorical variable that has two levels: picture naming and timed picture description. To obtain an average production value considering both tasks, we'll contrast code this variable, assigning –0.5 to picture naming and 0.5 to timed picture description (see Linck & Cunnings, 2015). This variable tests if participants produce different VOT values on the two tasks.
- Time × Task, an interaction term. This variable tests if the rate of change in VOT differs by task, that is, if participants show different rates of change for each task.

Our dependent variable is VOT, which we'll treat as a continuous dependent measure.

First, we plot the data to get a sense of how participants' VOT production changes. It's a good idea to plot the group data as well as a subset of individuals to examine the group trend and individual variability in change over time, so that's what we'll do (see the markdown for code to generate the plots). Figure 3.4 shows the group trajectory and Figure 3.5 trajectories for the first ten speakers. The group trajectory reveals several interesting patterns: (1) participants generally produced longer, more English-like VOT on the picture description task, that is, on the less controlled task; (2) there was significant improvement in VOT production over time, but the rate of change was not constant, insofar as the rate of improvement slowed down over time; (3) there appears to be a difference in the rate of change on each task, but that difference is subtle and may not be detectable (i.e., it may not be statistically and practically meaningful). The individual plots largely confirm these trends but add important information about

86 Researching the Production of Specific Features

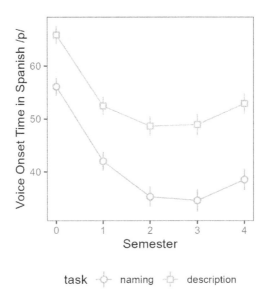

FIGURE 3.4 Group Changes in VOT as a Function of Session (Semester) and Task.

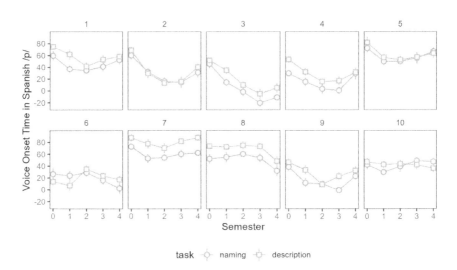

FIGURE 3.5 Changes in VOT as a Function of Session (Semester) and Task for a Subset of Speakers.

variability in the data set. For instance, s02 produced nearly identical VOT on both tasks, whereas the production patterns for the remaining speakers seem to conform to the group trend. Furthermore, most, but not all, speakers improved, and among those whose production improved, we can see individual differences in the rate and shape of change. All of this is perfectly normal and expected because the group trend need not be representative of any individual speaker in the data set.

Having inspected the data, we're now ready to analyze it. Unfortunately, with ANOVA, we cannot analyze speakers and items simultaneously. Instead, we need to collapse the data set. For our purposes, I'll carry out the speaker-level analysis and compare it to the mixed-effects model. To create the data set for this analysis, I computed a mean VOT for each speaker at each session on each task, reducing the data set from 3,000 observations to 300. I've included an example of how this can be done here, but there are many other ways to aggregate data in R.

```
data.vot.anova <- data.vot %>%
    group_by(participant, session, task) %>%
    summarise(vot = mean(vot))
```

We're now ready to run a 5×2 ANOVA, where 5 refers to the number of levels in Session and 2 to the number of levels in Task. At this point, we can begin checking some of the assumptions of ANOVA: normality and homogeneity of variances. We can create a histogram of VOT values to see if the data are normally distributed. For the assumption of sphericity, the variances of the difference scores between within-subjects effects should be equal. We can get a sense of whether this assumption may be violated by inspecting a boxplot and means and standard deviations grouped by Time and Task. We can formally test for sphericity using Mauchly's test. In our data set, the data are normally distributed, and based on the interquartile range of the boxplot and the standard deviations (see Table 3.1), it doesn't look like sphericity will be a problem. It's worth noting that violations of sphericity are common in repeated-measures designs. In that case, like we discussed in the previous chapter, a Greenhouse-Geisser correction can be applied to avoid Type 1 error inflation (false positives). I'd like to point out that there is another

TABLE 3.1 Descriptive Statistics for VOT over Time by Task

	Naming	*Description*
Session	*M (SD)*	*M (SD)*
0	56.10 (18.81)	65.88 (21.33)
1	42.02 (21.31)	52.47 (23.40)
2	35.32 (26.43)	48.66 (25.96)
3	34.62 (30.16)	48.95 (28.38)
4	38.54 (27.23)	52.92 (27.31)

88 Researching the Production of Specific Features

correction that is sometimes used, Huynh-Feldt. Most researchers use Greenhouse-Geisser by default, but that correction is more conservative and therefore more useful when there is a severe violation of sphericity. For the sake of demonstration, in this chapter, I'll apply both so that we can compare them.

To fit the ANOVA, we'll use the aov_car() function from the *afex* package (Singmann et al., 2023), as illustrated in the following chunk of code.

```
aov_car(vot ~ session * task + Error(participant/(session * task)),
        data = data.vot.anova)
```

After fitting the model, we request a summary of the analysis, which provides information on sphericity, using the summary() function on the model object we created. The outcome of this analysis shows that Session and Task are statistically significant, but the interaction term misses significance. A statistically significant value for Mauchly's test indicates a violation of sphericity. In our data, Session violated the assumption of sphericity and Session × Task nearly did. As a result, we need to apply either one of the two corrections we discussed to the degrees of freedom, using the new degrees of freedom to compute p values. To give you a sense of how the results could fluctuate under the different corrections, I report both uncorrected and corrected values in Table 3.2. For these data, statistical significance does not change, but it could in other data sets when the degrees of freedom are adjusted. It's worth mentioning that I made Table 3.2 for illustrative purposes, but you normally wouldn't make a table like this. For a more extensive explanation of how to apply sphericity corrections, see Larson-Hall (2016).

According to the generalized eta-squared effect size measure, Session explains about 7.50% of the variance in VOT, Task 5.90%, and Session × Task less than 1%. We can inspect the residuals of the model to check that they are normally distributed by using the residuals() function to generate them

TABLE 3.2 Summary of Uncorrected and Corrected Statistics for ANOVA

	Session			*Session × Task*		
	Df	*F*	*p*	*Df*	*F*	*p*
Baseline uncorrected	(4, 116)	17.71	<0.001	(4, 116)	2.13	0.082
GG corrected	(1.90, 54.99)	17.71	<0.001	(3.13, 90.87)	2.13	0.099
HF corrected	(2.03, 58.73)	17.71	<0.001	(3.56, 103.15)	2.13	0.090

and the hist() function to plot them, as shown in the following code. The plot suggests that the residuals are approximately normal.

```
residuals(vot.anova) %>%
  hist()
```

Based on our assessment of normality, sphericity, and the normality of residuals, it appears that all assumptions for the test are upheld (save sphericity, but we applied an appropriate correction for that violation), and we can therefore have confidence in our results. At this stage, we probably want to get estimated means for each task at each session, and we may want to create pairwise contrasts to see, for instance, if the rate of change was constant over time, that is, if there was significant development from one session to the next on each task. We know that rate of change was not constant over time—we saw as much in the plot—so generating pairwise contrasts allows us to assess the magnitude of change between adjacent levels of Session. We can generate pairwise contrasts using the *emmeans* package (Lenth, 2023). Our data set consists of five waves of data, in which case, we have a potential set of 30 comparisons, but we're not interested in comparing everything to everything else. Instead, we want to examine differences in rate of change between time points on each task. We can streamline our analysis by specifying a set of contrasts between adjacent waves on each task: 1 versus 2, 2 versus 3, 3 versus 4, and 4 versus 5.

First, we need to bring up a reference grid using the *emmeans* package so we can see the list of estimates. In the following code, we use the emmeans function on the model (vot_anova) ordering by Session then Task.

```
rgrid <- emmeans(vot.anova, ~ session * task)
```

That produces a reference grid of ten estimates, five for the picture description task and five for the naming task, in that order. We can then set our contrasts by setting one of the levels to –1, the other to 1, and all other levels to 0, as shown in the following chunk of code. Creating the contrasts in this way allows us to estimate the difference in VOT between adjacent levels of Session for each task.

```
vot.contrasts <- list(
naming_1v2 = c(-1, 1, 0, 0, 0, 0, 0, 0, 0, 0), # naming 1 v 2
naming_2v3 = c(0, -1, 1, 0, 0, 0, 0, 0, 0, 0), # naming 2 v 3
naming_3v4 = c(0, 0, -1, 1, 0, 0, 0, 0, 0, 0), # naming 3 v 4
naming_4v5 = c(0, 0, 0, -1, 1, 0, 0, 0, 0, 0), # naming 4 v 5
```

90 Researching the Production of Specific Features

description_1v2 = c(0, 0, 0, 0, 0, -1, 1, 0, 0, 0), # description 1 v 2
description_2v3 = c(0, 0, 0, 0, 0, 0, -1, 1, 0, 0), # description 2 v 3
description_3v4 = c(0, 0, 0, 0, 0, 0, 0, -1, 1, 0), # description 3 v 4
description_4v5 = c(0, 0, 0, 0, 0, 0, 0, 0, -1, 1)) # description 4 v 5

We then run the contrasts against the grid using the contrast function:
contrast(rgrid, vot.contrasts)

As shown in Table 3.3, pairwise estimates for earlier data points are statistically significant, whereas those for later data points are not, and the magnitude of the estimate is greater for earlier data points compared to later data points. From this analysis, we can conclude that the rate of change was not constant over the study, but rather waned over time. It also appears that participants experienced more improvement on the naming task than on the description task given that only one of the pairwise estimates for the description task was statistically significant. Thus, improvement seems to have waned more quickly on the description task than on the naming task. This type of analysis is uncommon because multi-wave longitudinal studies of pronunciation learning are uncommon, but Derwing and Munro (2013) is an excellent example of using pairwise comparisons to understand differences in rate of change over time.

In summary, based on this analysis, we know that participants produced different VOT values on each task, that VOT changed over time, and that the rate of change depended on the task, though the interaction term explained very little variance in the data and was not statistically significant. Based on the contrasts we set up for the post-hoc analysis, we also know that there was significant change in VOT between adjacent time points on both tasks over the first few sessions. And we know that the amount of change between adjacent sessions was not constant. Setting the pairwise contrasts allowed us to gain insight into curvilinear growth, but to be perfectly clear,

TABLE 3.3 A Priori Contrasts for ANOVA

Contrast	Estimate	95% CI	SE	t	p
naming_1v2	−14.08	[−19.26, −8.90]	2.53	−5.56	<0.001
naming_2v3	−6.71	[−10.57, −2.84]	1.89	−3.55	0.001
naming_3v4	−0.70	[−4.02, 2.63]	1.63	−0.43	0.672
naming_4v5	3.92	[−0.82, 8.65]	2.32	1.69	0.101
description_1v2	−13.41	[−18.99, −7.83]	2.73	−4.91	<0.001
description_2v3	−3.80	[−8.64, 1.04]	2.37	−1.61	0.119
description_3v4	0.29	[−3.11, 3.69]	1.66	0.17	0.865
description_4v5	3.97	[0.01, 7.93]	1.94	2.05	0.050

Note. df for all comparisons is 29.

we were not able to model it. We were also unable to estimate individual variability in intercepts and rates of change. Most importantly, we had to ignore variance in the items by creating participant-level averages by Session and Task. Mixed-effects modeling solves these problems, and, importantly, it allows us to model curvilinear change through the introduction of polynomial effects.

From our plots, we have already observed that there was substantial curvature in the group-level trajectory, which means that a linear term (i.e., a straight line) will not appropriately capture the developmental trend in the data. To model curvature, we can introduce polynomial terms, such as a quadratic term, which can approximate the growth curve. We could also test a cubic term, which would contain two turning points, but based on our preliminary analysis of the group trend and individual data, such a trajectory does not seem warranted. Polynomial growth terms will be correlated with one another. That is, the linear term and the derived quadratic term (i.e., squaring the linear term) will be strongly related to one another, which can be problematic for modeling. Fortunately, in R, there is an easy workaround. We can use the poly() function to create orthogonal linear and quadratic slopes, avoiding potential issues with multicollinearity: poly(session, 2). The syntax for this function takes the predictor, "Session" and creates new orthogonal polynomials based on the number provided: 2 yields a linear and a quadratic predictor, 3 a linear, quadratic, and cubic predictor, and so on. Entering poly(session, 2) into the model tests if there is a relationship between linear and quadratic rates of change and VOT. We're also interested in the effect of task, specifically if participants produce different VOT values depending on task and if the rate of change in VOT depends on task. Thus, we create an interaction term between Task, which we have contrast coded, and our polynomial growth term.

As I discussed in my notes on data analysis, there remains active debate around how to fit mixed-effects models, and depending on disciplinary background and training, researchers may opt for a variety of approaches. For our data, we have two general options for the fixed-effect structure. On the one hand, we could fit the most complex model we're interested in testing, which would include fixed effects for Task, the linear and quadratic versions of Session, and the interaction terms. On the other hand, we could build the model incrementally, comparing models to one another and, after reaching a final model, use the *lmerTest* package (Kuznetsova et al., 2017) to approximate degrees of freedom and generate a p value. Many researchers build and compare nested models to one another, so I want to show you that process. In my view, it's also sensible to take that approach here since we're essentially engaging in exploratory modeling with the goal of

92 Researching the Production of Specific Features

determining what polynomial growth components are needed to capture the curvature we observed in the plots. Crucially, when we're building and comparing models, we're engaging in a different type of testing where our goal is to identify the model that is the best representation of the data. When models differ by only one effect, if the model with that effect is statistically superior to the model without it, then we can tentatively conclude that the addition of that effect has significantly improved the model. Model comparisons of this type are done by performing a Chi-square test on the difference in their deviance statistics using the anova() function.

We also need to talk about random effects again because in this example all our predictor variables (Task, Linear Session, Quadratic Session, and the Task × Session interactions) are within-participants, which means that we could include all those predictors as by-participant random slopes. In my experience, complex random effects structures, especially random slopes for interactions, do not converge in pronunciation data sets, which tend to have small to medium sample sizes in terms of grouping units (e.g., 10–30 participants and 10–30 items). For this reason, I take a pragmatic approach to fitting random effects, following Brauer and Curtin's (2018) three rules for fitting random effects: random intercepts, random slopes for within-unit effects, and random slopes for within-unit interactions. In some cases, it's simply not possible to adhere to those three rules, in part because when I simulated the data I did not include random variance in the relevant estimates (e.g., in interactions). In short, then, I include random intercepts and try to fit random slopes for main predictors, but I don't try to model random slopes for interactions.

For the data set at hand, we have already descriptively observed substantial curvature in the group-level trajectories, curvature that is also evident at the individual level. We're specifically interested in evaluating this curvature, so we'll build and compare linear and quadratic growth models. Then, we'll integrate interaction terms with Task to see if there are different patterns of change on each task. Finally, we'll turn to the by-participant and by-item random slopes. Rather than burying the lead, I'll state from the start that integrating the full set of random slopes is not possible for this data set. One thing to note is that in this analysis we'll use the contrast-coded version of Task (task.c, where -0.5 = picture naming and 0.5 = picture description).

First, we build and compare the unconditional growth models:

```
vot.mem.linear <- lmer(vot ~ scale(session) +
            (1 | participant) +
            (1 | item), data = data.vot)
vot.mem.quadratic <- lmer(vot ~ scale(poly(session, 2)) +
            (1 | participant) +
            (1 | item), data = data.vot)
```

Researching the Production of Specific Features   **93**

The comparison, executed using the anova() function, shows that the quadratic growth model is superior to the linear growth model ($\chi^2(1) = 173.73, p < 0.001$). I added the conditional effect of Task to this model by including it first in an interaction with the linear slope and then in an interaction with both the linear and quadratic slopes. The linear interaction model was a better fit than the unconditional growth model ($\chi^2(2) = 10.64, p = 0.005$), which shows that there was in fact a different rate of change on each task. However, the quadratic interaction model did not improve fit further ($\chi^2(1) = 0.27, p = 0.601$), which means that the difference in the rate of change on each task was predominantly constrained to the linear function. In other words, there was a difference in the rate of change but not the rate of curvature or inflection point. The model with the Task × Linear Session interaction is as follows.

```
vot.mem.c1 <- lmer(vot ~ task.c*scale(session) + scale(poly(session, 2)) +
            (1 | participant) +
            (1 | item), data = data.vot)
```

In this model, I have standardized the polynomial growth terms using the scale() function to make them more easily interpretable. R permits nesting, so I have nested the poly() function within the scale() function, which tells R to compute the polynomials first and then scale them. I have also listed random effects on separate lines to make the code easier to read. When running this model, R will give a warning that the "fixed-effect model matrix is rank deficient so dropping 1 column/coefficient." This is because the linear slope is specified twice: once in the interaction with task.c and once in the scaled polynomial term. This warning is simply a reminder that one of these coefficients is a duplicate and is dropped from the model.

Before summarizing the model, we should integrate and test random effects. We can try testing the maximal model for by-participant random effects. Even though we know it's very unlikely that this model will converge, it's still worth doing, if only for the sake of reminding ourselves what such a model would look like. The maximal by-participant random effects structure is:

```
vot.mem.rsmax <- lmer(vot ~ task.c *scale(session) + scale(poly(session, 2)) +
            (1 + task.c*scale(session) + scale(poly(session, 2) | participant) +
            (1 | item), data = data.vot)
```

It's not surprising that this model doesn't converge because it's overly complicated for the size of our data set. We could try the convergence remedies that Brauer and Curtin (2018) suggested, but that's beyond the scope of this chapter. For now, we'll simplify the random effects structure, prioritizing

94 Researching the Production of Specific Features

the slopes for by-participant effects (e.g., Task, Linear Session, Quadratic Session) without the interaction terms:

```
vot.mem.rs1 <- lmer(vot ~ task.c *scale(session) + scale(poly(session, 2)) +
            (1 + scale(poly(session, 2) + task.c | participant) +
            (1 | item), data = data.vot)
```

This model converged, and when I compared this model to the model without the random slopes, the random slopes model was a significantly better fit: $\chi^2(10) = 497.15$, $p < 0.001$. I have summarized the models that we fit, and the order in which we fit them, in Table 3.4. You probably wouldn't

TABLE 3.4 Summary of Mixed-Effects Models Fit to the VOT Data

Model	Model description			Test against prior model	
	Fixed Effects	*Participants*	*Items*	*Statistic*	*p*
vot.linear	intercept linear	intercept	intercept		
vot.quadratic	intercept linear quadratic	intercept	intercept	$\chi^2(1) = 173.31$	<0.001
vot.c1	intercept linear quadratic task task × linear	intercept	intercept	$\chi^2(2) = 10.64$	0.004
vot.c2	intercept linear quadratic task task × linear task × quadratic	intercept	intercept	$\chi^2(1) = 0.27$	0.601
vot.rsmax	mem.vot.c1	intercept linear quadratic task task × linear task × quadratic	intercept	*did not converge*	
vot.rs1	mem.vot.c1	intercept linear quadratic task	intercept	$\chi^2(10) = 497.15$	<0.001

Note. Fixed effects for vot.rsmax and vot.rs1 are the same as in the vot.c1 model. Models that did not improve fit (vot.c2) or did not converge (vot.rsmax), shown with gray shading, were excluded from comparisons. vot.rs1 was therefore compared to vot.c1.

Researching the Production of Specific Features **95**

include this type of table in the body of a manuscript, but you should include it in supplementary online materials so that researchers understand how you iterated through a series of models.

The best-fitting model, vot.rs1, is summarized in Table 3.5. According to the model summary, participants produced an average VOT of 47.55 ms. This intercept represents the grand mean because we contrast-coded Task, so to get the average VOT that participants produced on each Task, we need to take into account the coefficient for that predictor. On the picture-naming task (contrast code = −0.50), participants produced an average VOT of 41.33 ms (47.55 + −0.50 × 12.45), and on the timed picture description task, they produced an average VOT of 53.78 ms (47.55 + 0.50 × 12.45). Although the coefficient for Task is on the threshold of being considered statistically significant, the confidence interval did not cross zero, and the large positive upper limit suggests that the effect is reasonably robust at the group level. The significant negative coefficient for the linear effect of Session shows that VOT decreased, but the significant positive coefficient for its quadratic counterpart demonstrates that the rate of change slowed down over time. Finally, the significant positive coefficient for the interaction term between the linear effect of Session and the contrast-coded effect of Task shows that rate of change was slightly slower on the picture description task. As we did for the intercept on each task, we can also compute the linear rate

TABLE 3.5 Summary of Linear Mixed-Effects Model Fit to VOT Data

Fixed effects	*Estimate*	*SE*	*t*	*95% CI*	*p*
Intercept	47.55	5.17	9.20	[37.42, 57.68]	<0.001
Linear Session	−5.09	1.16	−4.40	[−7.35, −2.82]	<0.001
Quadratic Session	4.83	1.12	4.33	[2.65, 7.02]	<0.001
Task	12.45	6.17	2.02	[0.37, 24.54]	0.058
Linear Session × Task	1.85	0.65	2.87	[0.59, 3.12]	0.004
Quadratic Session × Task	−0.38	0.65	−0.59	[−1.64, 0.89]	0.559

Random effects	*SD*	*Correlation*			
Participants					
Intercepts	22.93				
Slopes: Linear Session	6.08	0.63			
Slopes: Quadratic Session	5.85	−0.32	−0.52		
Slopes: Task	6.04	0.04	−0.06	0.13	
Items					
Intercepts	13.49				

Note. Task was contrast coded (picture naming = −0.50, timed picture description = 0.50). The poly function was used to generate orthogonal linear and quadratic terms for Session, and these terms were standardized. P values have been generated using the Satterthwaite approximation included in the lmerTest package (Kuznetsova et al., 2017).

96 Researching the Production of Specific Features

of change on each task by taking the base rate of change and combining it with the coefficient for the interaction term: for the picture naming task, $-5.09 + (1.85 \times -0.50) = -6.02$, and for the timed picture description task, $-5.09 + (1.85 \times 0.50) = -4.17$ ms.

Turning to the random effects, the *SD* for the item intercepts (13.49) was roughly half the *SD* of the participant intercepts (22.93), suggesting more variation in participants than in items. The *SD* for the by-participant random slopes for the linear and quadratic effects of Session (6.08 and 5.85, respectively) were smaller but still indicate variability in participants' rate of change over time. These values show that some participants had a rate of change that was steeper than average, whereas others had a rate of change that was more shallow than average. In other words, the random effects represent random variation around the mean effect, which is represented by the fixed effect in the model. The same is true for Task. We also need to interpret the covariances. A positive value for the covariance indicates that higher values of one parameter are associated with higher values of the other. For instance, the positive covariance between the Intercept and Linear Session (0.63) demonstrates that individuals who began the study with a higher intercept experienced a higher rate of change. A negative value indicates the opposite, that is, that higher values of one parameter are associated with lower values of the other. The negative value for the covariance between the Intercept and Quadratic Session (−0.32) suggests that individuals who began the study with a higher intercept did not experience as much curvature in their rate of change. Both of these effects make sense: Participants who produced stops with longer VOT (i.e., more English-like VOT) at the outset of the study changed more and experienced less leveling off, presumably because they had more room to improve than individuals who already produced relatively Spanish-like VOT at the beginning of the study.

An important step in fitting and evaluating mixed-effects models is checking for normality, linearity, and the homogeneity of variance of model residuals. These assumptions can be formally tested, but it is more common to test them using simple plots. For normality, model residuals should fall on a straight line, and for our data set they do. For linearity, when residuals are plotted against observed values, there should be no pattern evident. In our data set, there appears to be a linear association between residuals and observed values. We could introduce additional terms into the model or transform the outcome variable, but the model is already relatively complex given that it includes polynomial growth terms, and if we transform the outcome variable then we can no longer interpret the intercept and rate of change in a straightforward way that gives us insight into how much participants improve over time. For these reasons, in my view, it makes more sense to report that the assumption of linearity may not be upheld in this data set. For homogeneity of variance, when we plot fitted values against residuals,

Researching the Production of Specific Features **97**

they should fall around a straight line, and in our data set they do. In summary, then, normality and homogeneity of variance are upheld, but there may be some problems with linearity.

Example 2: Vowel Intelligibility over Time

In research on specific features, it's common to use listener-based assessments of intelligibility by, for instance, presenting the words the speakers produced to listeners in an identification task. If the listener selects the word the speaker intended to produce, then the trial is coded as a hit (1), and if the listener selects a word other than the intended one, then the trial is coded as a miss (0). In this scenario, the outcome measure is a binary variable. To analyze these data using ANOVA, as with the stop consonant production example, we would need to collapse the data set. However, in this case, we would collapse over two dimensions of the data: listeners and items. In addition to the problems, this can cause due to unmodeled variance, it's also problematic because it prevents us from analyzing listener-level variables. In pronunciation research, we're often interested in examining the speaker-, listener-, and even item-level variables that affect the production of specific features, but pooling over listeners and items makes this impossible unless we run separate analyses. Furthermore, there is a disconnect between the data handling that ANOVA requires and the construct of intelligibility itself. ANOVA requires that mean scores be computed, but it's not clear what a mean intelligibility score would represent given that intelligibility is most appropriately conceptualized as a binary outcome. By modeling the binary, trial-level data, we can produce estimates that indicate the likelihood of the speaker producing an intelligible variant, which aligns well with how intelligibility is conceptualized. It bears mentioning that there is another pronunciation construct that allows for gradience in judgments: comprehensibility. Certainly, word-level comprehensibility could also be assessed (Martin & Sippel, 2021), but for the sake of illustration, I focus on intelligibility data, and I won't aggregate data for ANOVA. Instead, I proceed directly to the logistic mixed-effects model of the trial-level data.

For this example, we'll take Munro and Derwing (2008) as a model. We'll assume our participants are 30 L2 English speakers who have recently immigrated to an English-speaking country. We'll also assume that we collected data from them every two months over their first year of immersion, yielding six waves of data. Like Munro and Derwing (2008), we're interested in participants' production of L2 English vowels, especially the /i/-/ɪ/ contrast, which tends to be difficult for most L2 English speakers. We included ten target words in the study, five each for /i/ and /ɪ/. We extracted the words and saved them to individual audio files, and we presented these files to 13 untrained L1 English listeners for evaluation. Listeners heard the word

98 Researching the Production of Specific Features

and selected the word they heard from a minimal pair in a two-alternative forced-choice identification task. We'll assume that our listeners were generous with their time and evaluated all (1,800) tokens from the study.

In an ideal world, we would have a data set consisting of 23,400 observations (30 speakers $\times$ 2 sounds $\times$ 5 words $\times$ 6 waves $\times$ 13 listeners). However, complete data sets are rare in pronunciation research and rarer still in longitudinal pronunciation research. Most of the time, at least a few observations will be missing because the participant missed one or more sessions, skipped an item, or bumped the microphone, coughed, laughed, or made another noise that would compromise the quality of the item. From an analytical standpoint, missing data is not problematic for model fitting. Mixed-effects models are capable of modeling all available data even when data are missing. At the same time, missing data can affect power and alter model estimates. To illustrate this point, in simulating the data, I created two missing data variables that will allow us to analyze the complete and incomplete data sets and compare them.

Our independent, or predictor, variables in this data set are:

- Time, which we can treat as a continuous variable because the intervals are equally spaced at two-month intervals. This variable tests whether there is a relationship between Time and Intelligibility, or if there is significant change in the intelligibility of English /i/ and /ɪ/ over time.
- Vowel, a categorical variable that has two levels: /i/ and /ɪ/ (*heed* and *hid* in the data). As in the previous example, we will contrast code this variable, assigning –0.5 to *heed* and 0.5 to *hid*. This variable tests if vowel intelligibility varies as a function of the vowel target.
- Time $\times$ Vowel, an interaction term. This variable tests if the rate of change in intelligibility differs by vowel target.
- Missing.speakerwave, a dummy variable indexing the session at which the speaker dropped out of the study (and thus the session at which no more data is available from that speaker)
- Missing.speaker, a filtering variable that allows us to subset the data to simulate speaker-level missing using the following code: subset(missing. speaker == "no"))
- Missing.item, a filtering variable that allows us to subset the data to simulate item-level missing using the following code: subset (missing.item == "no"))

Our grouping variables are:

- Listeners, $n = 13$
- Speakers, $n = 30$
- Items, $n = 10$

Our dependent, or outcome, variable is Intelligibility, which is a binary measure (0/1) that refers to whether the listener selected the vowel the speaker intended to produce.

Our first step is plotting and descriptive statistics. There is no easy way to plot binary data over time. We simply have to aggregate, so we'll average over listeners and items so we can inspect the shape of the intelligibility curve for both vowels. Our group plot (Figure 3.6) suggests a high level of accuracy in the production of /i/ (as expected) and initially low but increasing accuracy in the production of /ɪ/. The individual data (Figure 3.7) shows that participants follow the group trend, but there is substantial variability in the trajectory of /ɪ/ development. We could try to capture that variability using a combination of polynomial terms, as we did for the first example, but for this example, we'll focus on modeling a linear rate of change over time.

Means and standard deviations over time by vowel are given in Table 3.6. The standard deviations are quite large, which coincides with the fact that starting points and trajectories for individual participants are highly variable. We're ready to model the data. The syntax for logistic models is nearly identical to the syntax for a linear model, except that we need to use the glmer() function and specify that the distribution of the outcome measure is binomial. For this round of modeling, we'll fit the maximal fixed-effect model, which includes the following predictors: Session, Vowel, and Session × Vowel.

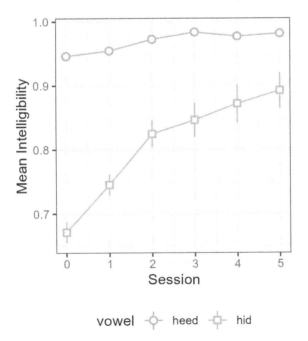

FIGURE 3.6   Group Changes in Intelligibility as a Function of Session and Vowel.

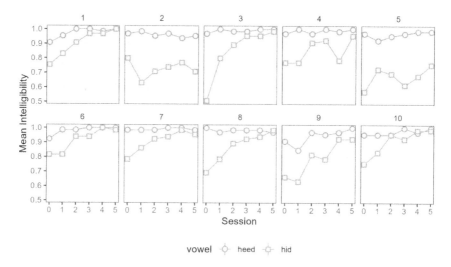

FIGURE 3.7 Changes in Intelligibility as a Function of Session and Vowel for a Subset of Speakers.

TABLE 3.6 Descriptive Statistics for Mean Intelligibility over Time by Vowel

Session	/i/	/ɪ/
1	94.61 (22.58)	67.12 (46.99)
2	95.43 (20.88)	74.51 (43.59)
3	92.23 (16.41)	82.46 (38.04)
4	98.36 (12.71)	84.62 (36.09)
5	97.69 (15.02)	87.18 (33.44)
6	98.15 (13.46)	89.23 (31.01)

We'll include by-listener, by-speaker, and by-item random intercepts, and then we'll incrementally test by-speaker random slopes unless we encounter convergence problems. As shown in Table 3.7, the most complex model with the by-speaker random slopes for the Session × Vowel interaction was singular, suggesting overfit, and the model with by-speaker random slopes for Session and Vowel (but no slopes for the interaction) did not improve fit over the simpler model with slopes for Session but not Vowel. We could conclude that the intel.rs2 model is not a good representation of the data because it did not improve fit, but we should probably retain it. As Brauer and Curtin (2018) and others have pointed out, including random slopes for fixed-effect predictors that are central to research questions is crucial for obtaining accurate estimates. Even though adding Vowel as a by-speaker random effect did not improve the fit of the model, we'll retain intel.rs2 as the best model that we can report on for this data set.

Researching the Production of Specific Features **101**

TABLE 3.7 Summary of Model Comparisons

Model	*Model description*				*Test against prior*	
Model	*Fixed Effects*	*Speaker*	*Listener*	*Item*	*Statistic*	*p*
intel	Intercept session vowel sess. × vowel	Intercept	intercept	intercept		
intel.rs1	Intel	intercept session	intercept	intercept	$\chi^2(2)=412.30$	<0.001
intel.rs2	intel	intercept session vowel	intercept	intercept	$\chi^2(3)=4.64$	0.200
intel.rs3	Intel	intercept session vowel sess. × vowel	intercept	intercept	*singular*	

TABLE 3.8 Summary of Logistic Mixed-Effects Model Fit to the Intelligibility Data

Fixed effects	*OR*	*SE*	*z*	*95% CI*	*p*
Intercept	6.24	0.84	13.65	[4.80, 8.12]	<0.001
Vowel	0.11	0.02	−10.65	[0.07, 0.17]	<0.001
Session	1.59	0.10	7.19	[1.40, 7.19]	<0.001
Session × Vowel	1.00	0.04	0.07	[0.93, 1.08]	0.946

Random effects	*SD*	*Correlation*	
Speakers			
Intercepts	0.27		
Slopes: Session	0.33	0.06	
Slopes: Vowel	0.24	−0.07	0.32
Listeners			
Intercepts	0.26		
Items			
Intercepts	0.28		

Table 3.8 gives a summary of the final model. In this table, I have converted log odds to odds ratios (*OR*) using the tab_model() function from the *sjPlot* package (Lüdecke, 2022), where an $OR > 1$ favors the outcome and an $OR < 1$ disfavors it. In this analysis, we contrast coded the Vowel predictor (/i/ = −0.50, /ɪ/ = 0.50). Contrast coding Vowel means that the intercept represents the average likelihood of an intelligible production at

the outset of the study, considering both vowels. Had we let R set, for instance, /i/ as the reference level, then the intercept would represent the initial intelligibility of /i/. The same holds for Session. Our contrast-coded vowel variable means that the estimate for Session represents the average effect of Session on intelligibility, or the average rate of change in likelihood, considering both vowel targets. We can do some math to get the intercept and rate of change for each vowel, or we can use the *emmeans* package (Lenth, 2023) to extract those estimates, but we'll get to that in a moment.

Overall, taking into account both vowels, speakers were fairly likely to produce an intelligible variant at the outset of the study. In fact, there was about an 86% chance that speakers would produce an intelligible variant at the first data point (an *OR* of 6.24 corresponds to a probability of roughly 86%). We must keep in mind that this was for both vowels, and in light of that information, the high probability makes sense because speakers showed near-ceiling intelligibility for /i/ and moderate intelligibility for /ɪ/. In short, then, the high performance on /i/ made up for the low performance for /ɪ/. This is clearly evident in the effect for Vowel, which showed a very small *OR*. Because /ɪ/ was coded as the positive value (0.50), this means that the probability of producing an intelligible /ɪ/ was well below that of /i/ and below the intercept. The *OR* for Session was greater than 1.00, which means that the probability of producing an intelligible variant increased over time. Finally, the interaction term did not reach statistical significance, the *OR* was exactly 1.00, and the corresponding 95% *CI* showed a narrow range around 1.00, indicating no effect of vowel on rate of change. We can also interpret the covariances. For instance, the covariance between by-speaker intercepts and slopes for Session was negligible (0.06), suggesting virtually no relationship between the intercept and rate of change. This is atypical and somewhat surprising because normally there would be some sort of relationship. However, I didn't specify it in the simulation, so this is simply the way the data turned out.

Logistic mixed-effects models do not impose the same assumptions as linear models, but we still need to check for linearity and outliers that could potentially have a strong influence on model estimates. The *DHARMa* package (Hartig, 2017) is specifically designed to produce residual diagnostics for logistic models. We can use this package to simulate residuals based on our model and then check assumptions on the simulation. To simulate residuals, we use the simulateResiduals() function with our model object as the input.

sim.residuals <- simulateResiduals(fittedModel = glm.intel.rs2)

We can then get diagnostics by plotting the DHARMa object we have created.

```
plot(sim.residuals)
```

This function produces a QQ plot comparing observed and expected residuals (like the QQ plot for a linear model, the points should fall on a diagonal line) and a residual plot comparing residuals and predicted values. It also returns p values for the Kolmogorov-Smirnov goodness-of-fit test and dispersion and outlier tests. For our simulated data, $p > 0.05$ for all tests, which indicates that our model performs well. It is also worthwhile to create residual plots for individual predictors, which in our case would be Session and Vowel:

```
plotResiduals(sim.residuals, form = data.vowels$session)
plotResiduals(sim.residuals, form = data.vowels$vowel)
```

The variance at each level of the predictor should be approximately equal, and the plot will return a boxplot and Levene's test for homogeneity of variance. The test shows that in our data there is no problem with homogeneity of variance.

In practice, it is not uncommon to find that your model does not perform well on at least one of these tests. If one or more tests show serious problems with your model, you may need to fit a different type of model altogether, or you may need to include additional predictors. In my experience, correcting for these problems can be a real challenge and often involves fitting models that are not common in the field (e.g., a zero-/one-inflated beta model). In this case, you should report the original model along with any problems you encounter so that researchers understand that they should interpret your estimates with caution. You can also explore alternative models and report on them in an endnote or appendix. In this way, you report on the model the field is familiar with, laying the groundwork for meaningful comparison in future studies, while also attempting to fit an alternative model that may correct for some of the issues in the original model.

Summary and Recommendations

In this chapter, we have examined approaches to studying the production of specific features, such as individual vowels and consonants. We have discussed why researchers choose to examine specific features and how they pick a good target structure that aligns with their research questions.

104 Researching the Production of Specific Features

We have also discussed the tasks used to elicit production data and how those data are subsequently processed, coded, and statistically analyzed. Below is a summary of recommendations for conducting research in this area.

- Know what you are interested in studying: development over time, controlled and spontaneous production knowledge, production in different phonetic environments or in different types of words, etc. Knowing what conceptual area you want to study has an impact on the target structure you select and how you approach its measurement.
- Know why you have selected a target structure: Have you selected the target structure because L2 speakers struggle to produce it? If so, is it an intelligibility problem or do they produce intelligible variants that show interesting acoustic properties? Alternatively, have you selected the structure because it is well studied and offers the opportunity to study subtle patterns of crosslinguistic interaction, which may only be evident through a fine-grained acoustic analysis?
- Carefully consider the pros and cons of production tasks: Include controlled and spontaneous production tasks to obtain a more representative sample of speech under different processing conditions. Speakers may produce intelligible and accurate variants in controlled speech, but that does not mean they will do so in spontaneous speech.
- Include at least 5–10 tokens per target structure, considering other grouping variables such as task and phonetic environment. More observations are not always better, but having more observations will allow for more robust modeling of the data, especially because at least some missing data is common in pronunciation research (e.g., 5–10% in most studies, up to 30% in longitudinal studies).
- Use mixed-effects models so that you can simultaneously estimate listener-, speaker-, and item-level effects and understand variance in all three layers of data structure. Mixed-effects models also allow for the quantification of individual differences via random effects.
- Aim for transparency: Make materials, data, and analysis code publicly available whenever possible.

Chapter Questions

1. What are the ways in which production accuracy can be measured? How are these approaches related to the notion of phonological versus phonetic accuracy?
2. Considering the languages you know and/or have studied, design a research question addressing the production of a specific feature. Explain why that feature is a good candidate for research.

Researching the Production of Specific Features **105**

TABLE 3.9 Summary of Fixed-Effect Estimates for Complete and Missing Data

Fixed effects	OR	SE	z	95% CI	p
Complete					
Intercept	6.24	0.84	13.65	[4.80, 8.12]	<0.001
Vowel	0.11	0.02	−10.65	[0.07, 0.17]	<0.001
Session	1.59	0.10	7.19	[1.40, 7.19]	<0.001
Session × Vowel	1.00	0.04	0.07	[0.93, 1.08]	0.946
Missing-by-Item					
Intercept					
Vowel					
Session					
Session × Vowel					
Missing-by-Speaker					
Intercept					
Vowel					
Session					
Session × Vowel					

3. Design a data collection and coding procedure that would be appropriate for the research question you generated for (2).
4. Reanalyze the vowel production data using the two missingness variables. Start with the item-level missingness, which should be easier to model given that there is less missing data overall. Then, try modeling the data with speaker-level missingness.

   a) What problems do you encounter? How do you propose to overcome them and/or report on them?
   b) Fill in Table **3.9** with the revised estimates (as possible) for the models fit to the two types of data with missing observations. How do the estimates change? Think about the point estimate, its confidence interval, and the *p* value.

References

Abrahamsson, N. (1999). Vowel epenthesis of /sC(C)/ onsets in Spanish/Swedish interphonology: A longitudinal case study. *Language Learning, 49*(3), 473–508. https://doi.org/10.1111/0023-8333.00097

Abrahamsson, N., & Hyltenstam, K. (2009). Age of onset and nativelikeness in a second language: Listener perception versus linguistic scrutiny. *Language Learning, 59*(2), 249–306. https://doi.org/10.1111/j.1467-9922.2009.00507.x

Abramson, A. S., & Whalen, D. H. (2017). Voice Onset Time (VOT) at 50: Theoretical and practical issues in measuring voicing distinctions. *Journal of Phonetics, 63*, 75–86. https://doi.org/10.1016/j.wocn.2017.05.002

Amengual, M. (2012). Interlingual influence in bilingual speech: Cognate status effect in a continuum of bilingualism. *Bilingualism: Language and Cognition*, *15*(3), 517–530. https://doi.org/10.1017/S1366728911000460

Andringa, S. (2014). The use of native speaker norms in critical period hypothesis research. *Studies in Second Language Acquisition*, *36*(3), 565–596. https://doi.org/10.1017/s0272263113000600

Baart, J. (2009). *A field manual of acoustic phonetics*. SIL International.

Best, C. T., & Tyler, M. D. (2007). Nonnative and second-language speech perception: Commonalities and complementarities. In M. J. Munro & O.-S. Bohn (Eds.), *Second language speech learning: The role of language experience in speech perception and production* (pp. 13–24). John Benjamins.

Birdsong, D. (2018). Plasticity, variability and age in second language acquisition and bilingualism. *Frontiers in Psychology*, *9*. https://www.frontiersin.org/articles/10.3389/fpsyg.2018.00081

Bongiovanni, S., Long, A. Y., Solon, M., & Willis, E. W. (2015). The effect of short-term study abroad on second language Spanish phonetic development. *Studies in Hispanic and Lusophone Linguistics*, *8*(2), 243–283. https://doi.org/10.1515/shll-2015-0010

Brauer, M., & Curtin, J. J. (2018). Linear mixed-effects models and the analysis of nonindependent data: A unified framework to analyze categorical and continuous independent variables that vary within-subjects and/or within-items. *Psychological Methods*, *23*(3), 389–411. https://doi.org/10.1037/met0000159

Casillas, J. V. (2020). Phonetic category formation is perceptually driven during the early stages of adult L2 development. *Language and Speech*, *63*(3), 550–581. https://doi.org/10.1177/0023830919866225

Cho, T., Whalen, D. H., & Docherty, G. (2019). Voice Onset Time and beyond: Exploring laryngeal contrast in 19 languages. *Journal of Phonetics*, *72*, 52-65. https://doi.org/10.1016/j.wocn.2018.11.002

Colantoni, L., & Steele, J. (2007). Acquiring /ɾ/ in context. *Studies in Second Language Acquisition*, *29*, 381–406. https://doi.org/10.1017/S0272263107070258

Colantoni, L., Steele, J., & Escudero, P. (2015). *Second language speech: Theory and practice*. Cambridge University Press.

Derwing, T. M. (2010). Utopian goals for pronunciation teaching. In J. Levis & K. LeVelle (Eds.), *Proceedings of the 1st Pronunciation in Second Language Learning and Teaching Conference* (pp. 24–37). Iowa State University.

Derwing, T. M., & Munro, M. J. (2013). The development of L2 oral language skills in two L1 groups: A 7-year study. *Language Learning*, *63*(2), 163–185. https://doi.org/10.1111/lang.12000

Earle, F. S., & Myers, E. B. (2014). Building phonetic categories: An argument for the role of sleep. *Frontiers in Psychology*, *5*, 1192. https://doi.org/10.3389/fpsyg.2014.01192

Earle, F. S., & Myers, E. B. (2015a). Sleep and native language interference affect nonnative speech sound learning. *Journal of Experimental Psychology: Human Perception and Performance*, *41*(6), 1680–1695. https://doi.org/10.1037/xhp0000113

Earle, F. S., & Myers, E. B. (2015b). Overnight consolidation promotes generalization across talkers in the identification of nonnative speech sounds.

Journal of the Acoustical Society of America, 137(1), EL91–EL97. https://doi. org/10.1121/1.4903918

Eddington, D. (2011). What are the contextual phonetic variants of in colloquial Spanish? *Probus, 23*(1), 1–19. https://doi.org/doi:10.1515/prbs.2011.001

Face, T. L. (2006). Intervocalic rhotic pronunciation by adult learners of Spanish as a second language. In C. A. Klee & T. L. Face (Eds.), *Selected Proceedings of the 7th Conference on the Acquisition of Spanish and Portuguese as First and Second Languages* (pp. 47–58). Cascadilla Proceedings Project.

Flege, J. E. (1987). The instrumental study of L2 speech production: Some methodological considerations*. *Language Learning, 37*(2), 285–296. https://doi. org/10.1111/j.1467-1770.1987.tb00569.x

Flege, J. E. (1995). Second language speech learning: Theory, findings, problems. In W. Strange (Ed.), *Speech perception and linguistic experience: Issues in cross-language research* (pp. 233–277). York Press.

Flege, J. E., & Bohn, O.-S. (2021). The revised speech learning model. In R. Wayland (Ed.), *Second language speech learning: Theoretical and empirical progress* (pp. 3–83). Cambridge University Press.

Flege, J. E., Yeni-Komshian, G. H., & Liu, S. (1999). Age constraints on second-language acquisition. *Journal of Memory and Language, 41*(1), 78–104. https:// doi.org/10.1006/jmla.1999.2638

Hartig, F. (2017). DHARMa: Residual Diagnostics for Hierarchical (Multi-Level / Mixed) Regression Models. R package version 0.1.5. <http://florianhartig. github.io/DHARMa/>.

Johnson, K. (2011). *Acoustic and auditory phonetics* (3rd ed.). Wiley-Blackwell.

Kartushina, N., & Frauenfelder, U. H. (2014). On the effects of L2 perception and of individual differences in L1 production on L2 pronunciation. *Frontiers in Psychology, 5*, 1246. https://doi.org/10.3389/fpsyg.2014.01246

Kuznetsova, A., Brockhoff, P. B., & Christensen, R. H. B. (2017). "lmerTest Package: Tests in Linear Mixed-effects models." *Journal of Statistical Software, 82*(13), 1–26. https://doi.org/10.18637/jss.v082.i13.

Larson-Hall, J. (2016). *A guide to doing statistics in second language research using SPSS and R*. Routledge.

Lenneberg, E. H. (1967). *Biological foundations of language*. Wiley.

Lenth, R. (2023). _emmeans: Estimated Marginal Means, aka Least-Squares Means_. R package version 1.8.4-1, <https://CRAN.R-project.org/package=emmeans>.

Linck, J. A., & Cunnings, I. (2015). The utility and application of mixed-effects models in second language research. *Language Learning, 65*(S1), 185-207. https://doi.org/10.1111/lang.12117

Lisker, L., & Abramson, A. S. (1964). A cross-language study of voicing in initial stops: Acoustic measurements. *Word, 20*(3), 384–422. https://doi.org/10.10 80/00437956.1964.11659830

Long, M. H. (1990). Maturational constraints on language development. *Studies in Second Language Acquisition, 12*(3), 251–285. https://doi.org/10.1017/ S0272263100009165

Lüdecke, D. (2022). _sjPlot: Data Visualization for Statistics in Social Science_. R package version 2.8.11, <https://CRAN.R-project.org/package=sjPlot>.

Maddieson, I. (1984). *Patterns of sounds*. Cambridge University Press.

Major, R. C. (1987). English voiceless stop production by speakers of Brazilian Portuguese. *Journal of Phonetics, 15*(2), 197–202. https://doi.org/10.1016/S0095-4470(19)30560-1

Martin, I. A., & Sippel, L. (2021). Is giving better than receiving? *Journal of Second Language Pronunciation, 7*(1), 62–88. https://doi.org/10.1075/jslp.20001.mar

Meteyard, L., & Davies, R. A. I. (2020). Best practice guidance for linear mixed-effects models in psychological science. *Journal of Memory and Language, 112*, 104092. https://doi.org/10.1016/j.jml.2020.104092

Munro, M. J. (2021). On the difficulty of defining "difficult" in second-language vowel acquisition. *Frontiers in Communication, 6*(53). https://doi.org/10.3389/fcomm.2021.639398

Munro, M. J., & Derwing, T. M. (1995). Processing time, accent, and comprehensibility in the perception of native and foreign-accented speech. *Language and Speech, 38*(3), 289–306. https://doi.org/10.1177/002383099503800305

Munro, M. J., & Derwing, T. M. (2008). Segmental acquisition in adult ESL learners: A longitudinal study of vowel production. *Language Learning, 58*(3), 479–502. https://doi.org/10.1111/j.1467-9922.2008.00448.x

Munro, M. J., Derwing, T. M., & Thomson, R. I. (2015). Setting segmental priorities for English learners: Evidence from a longitudinal study. *International Review of Applied Linguistics in Language Teaching, 53*(1), 39–60. https://doi.org/10.1515/iral-2015-0002

Nagle, C. L. (2018). Examining the temporal structure of the perception-production link in second language acquisition: A longitudinal study. *Language Learning, 68*(1), 234–270. https://doi.org/10.1111/lang.12275

Nagle, C. L. (2021a). Assessing the state of the art in longitudinal L2 pronunciation research. *Journal of Second Language Pronunciation, 7*(2), 154–182. https://doi.org/10.1075/jslp.20059.nag

Nagle, C. L. (2021b). Revisiting perception–production relationships: Exploring a new approach to investigate perception as a time-varying predictor. *Language Learning, 71*(1), 243–279. https://doi.org/10.1111/lang.12431

Nagle, C. L., Huensch, A., & Zárate–Sández, G. (2023). Exploring phonetic predictors of intelligibility, comprehensibility, and foreign accent in L2 Spanish speech. *The Modern Language Journal, 107*(1), 202–221. https://doi.org/10.1111/modl.12827

Olson, D. J., & Offerman, H. M. (2021). Maximizing the effect of visual feedback for pronunciation instruction. *Journal of Second Language Pronunciation, 7*(1), 89–115. https://doi.org/10.1075/jslp.20005.ols

Rehman, I. (2021). *Real-time formant extraction for second language vowel production training.* (Publication No. 28417633) [Doctoral dissertation, Iowa State University]. ProQuest Dissertations & Theses Global.

Riney, T. J., & Takagi, N. (1999). Global foreign accent and voice onset time among Japanese EFL speakers. *Language Learning, 49*(2), 275–302. https://doi.org/10.1111/0023-8333.00089

Rose, M. (2010). Intervocalic tap and trill production in the acquisition of Spanish as a second language. *Studies in Hispanic and Lusophone Linguistics, 3*(2), 379–419. https://doi.org/10.1515/shll-2010-1080

Saito, K., & Plonsky, L. (2019). Effects of second language pronunciation teaching revisited: A proposed measurement framework and meta-analysis. *Language Learning*, *69*(3), 652–708. https://doi.org/10.1111/lang.12345

Saito, K., & van Poeteren, K. (2017). The perception–production link revisited: The case of Japanese learners' English /ɹ/ performance. *International Journal of Applied Linguistics*, *28*(1), 3–17. https://doi.org/10.1111/ijal.12175

Sakai, M. (2018). Moving towards a bilingual baseline in second language phonetic research. *Journal of Second Language Pronunciation*, *4*(1), 11–45. https://doi.org/10.1075/jslp.00002.sak

Schoonmaker-Gates, E. (2015). On voice-onset time as a cue to foreign accent in Spanish: Native and nonnative perceptions. *Hispania*, *98*(4), 779–791. https://doi.org/10.1353/hpn.2015.0110

Shea, C. E., & Curtin, S. (2011). Experience, representations and the production of second language allophones. *Second Language Research*, *27*(2), 229–250. https://doi.org/10.1177/0267658310375753

Singmann, H., Bolker, B., Westfall, J., Aust, F., & Ben-Shachar, M. (2023). _afex: Analysis of Factorial Experiments. R package version 1.2-1, <https://CRAN.R-project.org/package=afex>.

Stölten, K., Abrahamsson, N., & Hyltenstam, K. (2015). Effects of age and speaking rate on voice onset time. *Studies in Second Language Acquisition*, *37*(1), 71–100. https://doi.org/10.1017/s0272263114000151

4

RESEARCHING THE PERCEPTION-PRODUCTION LINK

Introduction

Why are researchers interested in the perception-production link at all? From a theoretical perspective, examining how perception and production are related to one another can shed light on what the basic units and mechanisms of speech perception and production are. Simply put, what are people learning when they learn to perceive a sound, and what are they learning when they learn to produce it? Are they learning the same type of information? If so, what does that information consist of? If not, how is perceptual information converted into a format suitable for production and on what timeline does this occur? Traditionally, researchers have assumed that people are learning categories, but that may not be the case, especially in L2 (Baese-Berk et al., 2022). These theoretical questions have practical implications. For instance, if perception and production are related, then it stands to reason that training perception could have a wash over effect on production and vice versa, though production-to-perception transfer has not been studied as extensively as its perception-to-production counterpart (Sakai & Moorman, 2018). From a developmental perspective, investigating the strength of the link over time can shed light on how transfer between modalities can be optimized, that is, how perception-to-production transfer from perception training can be quickened and/or magnified. To be clear, it's uncontroversial that perception and production are related, and it's relatively uncontroversial that there is a time lag between learning in one modality and the other. There is also consensus that many variables affect production, perception being but one of them (Kissling, 2014). Still, it's

DOI: 10.4324/9781003279266-4

easy to imagine how the strength of the perception-production link might change over time and the implications these changes could have for language learning. For example, during the initial stages of learning, perception could be the strongest regulator of production learning, constraining how accurately learners produce L2 sounds. Then, it could become one of several predictors, and finally, its influence might diminish. It's also easy to imagine the opposite. During the initial stages of learning, when the connection between the two modalities is tenuous—assuming that it is— then perception might not influence production much at all, in which case there would be little cross-modality transfer. Then, as learning progresses, and as the perception-production link is forged and becomes more robust, the pace and strength of transfer might increase. As these hypotheses illustrate, many questions remain about the link itself, and empirically robust perception-production research capable of addressing these questions is just beginning to emerge.

Part of the challenge of working on the perception-production link is that doing so demands an understanding of both perception and production, including how each modality is measured and evaluated. Yet, this knowledge is not enough to carry out robust perception-production work. Perception-production research is its own strand with its own set of theories and methods. The main conceptual challenge in this area is understanding how the two modalities are connected and how that connection emerges and develops during L2 learning. The main methodological challenge is developing tasks and evaluation schemes that allow the two modalities to be compared. To date, in many cases, researchers have collected perception and production data and analyzed performance in each modality independently, treating the perception-production link as an add-on or an after-thought to be addressed using relatively simple analytical techniques such as rank-ordering participants in terms of observed patterns (perception > production, production > perception, etc.) or using correlation to quantify the relationship between perception and production performance at a single point in learners' developmental trajectory. While a sensible starting point for perception-production research, the state of the art has evolved significantly, and researchers now have the methodological and statistical tools to carry out more conceptually interesting and empirically rigorous analyses.

There is little doubt that L2 speech perception and production are related. Models of L2 speech learning such as the Speech Learning Model (Flege, 1995; Flege & Bohn, 2021) argue that perception and production influence one another and co-evolve, and the (L2) Perceptual Assimilation Model (Best, 1995; Best & Tyler, 2007) takes the articulatory gesture as the basic unit of speech perception (i.e., according to this model, what speakers perceive are the invariant articulatory gestures that give rise to the complex, multimodal acoustic reality of speech), which means that perception and production should be tightly coordinated because they share the same underlying representation. Empirically, there is a large body of research demonstrating a link between the two modalities. In their meta-analysis of perception training studies, Sakai and Moorman (2018) found that perception training leads to small but reliable gains in production, but the magnitude of the gain across modalities was not significantly related. Put another way, improved perception led to improved production, but the amount of improvement in perception was not related to the amount of improvement in production. Sakai and Moorman's (2018) work also shed light on several important moderator variables, such as the length of the training and its focus (i.e., training obstruents vs. liquids vs. vowels). Meta-analytic findings such as these are useful because they reveal the average effect that can be expected, aggregating over individual research reports. They also account for variability in results via moderator analyses. At the same time, meta-analysis cannot account for what was never there in the first place, which means that any systematic gap in the literature remains unresolved. Furthermore, perception-production research seems to show greater variability than perhaps other areas of L2 pronunciation because it sits at the intersection of two research domains, each with its own set of traditions and methods.

Certainly, researchers should continue to rely on meta-analysis as a tool for systematizing and understanding the state of the art; it would be interesting and worthwhile, for example, to have a meta-analysis focusing on observational research, where the goal would be to obtain an estimate of the average correlation coefficient that can be expected in perception-production work. However, to advance the state of the art, researchers also need to revisit perception-production research methods to design perception-production studies that are as comparable to one another as possible (Nagle & Baese-Berk, 2021). In perception-production work, there is variability in research design, notably whether researchers take an experimental or observational approach and whether within an observational paradigm they examine the link cross-sectionally or longitudinally; variability in concept/focus, insofar as researchers have examined a range of speaker populations, proficiencies, and target structures; and variability in measurement, in terms of the tasks, outcome measures, and analytical procedures that researchers have used. Most of the time, studies differ along several parameters, making it difficult, if not impossible, to determine the source of perception-production differences in the existing literature. In my view, it's essential that researchers approach the perception-production link more systematically and incrementally, designing maximally comparable studies by manipulating one or two variables while holding all others constant.

It bears mentioning here that not all features should be manipulated/ tested, nor should all combinations of features. At this stage of perception-production research, much more longitudinal work is needed. As such, cross-sectional work should be undertaken cautiously, if at all. One area where cross-sectional research could be helpful would be in the systematic manipulation of measurement features, where a one-shot design could be used to test what the perception-production link looks like (i.e., how it manifests) under a variety of task conditions (for perception, discrimination and identification; for production, controlled and spontaneous speech) and considering various perspectives on accuracy (for production, listener-based intelligibility vs. acoustic analysis). Such a study could provide baseline data that could speak to the measurement conditions under which perception and production appear to be more strongly aligned with one another. If combined with other levers in the system, for instance, a range of L1-L2 pairings and target structure, then such data could provide additional insight into how language pairings and target structures shape the link (i.e., what the perception-production link looks like for different types of target structures, language pairings, tasks). Ultimately, however, L2 speech research is fundamentally about understanding development, which in this case means understanding how perception and production interact and shape one another throughout the L2 learning process. For that, longitudinal data is necessary.

Current Approaches to the Link

Before we examine each group of study features and how they can be meaningfully combined to shed light on the perception-production link, as a starting point, it's useful to look at the types of studies that researchers have carried out. For this purpose, I distinguish between experimental studies in which perception or production was trained and gains were measured in the untrained modality (e.g., the studies that Sakai and Moorman (2018) synthesized in their meta-analysis), and observational studies, in which the researcher collected perception-production data without providing training in either modality. Experimental research is nearly always longitudinal, insofar as it corresponds to a pre-post(-delayed) design. However, in some cases, with novice L2 learners who have no experience with the L2 or target structure, researchers may forgo pre-testing, collecting only post-training data. I don't recommend this approach because even when participants have no knowledge of and have had no exposure to the target structure, there are likely to be important differences in baseline perception and production that should be taken into account. Likewise, on the other side of the testing procedure, it is important to consider implementing one—or several—delayed

114 Researching the Perception-Production Link

post-tests (Nagle, 2022), which can speak to the extent to which training leads to cross-modality gains that are durable (i.e., that do not rapidly diminish after training). This question is an interesting one because even if training perception leads to gains in production at post-test (Sakai & Moorman, 2018), the transfer may fade rapidly. In other words, cross-modality learning may be ephemeral.

Observational studies may be either cross-sectional or longitudinal. In a cross-sectional design, perception and production data are collected at a single point in time. To get at developmental issues, data may be collected from several groups. For instance, to understand how age of onset of L2 learning, length of L2 residence, and quantity and quality of L2 use affect performance in each modality and the strength of the link, researchers may collect one-shot data from participants who fall along a continuum on each variable. Jia et al. (2006) compared three groups of L1 Mandarin speakers who were learning L2 English: (1) learners studying English in China, (2) learners who had recently arrived in the United States, and (3) learners who had been living in the United States for a longer period. Learners of varying ages were represented in all groups, which allowed the authors to examine how age, context of learning, and amount of exposure affected learners' perception and production of English vowel categories, including the perception-production link. In other cases, researchers may cross variables, creating categories of participants (e.g., early age of L2 onset, high amount of L1 use vs. early age of L2 onset, low amount of L1 use), setting up categorical contrasts that are theoretically interesting. In fact, this is how early perception-production work began, and much of this work informed the first version of the Speech Learning Model (Flege, 1995). However, even in the first formulation of the model, Flege underscored the importance of longitudinal data: "If the perception of L2 sounds does change, we need to know *how* [original emphasis] it changes, and what impact perceptual changes have on L2 speech production" (1995, p. 269). In the revised model, Flege and Bohn made an even stronger case for investigating the link longitudinally. If "L2 segmental production and perception coevolve without precedence" (2021, pp. 28–29), then the only way to advance the state of the art is to examine how the two modalities fluctuate and interact over time. This conceptualization necessitates a shift in current research practices. Methodologically, to examine coevolution, researchers will need to collect several waves of perception and production data (see, e.g., the longitudinal study that Flege and Bohn (2021) proposed), and analytically, it will be necessary to adopt more sophisticated modeling techniques capable of relating change in one modality to change in another.

Several studies have already made strides in this area. In Nagle (2018), I collected five waves of stop consonant perception and production data from English-speaking learners of Spanish. Participants completed an identification task and two production tasks, a sentence formation task and a sentence reading task, which I designed to tap into more spontaneous and more controlled production, respectively. I analyzed the timing of the link, finding that changes in perception predicted changes in production at the subsequent data point. In another study, I analyzed stop consonant perception and production over eight waves in a similar sample of learners (Nagle, 2021). My goal in that study was to examine if within-subjects changes in perception were related to within-subjects changes in production. In other words, I investigated whether improvements in perception were associated with improvements in production. Surprisingly, I found that good perceivers tended to be good producers, but improved perception was not related to improved production. While the 2018 and 2021 studies are conceptually and methodologically similar in many ways, they still show important differences in measurement. For instance, in the 2021 study, I used a different set of tasks to define perception and production ability: oddity for perception and delayed word repetition and timed picture description to tap into controlled and spontaneous production ability. Casillas (2020) is another study examining stop consonant perception and production in a group of English-speaking learners of Spanish who were enrolled in a domestic immersion program. He collected data over eight weekly sessions, using a labeling task to measure participants' perception and picture naming to measure their production. He found evidence for changes in both modalities, but changes in perception preceded changes in production.

These studies raise questions about how similar studies need to be in order to be directly comparable. Relevant study features are summarized in Table 4.1. All three studies dealt with English-speaking learners of Spanish, but in my studies I examined classroom learners, whereas Casillas investigated learners in a domestic immersion program. Due to the inherent timing characteristics of these contexts—with classroom learners on an academic schedule and domestic immersion learners in a short-term, intensive summer program—the duration of the studies and spacing of data points were different. All three used different perception and production tasks, but they operationalized accuracy in similar ways (e.g., voice onset time (VOT) as a measure of acoustic accuracy for the production data). They used sophisticated but slightly different analytical approaches to examine the perception-production link. In Nagle (2018), I tested different levels of perception-production synchronization by fitting linear mixed-effects models with different amounts of lag applied to the production data relative to perception. In Nagle (2021), I fit a perception model, extracted within-subjects residuals, and then incorporated those perception residuals as a time-varying predictor of production accuracy, again

116 Researching the Perception-Production Link

TABLE 4.1 Summary of Study Features in Nagle (2018, 2021) and Casillas (2020)

	Nagle (2018)	*Nagle (2021)*	*Casillas (2020)*
L2 sample size	26	37	10
Context of learning	Classroom	Classroom	Domestic immersion
Number of waves	5	7	8
Spacing of waves	Every half semester	Monthly	Weekly
Total duration	12 months	8 months	7 weeks
Target structure	Word-initial /b, p/	Word-initial /b, p/	Word-initial /b, d, g, p, t, k/
Perception tasks	Identification	Oddity	VOT continuum labeling
Perception accuracy	d prime	Model-estimated probabilities	Crossover boundary
Production tasks	Sentence reading Sentence formation	Delayed repetition Picture description	Delayed repetition
Production accuracy	Acoustic (VOT)	Acoustic (VOT)	Acoustic (VOT)

Note. In Nagle's studies, there was substantial participant attrition over the course of the study, resulting in a progressively smaller sample size at each data point, particularly across semesters.

using mixed-effects models. Casillas (2020) used a generalized additive mixed-effects model to examine phoneme boundaries in perception and production. This is particularly noteworthy because by operationalizing development in terms of phoneme boundaries in both modalities, he was able to analyze highly comparable outcome measures. Thus, these studies are highly similar in some ways but quite different in others, which begs the question: How do we go about investigating the perception-production link in a comprehensive and systematic way? Before we get to this question, we need to talk about measurement.

Perception-Production Measurement Issues

In perception-production research, measurement issues occur at two levels. First, we must decide how to elicit and score data in each modality, but perception-production measurement also demands that we go beyond considering measurement in each modality independently. One of the central tasks of perception-production research is establishing conceptual and methodological parity between perception and production tasks and measures. For instance, if perception is defined as the ability to correctly identify L2 sounds, then production should be operationalized on similar grounds, as the ability to produce identifiable L2 sounds. In this case, a listener-based measure of production accuracy, such as intelligibility, could be used. Yet, although this approach is intuitively appealing, speakers may produce intelligible contrasts in a variety of nonnativelike ways. They may use different cues than native speakers use, a combination of native and nonnative cues, or native cues that are weighted in a different way. Saito and van Poeteren (2017) showed that L1 Japanese speakers used F2 and duration to differentiate between English /l/ and /ɹ/, and the best predictor of intelligibility, as assessed by native English listeners, was F2, even though in native speech the /l/-/ɹ/ contrast is predominantly cued by differences in F3. The point is, given that perception stimuli are nearly always produced by native speakers, the phonetic cues that are the target of perception research may not match the phonetic cues that nonnative speakers use when producing the contrast. Thus, a relevant question is, should the phonetic cues that listeners are sensitive to in perception be related to the phonetic cues they use in production? The answer to that question appears to be a tentative yes. Flege et al. (1997) found that cue use in perception was related to cue use in production, but perception cue use did not account for all variance in production, suggesting that perception accuracy was an important predictor of production accuracy, but not the sole predictor. Researchers need to keep in mind that there is an upper limit on the strength of the perception-production relationship in any study because production depends on perception and many other factors. In speech research, we tend to treat L1 speakers as a highly homogenous group in terms of their perception and production, and in this section, I have partially adopted this view. However, even among L1 speakers, there is tremendous variation in the perception and production of sounds (e.g., Escudero & Boersma, 2004; Schertz et al., 2015), so it shouldn't come as a surprise that L2 speakers also show a high amount of variability. What can be said, however, is that variability is likely to be more constrained for L1 speakers than it is for L2 speakers.

In his examination of stop consonant perception and production, Casillas (2020) measured perception using a labeling task, using the resulting data to derive a perceptual crossover boundary for each participant (i.e., the point on the VOT continuum at which voiced stops were perceived as voiceless). He elicited production data using a picture naming task, which he also used to derive a production crossover boundary. In his analysis, he found that changes in perception boundaries preceded changes in production boundaries. His study, as well as Flege et al.'s (1997), underscores the importance of developing perception and production variables that are comparable. If no perception-production relationship is found, it may be because the perception and production measures were not very comparable. In other words, in some cases, no relationship between the measures

118 Researching the Perception-Production Link

would be expected because the measures themselves are inherently different. Surprisingly, to date, there has been no comprehensive methodological analysis of perception-production relationships involving different tasks and perspectives on accuracy. Such baseline research would benefit the field by providing data on the conditions under which researchers can expect to find a perception-production link and how its strength may vary according to the measurement features of the research design. I return to this point in the next section.

Perception ability is commonly quantified using a sensitivity index such as d prime, which represents the listener's sensitivity to the target contrast. Yet, it's unclear how such a measure should be related to production ability. In production, the speaker produces a single item, the accuracy of which can be quantified using acoustic analysis or listener judgment. How can researchers relate a sensitivity index, which inherently involves two sounds, to a production measure involving only one? One potential that has yet to be explored is defining production accuracy as a listener-based d prime measure. That would involve using speaker tokens as the stimuli for a discrimination test given to native listeners, in which case a production d prime score could be derived. This score would represent the speaker's ability to produce a clear contrast between two sounds. Regardless of whether such an approach ultimately proves fruitful, the point remains: As researchers, we must carefully consider and justify the perception and production tasks and outcome measures we include in our work, and this explanation must include an exploration of why the measures we have selected actually warrant comparison. Minimally, even when measurement issues are not the focus of empirical work, including multiple tasks and measures can help increase current knowledge by providing insight into how perception-production relationships fluctuate depending on the measurement decisions we make. I'm fully aware of the fact that I'm presenting more "problems" and questions than answers, but this is a reflection of the state of the art in perception-production research.

A Systematic Approach to the Link

There are still many unresolved questions about how the perception-production link works in L2 learning. To understand the link, it's critical that researchers develop studies that are maximally comparable by systematically manipulating variables of interest while controlling all other elements of methodology. There are three potential sets of variables that researchers can consider: (1) measurement issues, which encompass the tasks used to elicit data and how they are scored, that is, how perception and production abilities are operationalized; (2) sampling issues, which are related to participant characteristics such as L2 proficiency at the time of testing, the L1-L2 pairing, and target structure, which together set the nature and difficulty of the learning task in both modalities; and (3) training issues, which in experimental, training-based studies correspond to the type and structure of training, such as whether the training focuses on perception, production, or both, the number of trials per training session, and the frequency and spacing of sessions, among other training-relevant variables. In this chapter, I focus on measurement and sampling issues because I address training (i.e., experimental) research extensively in Chapter 6.

The first goal of perception-production research should be to understand how the link manifests in different learning scenarios. In Nagle and Baese-Berk (2021), we discussed several potential learning scenarios, which take into account the number of categories in the L1 and L2 and the phonetic cues with which they are implemented. In a boundary shift scenario, the L1 and L2 have the same number of categories and use the same cue but place the phonological boundary between categories at a different location on the phonetic continuum. Thus, this scenario is not about learning new categories or cues but rather requires learning how the L2 divides up the phonetic continuum with respect to its phonological categories. In a new category, same cue scenario, the L2 has more categories than the L1, but the phonetic cue is the same. In this case, then, the L2 learner needs to create a new category using a known/familiar phonetic cue. Finally, in a new category, new cue scenario, the L2 has more categories than the L1, and those categories are implemented using a new cue that is not used contrastively in the L1, which means that the L2 learner must add a new category by learning to attend to a novel phonetic cue (while simultaneously adjusting the familiar cue). In their meta-analysis, Sakai and Moorman (2018) laid out several additional possibilities, including phonotactic constraints, where the L2 allows contrasts to occur in positions that are disallowed in the L1 (e.g., word-final stop consonants in English). Regardless of whether these hypothesized scenarios are borne out empirically, the takeaway is that we must consider what L2 category learning entails and investigate how perception-production unfolds under those different conditions.

In Nagle and Baese-Berk (2021), we developed a set of learning scenarios considering crosslinguistic differences in stop consonant systems. Table 4.2 provides an overview of stop consonants in several languages. In English, Spanish, Thai, and Korean, VOT is one of the primary cues to stop consonant contrasts, but each language divides the VOT continuum in a different way. In English and Spanish there are two stop categories, whereas in Thai and Korean there are three. Furthermore, in Korean, in addition to VOT, F0 is also necessary to fully differentiate the three stop categories. Applying the taxonomy we presented in the 2021 article, for English speakers,

120 Researching the Perception-Production Link

TABLE 4.2 Potential Crosslinguistic Learning Categories for Stop Consonants

Language	Phonological Categories	Primary Phonetic Cues	Cue Type
English	2	VOT	Temporal
Spanish	2	VOT	Temporal
Thai	3	VOT	Temporal
Korean	3	VOT, F0	Temporal, Spectral

Spanish would be a boundary shift (same number of categories, same phonetic cue, different phonetic configuration), Thai would be a new category, same cue, and Korean would be a new category, new cue. This principally applies to word-initial (and utterance-initial) stops.

How else could this taxonomy be expanded and tested? For one, the phonetic cues are either temporal (VOT) or spectral differences (F0). Another temporal cue could be tested to determine the extent to which temporal cues pattern together. For instance, English speakers' perception and production of Japanese geminate stops, which occur in word-medial position and principally show differences in closure duration, could be tested. And for that matter, English speakers' perception and production of word-medial Spanish stops, where closure duration is also a cue to stop consonant voicing, could also be tested (see, e.g., Zampini & Green, 2001). Perception and production of novel place contrasts could be examined by, for instance, examining English speakers' perception and production of the Hindi dental-retroflex contrast. In outlining these possibilities, I have framed research in terms of English speakers' perception and production of additional languages, but it bears mentioning that English doesn't need to be the L1 or L2. Indeed, it would be profitable to expand to language pairs that don't involve English at all.

The point I'm trying to make is to take a principled approach to establishing meaningful comparisons, abstracting away from particular language pairings and target structures whenever possible to understand perception-production under different types of crosslinguistic phonological and phonetic similarity. To that point, some of the languages reviewed also present similar contrasts in their fricative systems. Japanese has geminate fricatives, and Korean has a tense-plain-aspirated affricate system that mirrors its stop consonant system. Korean also has plain and tense fricatives. Would the perception-production of Korean stops look similar to perception-production of Korean affricates and fricatives? Regardless of the answer to that question, the data can shed important light on contrast-specific versus contrast-general forms of learning. For instance, if learners are trained on the Korean stops, does that training generalize to affricates, considering perception, production, and the perception-production link? And in the absence of training, how does learners' perception and production of Korean stops, affricates, and fricatives develop?

Another important issue is systematicity in measurement. The tasks that we select and how we define performance in each modality certainly affect perception-production findings. In fact, a consistent theme in perception-production research is that findings are task-dependent, and in some cases, researchers have called into question whether perception and production measures can be compared at all. In other words, are we comparing apples to oranges, or is there a way to establish conceptually and empirically valid comparisons? It is my view that we don't yet have enough information on within- and cross-modality relationships for a variety of languages and target structures. How do different forms of discrimination relate to one another, and how do they relate to identification? Likewise, to what extent is performance on different production tasks correlated? And, most importantly for the perception-production link, to what extent is performance on a range of perception tasks related to performance on a range of production tasks? Rather than manipulating tasks across studies, I think it would be beneficial to include multiple tasks in each study, which would provide more robust measurement of both modalities. There is also a sound theoretical basis for doing so. According to the Speech Learning Model (Flege, 1995; Flege & Bohn, 2021), learners must notice a difference between crosslinguistically similar sounds before they begin to form a phonetic category for a new L2 sound. To test the developmental sequence that Flege and Bohn (2021) laid out in the revised model, researchers would need to examine learners' ability to discriminate L1-L2 pairs alongside their ability to identify L2 sounds, and they would need to do so longitudinally, documenting relationships among discrimination, identification, and production accuracy.

In this section, I have attempted to provide general guidelines that should inform perception-production research. These guidelines can be interpreted as bumper lanes at a bowling alley, insofar as they establish boundary conditions for carrying out conceptually and methodologically sound perception-production work that is likely to advance the state of the art. The examples I have given should be interpreted not as hard-and-fast rules of studies to be carried out but rather as examples. Certainly, many other facets of sampling, measurement, and training can be meaningfully combined and tested. The main takeaway is that, as researchers, we should take care not to change too much from one study to the next and to have a specific rationale for making the research decisions we have made. If we (continue to) change many variables simultaneously, it will be difficult to isolate the

122 Researching the Perception-Production Link

effect each variable has on the perception-production link. And if we do not have a clear rationale for doing what we are doing, then we may engage in research that is low-impact or altogether methodologically unsound. Replication research, including close replications, could therefore be especially useful in clarifying perception-production relationships. To my knowledge, there have not been any close replications in perception-production research, even though such replications could provide detailed insight into variability across studies when methods are held constant.

Statistical Analysis

One of the challenges of working with perception-production data, especially longitudinal data, is figuring out a way to relate two dynamic measures. The principal goal of contemporary perception-production research is to understand how changes in one modality map onto changes in the other. In other words, perception-production data analysis is about relating two processes of change. Traditional analyses like ANOVA do not support time-varying predictor variables, which are independent variables that take on unique values at each data point. However, mixed-effects models and structural equation models do. Structural equation models can also be beneficial for looking at the relationship between the slope of change in perception and the slope of change in production. I focus on one statistical analysis example in this chapter, analyzing the data two ways: using a mixed-effects model and using a structural equation model. To do so, I combine and reformulate the vowel perception and production data discussed in Chapters 2 and 3.

Example 1: Mixed-Effects Model

As is the case with most data, we have several analytical pathways that we could pursue, each with its own complexities. My goal in the data portion of this chapter is to present some new analyses researchers may not have considered and to point to resources for carrying out more advanced analyses. The first thing I'd like to illustrate is how we can use the mixed-effects models we built in the previous chapters to extract by-subject random slopes for time, which quantify individual developmental trajectories, and then use those estimates in a correlation analysis to determine if the rate of change in perception and the rate of change in production are related to one another. I start with this analysis because researchers are likely familiar with correlation analysis, but this analysis represents a step up from a simple analysis of perception and production data at one time point.

Researching the Perception-Production Link **123**

A model-based approach is advantageous compared to other simpler approaches. One option would be to calculate a gain score from the first to the last data point in perception and production, treating that gain score as an estimate of the slope of learning in each modality. Using simple gain scores is not a good option for two reasons. First, if we were to use some form of gain score, we would be forced to use only two data points, the first and the last, ignoring all other available data points, which should contribute to the calculation of the rate of change over time. Perhaps we could adopt a more sophisticated approach, using more advanced mathematical techniques to estimate the slope over several data points, but that is precisely what the model does for us. Second, if we use the raw data, we assume that there is no measurement error, which is especially problematic if we limit ourselves to gain scores based on two data points. Briefly stated, the more measurements we have, the better we can estimate within-subjects variability in performance over time, which increases measurement precision. Remember that at any given data point, we have several perception and production trials for each target structure. If we aggregate this data into a time-specific mean for each participant and use those means to compute a gain score, we ignore item-/ trial-level variance, but if we use a model to build and extract by-subject trajectories, we specifically account for the item-level variance, making our estimates more precise. Furthermore, on a conceptual level, because development is a latent construct that we cannot directly measure but rather must infer from performance slices collected over time, we must be cognizant of the fact that we need to collect enough slices to estimate a latent developmental slope reliably. For all these reasons, a model-based approach is superior to simple computation of mean scores based on aggregated raw data.

One issue we can run into with this approach—and an issue that can also affect our ability to model perception as a time-varying predictor of production—is the fact that in some cases, we may not be able to fit by-subject random slopes for time. If we do not have a sufficiently large sample, in terms of participants, data points, and observations (i.e., trials or items), then the model may not converge, or it could be singular. In that case, this analysis will not be possible because the by-participant random slopes cannot be modeled. For the sake of this example, we'll assume that we can fit the by-participant random slopes.

I'll repeat some of the analyses from the relevant chapters for the sake of completeness and because I'll emphasize different aspects of the models than what I presented originally. Our plan is to fit separate models to the perception and production data. In fitting these models, our primary objective is to integrate a fixed effect for Time as well as the corresponding by-subject random effect. Then, we use these models to extract the

124 Researching the Perception-Production Link

random effects, bind them to a new data frame, and run a correlation to see if model-estimated developmental trajectories in perception (as opposed to simple gain scores) are related to model-estimated developmental trajectories in production.

In Chapter 2, we analyzed participants' identification of two English vowel contrasts, /i/-/ɪ/ and /æ/-/ɛ/, over six sessions. In Chapter 3, we analyzed participants' production of English /i/ and /ɪ/ over six sessions. We operationalized production accuracy as intelligibility, that is, whether listeners correctly identified the word the speaker intended to produce. Thus, these two data sets are conceptually linked, insofar as both perception and production are grounded in identification accuracy (participants' identification of the target sound and listeners' identification of what participants actually produced). The perception data set contained data for four vowels across two contrasts, so to make it comparable to the production data, we need to subset it to a data set consisting of only data for /i/-/ɪ/ (see the R markdown for how to subset the data) and refit the perception model with Session as both a fixed effect and a by-participant random effect.

```
fm.perception <- glmer (correct ~ session +
                  (1 + session | participant) +
                  (1 | trial), data = data.perception, family = "binomial")
```

Then, we extract the by-participant random effects, bind them to a data frame, and clean them up so that the final data frame contains two variables: a participant index variable and the by-subject estimates for the effect of Session (see the R markdown for this chapter for relevant code). As a reminder, there is much more that we could extract from the model, but here, we're only extracting the information we need for the perception-production slope analysis. We repeat this procedure for the production data.

```
fm.production <- glmer (correct ~ session +
                  (1 | listener) +
                  (1 + session | speaker) +
                  (1 | item), data = data.production, family = binomial)
```

Like we did for the perception data, we extract the production estimates for the by-participant (by-speaker) random slopes, bind them to a data frame, and tidy it up. We're nearly ready to correlate the by-subject estimated slopes in perception and production learning. We need to merge the two sets of random effects into a single data frame. We should also add the fixed effect to the random effect. The random effect estimates represent the deviation from the fixed effect, that is, each individual estimate represents how different that individual is from the group. For this reason, the random effects can be negative or positive. In the context of our analysis, a negative individual estimate would represent a rate of change that was slower than the group average, and a positive estimate would represent a rate of change that was faster than the group average. To be clear, a negative estimate does not mean a negative growth trajectory, but rather a growth trajectory that was below the average estimated trajectory. We could correlate the random effect estimates without adding in the fixed effect, but I prefer to add the fixed effect to avoid confusion. Note that the correlation between the random effects with and without the fixed effect added will be the same, so we're not altering the perception-production relationship in any way. We're simply making the analysis more transparent and interpretable. I'll create new variables in the data frame by adding the fixed effects for Session from the perception and production models to the random effects.

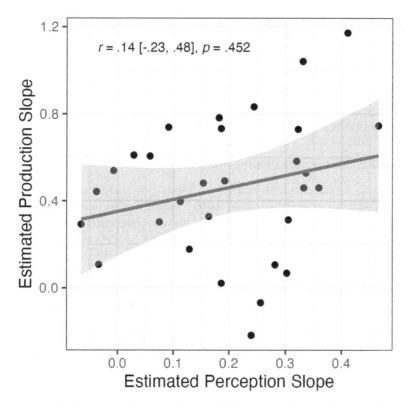

FIGURE 4.1 Relationship between Rate of Change in Perception and Rate of Change in Production.

```
data.perprod <- data.perprod %>%
  mutate(per.estimate2  = per.estimate  + .20166,
         prod.estimate2 = prod.estimate + .46680)
```

Once we correlate the measures, we see that the rate of change in perception and the rate of change in production show a small correlation, but the coefficient isn't statistically significant ($r = 0.24$, 95% CI = $[-0.13, 0.55]$, $p = 0.196$). However, it's worth noting that the 95% CI suggests that the effect could be as large as 0.55, which would be a medium-to-large effect. Although this value is less compatible with the data because it lies at the upper limit of the 95% CI, it's not impossible. Figure 4.1 plots the data.

From this analysis, we can conclude that (1) participants improved significantly in their identification and production of the English /i/-/ɪ/ contrast but (2) the rate of change in perception learning (i.e., in their identification) was not related to the rate of change in production learning (i.e., the identifiability, or intelligibility, of their production). Admittedly, this analysis is still somewhat simple because it does not consider the dynamic, or time-varying, effect of perception on production. Presenting a full time-varying approach is beyond the scope of this book, but I have reported on a variety of techniques that could be used to analyze perception-production techniques longitudinally (Nagle, 2018, 2021). Interested readers can also refer to Casillas (2020), which is a longitudinal study on stop consonant perception and production and the perception-production link.

Example 2: Multivariate Latent Growth Curve Model

Until now, we have used mixed-effects models to analyze data, but we can also use structural equation models to analyze development, treating the intercept and slope as latent factors. In my view, structural equation models present certain advantages over mixed-effects models when it comes to perception-production data. Notably, we can simultaneously model the perception and production data, using the structural equation model to examine both within- (e.g., the relationship between the perception intercept and the perception slope) and cross-modality relationships (i.e., the relationship between the perception slope and the production slope, which is our primary interest in this chapter). The structural equation model is advantageous because we can run the full analysis in a single model without the need to extract and analyze the random effect estimates separately, as we did with the mixed-effects models. Beyond their utility for analyzing perception-production relationships, structural equation models are widely used for analyzing latent individual difference constructs and so presenting them here will lay the groundwork for discussing them again in Chapter 7, which deals with individual differences in pronunciation learning. At the same time, we've been focusing on mixed-effects models up to this point, so if structural equation modeling feels overwhelming at this stage, feel free to skip this section.

To build this analysis from the ground up, we will fit separate structural equation models to the perception and the production data. Then, we will combine those models to fit a single model to assess the perception-production relationship. One of the challenges we face with this type of analysis is what to do with the individual trials or items. We could incorporate them into the model, which would yield a doubly-latent model where (1) performance at each time point is modeled as a latent construct based on the items tested at that time point and then (2) the intercept and slope are modeled as latent factors based on the latent performance variables. As you can see, this analysis is complicated (and data intensive), so for the sake of demonstration, I won't fit this model here. Instead, we will work with mean accuracy scores in perception and production, pooling over trials and items. To be clear, pooling the data in this way has its disadvantages, but doing so is necessary for the structural equation models we will fit. A streamlined version of the model we are attempting to build is given in Figure 4.2. In this simplified illustration, the latent intercepts and slopes give rise to the time-specific indicators. We define the latent intercept by setting all factor

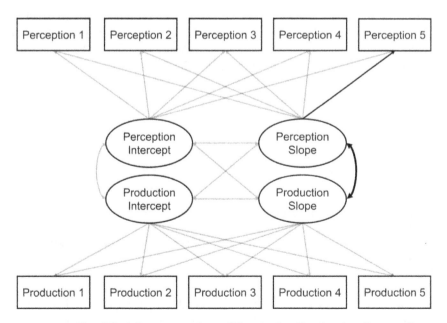

FIGURE 4.2 Simplified Representation of Perception-Production Latent Curve Model.

128 Researching the Perception-Production Link

loadings to 1, and we define the latent slope by numbering factor loadings in ascending order, beginning with 0. In terms of the latent factors, I have included covariances between (1) the latent intercepts, (2) the latent slopes, and (3) the latent intercept and slope, within (e.g., perception intercept with perception slope) and across (e.g., perception intercept with production slope) modalities. The key estimate we are trying to obtain is shown as the boldest black line: the covariance between the latent perception slope and the latent production slope.

In an ideal world, we would be able to recycle the data from the first two chapters for structural equation modeling. However, if we do that, the model is likely to show serious problems with fit because when I simulated those data sets I didn't take into account the parameters that need to be simulated for a structural equation model. In short, the only surefire way to generate structural equation model data suitable for analysis is to simulate the structural equation model itself, letting the model dictate the data structure. So, for this analysis, we'll use a new data set. In this data set, the variables don't look like what you're accustomed to seeing. Remember that our outcome variable was binary, $0/1$. If we aggregated the data, then we would expect a score ranging from 0 to 1, reflecting the proportion of correct responses for a given participant at a given session. The simulated structural equation model data doesn't conform to this property, but the structural equation model does conform to the parameters I input. As a result, for this example, we'll focus on the steps required for this analysis rather than the actual numbers in the data set. Lastly, I should point out that I increased sample size for this analysis, simulating data for 100 participants. Structural equation models tend to be data intensive.

The *lavaan* (Rosseel, 2012) package is used for structural equation modeling in R. The basic procedure for fitting a structural equation model is to define the model, fit it to the data, and then assess its fit. Fortunately, the models we will fit first are relatively simple. To create an intercept term, we premultiply the columns indicating participants' score at each session by 1, and to create a slope term, we premultiply those columns by 0–5, in order.

```
lcm.per <- "
perception.int =~ 1*perception1 + 1*perception2 + 1*perception3 + 1*percep-
tion4 + 1*perception5 + 1*perception6
perception.slp =~ 0*perception1 + 1*perception2 + 2*perception3 + 3*percep-
tion4 + 4*perception5 + 5*perception6
"
```

Notice two conventions. First, the entire model appears in quotation marks, and second, when we specify a latent factor, such as the latent intercept or slope, we use an equal sign and a tilde (=~). We have specified the model, so we can now fit it to the data using the growth() function and call a summary of it using the summary() function.

```
lcm.per.fit <- growth(model = lcm.per, data = data.perception, missing = "ML")
summary(lcm.per.fit, fit.measures = T, standardized = T)
```

We repeat this procedure for the production data. Before we move forward with the full model of the perception-production data, we need to review the model fit indices for the simple latent curve models we fit to the perception and production data. Both models are summarized in Table 4.3.

Overall, the fit indices look reasonable. The Comparative Fit Index (CFI) and the Tucker–Lewis Index (TLI) are above 0.90, and the Standardized Root Mean Squared Residual (SRMR) <0.10. The Root Mean Square Error of Approximation (RMSEA) is a bit on the high side for both models. Ideally, RMSEA <0.05, but values <0.10 are acceptable. It's odd that the estimated latent slope for the production data is negative because we wouldn't expect it to be, but it's not a problem for our analysis. The full model is simply a combination of the independent models.

```
lcm.perpro <- "
perception.int =~ 1*perception1 + 1*perception2 + 1*perception3 + 1*perception4 + 1*perception5 + 1*perception6
perception.slp =~ 0*perception1 + 1*perception2 + 2*perception3 + 3*perception4 + 4*perception5 + 5*perception6
production.int =~ 1*production1 + 1*production2 + 1*production3 + 1*production4 + 1*production5 + 1*production6
production.slp =~ 0*production1 + 1*production2 + 2*production3 + 3*production4 + 4*production5 + 5*production6
"
```

TABLE 4.3 Summary of Perception and Production Latent Curve Models

Model Statistic	Perception Model	Production Model
$\chi^2(16)$	27.89	28.32
CFI	0.987	0.988
TLI	0.988	0.989
RMSEA	0.086 [0.025, 0.138]	0.088 [0.028, 0.140]
SRMR	0.047	0.039
Latent intercept	0.322	0.633
Latent slope	0.118	−0.084
Intercept-slope correlation	−0.134	−0.453

Note. The confidence interval given for RMSEA is a 90% interval.

130 Researching the Perception-Production Link

The fit indices look good: CFI = 0.986, TLI = 0.985, RMSEA = 0.068 [0.035, 0.097], and SRMR = 0.037. There is virtually no change in the estimated latent intercepts and slopes. For perception, the intercept = 0.328 and the slope = 0.116, and for production, the intercept = 0.632 and the slope = –0.084. I won't summarize the whole set of covariances here (interested readers can refer to the model in the R markdown). Instead, we'll focus on the correlation between the latent slopes: $r = 0.68$. This would be considered a large effect according to Plonsky and Oswald's (2014) benchmarks for SLA research. This coefficient suggests a strong relationship between the rate of change in perception and the rate of change in production. Remember that this data set is a new data set that I simulated, so we wouldn't expect the correlation in the structural equation model to mirror the correlation that we observed when we correlated the random effect estimates we extracted from the mixed-effects models.

I have intentionally kept this discussion of the structural equation models brief. Readers who are interested in learning more about structural equation modeling can consult Kline (2023) and Schoonen (2015). Kline (2023) is an excellent, comprehensive overview, and Schoonen (2015) is a good discussion of structural equation modeling in SLA.

Summary and Recommendations

- Whenever possible, include multiple perception and production tasks in your perception-production research; be clear about the strengths and limitations of each task and the ways in which they differ.
- Perception and production tasks and outcome measures should be comparable; think about what measures should be compared. If perception is based on identification, then production should be based on identification; if perception is quantified via cue weights, then production should also be quantified via cue weights. Avoid apples-to-oranges comparisons.
- Use a longitudinal design. Understanding the perception-production link demands an understanding of how performance in each modality changes and the impact perceptual changes have on production (and vice versa). Longitudinal designs can be applied in observational or experimental studies.
- Use appropriate analyses; in most cases, simple correlation is not a viable analytical approach for longitudinal data, and even if it is, it's unlikely to provide novel insight into perception-production relationships. Analysis is not an afterthought but requires an investment of time and energy like any other aspect of research methodology. Take the time needed to learn about and conduct an appropriate analysis for longitudinal perception-production data.

Researching the Perception-Production Link **131**

- Consider replication. Conduct a close replication of your own research or another perception-production study whose methods have been reported clearly and transparently. By the same token, aim for transparency and open science. Open science is beneficial for all research areas but has the chance to make a substantial impact on perception-production research, where complex decisions must be made related to each modality and to the link itself. If you closely replicate your own work, then you can also consider combining methodologically identical data sets, which may present opportunities for more complex and robust analyses than those that would have been possible on the original, smaller-n data sets.

Chapter Questions

1. Find at least two studies investigating the perception and production of the same target structure, ideally in the same learner population. Use Table 4.1 to compare the studies. In what ways are they similar and different? How might the decisions the authors made affect their findings? What limitations did the authors acknowledge in the manuscript regarding their task and measurement choices?
2. Think about an additional language you know. Design a longitudinal study on the perception-production link, justifying your selection of target structure, tasks, and coding procedures.
3. Find a study on the perception-production link published in the last five years. Could you replicate it? That is, are the tasks and procedures described in sufficient detail to allow for replication? Have the authors made their materials, experimental procedures, data, and analyses available?
4. Using the stop consonant data from the first two chapters, follow the first analysis to fit mixed-effects models to the stop perception and production data. Then, extract the random effect estimates and correlate them. How strongly is the rate of change in stop consonant perception related to the rate of change in stop consonant production?

References

Baese-Berk, M. M., Chandrasekaran, B., & Roark, C. L. (2022). The nature of nonnative speech sound representations. *The Journal of the Acoustical Society of America*, 152(5), 3025–3034. https://doi.org/10.1121/10.0015230

Best, C. T. (1995). A direct realist view of cross-language speech perception. In W. Strange (Ed.), *Speech perception and linguistic experience: Issues in cross-language research* (pp. 171–204). York Press.

Best, C. T., & Tyler, M. D. (2007). Nonnative and second-language speech perception: Commonalities and complementarities. In M. J. Munro & O.-S. Bohn (Eds.), *Second language speech learning: The role of language experience in speech perception and production* (pp. 13–24). John Benjamins.

Casillas, J. V. (2020). Phonetic category formation is perceptually driven during the early stages of adult L2 development. *Language and Speech*, *63*(3), 550–581. https://doi.org/10.1177/0023830919866225

Escudero, P., & Boersma, P. (2004). Bridging the gap between L2 speech perception research and phonological theory. *Studies in Second Language Acquisition*, *26*(4), 551–585. https://doi.org/10.1017/s0272263104040021

Flege, J. E. (1995). Second language speech learning: Theory, findings, problems. In W. Strange (Ed.), *Speech perception and linguistic experience: Issues in cross-language research* (pp. 233–277). York Press.

Flege, J. E., & Bohn, O.-S. (2021). The revised speech learning model. In R. Wayland (Ed.), *Second language speech learning: Theoretical and empirical progress* (pp. 3–83). Cambridge University Press.

Flege, J. E., Bohn, O.-S., & Jang, S. (1997). Effects of experience on nonnative speakers' production and perception of English vowels. *Journal of Phonetics*, *25*(4), 437–470. https://doi.org/10.1006/jpho.1997.0052

Jia, G., Strange, W., Collado, J., & Guan, Q. (2006). Perception and production of English vowels by Mandarin speakers: Age-related differences vary with amount of L2 exposure. *Journal of the Acoustical Society of America*, *119*(2), 1118–1130. https://doi.org/10.1121/1.2151806

Kissling, E. M. (2014). What predicts the effectiveness of foreign-language pronunciation instruction? Investigating the role of perception and other individual differences. *The Canadian Modern Language Review*, *70*(4), 532–558. https://doi.org/10.3138/cmlr.2161

Kline, R. B. (2023). *Principles and practice of structural equation modeling* (5th ed.). Guilford Press.

Nagle, C. (2022). Rethinking pronunciation posttesting. *Journal of Second Language Pronunciation*, *8*(2), 161–167. https://doi.org/10.1075/jslp.22019.nag

Nagle, C. L. (2018). Examining the temporal structure of the perception-production link in second language acquisition: A longitudinal study. *Language Learning*, *68*(1), 234–270. https://doi.org/10.1111/lang.12275

Nagle, C. L. (2021). Revisiting perception–production relationships: Exploring a new approach to investigate perception as a time-varying predictor. *Language Learning*, *71*(1), 243–279. https://doi.org/10.1111/lang.12431

Nagle, C. L., & Baese-Berk, M. M. (2021). Advancing the state of the art in L2 speech perception-production research: Revisiting theoretical assumptions and methodological practices. *Studies in Second Language Acquisition*, *44*(2), 580–605. https://doi.org/10.1017/s0272263121000371

Plonsky, L., & Oswald, F. L. (2014). How big Is "big"? Interpreting effect sizes in L2 research. *Language Learning*, *64*(4), 878–912. https://doi.org/10.1111/lang.12079

Rosseel, Y. (2012). "lavaan: An R Package for Structural Equation Modeling." *Journal of Statistical Software*, *48*(2), 1–36. https://doi.org/10.18637/jss.v048.i02.

Saito, K., & van Poeteren, K. (2017). The perception–production link revisited: The case of Japanese learners' English /ɹ/ performance. *International Journal of Applied Linguistics*, *28*(1), 3–17. https://doi.org/10.1111/ijal.12175

Sakai, M., & Moorman, C. (2018). Can perception training improve the production of second language phonemes? A meta-analytic review of 25 years of perception training research. *Applied Psycholinguistics*, *39*(1), 187–224. https://doi.org/10.1017/s0142716417000418

Schertz, J., Cho, T., Lotto, A., & Warner, N. (2015). Individual differences in phonetic cue use in production and perception of a nonnative sound contrast. *Journal of Phonetics, 52*, 183–204. https://doi.org/10.1016/j.wocn.2015.07.003

Schoonen, R. (2015). Structural equation modeling in L2 research. In L. Plonsky (Ed.), *Advancing quantitative methods in second language research* (pp. 213–242). Routledge.

Zampini, M., & Green, K. P. (2001). The voicing contrast in English and Spanish: The relationship between perception and production. In J. Nicol (Ed.), *One mind, two languages* (pp. 23–48). Wiley-Blackwell.

5
RESEARCHING THE PRODUCTION OF GLOBAL FEATURES

Introduction

In research on speech production, researchers tend to focus on the speaker. However, speech is also in the ear of the listener, and listeners have played an important role in speech research. For instance, in early work, L1 listeners were recruited to rate the accentedness of L2 speakers, with the goal of determining who had a nativelike accent in the L2. Since that early work centering on nativelikeness, listener-based ratings have expanded. In Chapter 3 on the production of specific features, I introduced transcription and forced choice tasks as a means of quantifying word-level intelligibility (e.g., Does the listener hear the word the speaker intended to produce?). In this chapter, I discuss four prominent listener-based constructs that have been applied to longer stretches of L2 speech: intelligibility, comprehensibility, fluency, and accentedness.

Intelligibility refers to actual understanding of speech, irrespective of processing effort, whereas comprehensibility represents ease of understanding and is therefore a subjective measure of the amount of effort the listener must invest to understand the speech (and, by extension, the speaker). Accentedness represents the nativelikeness of speech, as assessed by the listener in reference to a native, often local, variety of the target language. Perceived fluency is a measure of the listener's perception of the rhythm and flow of speech. In recent years, research on global dimensions of speech has increased exponentially, but, as I mentioned in the opening paragraph, listener-based ratings were included in some of the earliest studies in second language acquisition (SLA). As a means of providing background

DOI: 10.4324/9781003279266-5

on the trajectory of work in this area, I divide research into three general periods: (1) early work examining relationships between the global features, (2) a second wave of research (2010–2020) examining linguistic predictors of comprehensibility and accentedness, and (3) a recent wave of research (2018–) that has begun to examine listener-based dimensions from dynamic and interactive perspectives. This area continues to generate intense scholarly interest (e.g., Crowther & Isbell, 2023), so I have no doubt that by the time this book is published, a new strand of global features research will have emerged. It also bears mentioning that this research sits at the intersection of several disciplines, including social psychology (Fuertes et al., 2012) and communication studies (Dragojevic & Giles, 2016; Dragojevic et al., 2017). I don't have the space to address this point extensively in this chapter, but I wanted to mention it because I think it's important to understand that researchers from diverse disciplinary backgrounds are interested in listeners' perceptions. I suspect as work in this area continues to evolve, it will become increasingly interdisciplinary, so I encourage speech researchers interested in this area to read and draw upon literature in adjacent fields.

Gass and Varonis were perhaps the first SLA researchers to investigate the relationship between various aspects of linguistic competence and comprehensibility, which they defined as "how easy it is to interpret the message" (1984, p. 125). They ran a series of experiments to examine how the grammaticality and pronunciation of an utterance affected native speaker perception. Presaging more recent studies examining linguistic predictors of comprehensibility and the subtle ways in which various aspects of linguistic performance interact to shape listener judgments, they found that nonnative pronunciation was more often categorized as "bad" in ungrammatical utterances, which were also rated as less comprehensible. In Munro and Derwing's (1995, 2020) landmark study on the interrelationships among intelligibility, comprehensibility, and accentedness, a study which effectively defined research methodology for global dimensions, L2 English speakers recorded a short picture narration task from which two utterances were sampled and presented to listeners for transcription (intelligibility) and rating (comprehensibility and accentedness). The authors also coded the utterances for several linguistic variables, including grammatical and phonemic errors, to examine the relationship between those features and the global ratings. Findings showed that (1) intelligibility and comprehensibility were more strongly associated with one another than they were with accentedness, (2) utterances transcribed with perfect accuracy were generally comprehensible but showed varying degrees of accentedness, and (3) a range of linguistic features had an impact on all three listener-based dimensions (see also Derwing & Munro, 1997). The fact that even a moderate-to-strong accent did not necessarily affect listener understanding (intelligibility) sparked a shift toward intelligibility rather than nativelikeness in pronunciation research and teaching (Levis, 2005, 2020).

Since those initial studies, global dimensions have experienced a theoretical and methodological renaissance. In one strand of work, researchers have concentrated on understanding the linguistic variables that underpin listeners' comprehensibility and accentedness judgments. Importantly, comprehensibility, instead of intelligibility, has risen to the forefront of this body of literature as the primary metric of listener understanding because it's easy to assess using scalar ratings and, as such, is applicable to a variety of teaching and research settings. In Trofimovich and Isaacs (2012), listeners evaluated 30-second samples of spontaneous speech, which the authors coded for 19 linguistic variables spanning pronunciation, fluency, lexis and grammar, and discourse. In agreement with Munro and Derwing (1995), their findings provided another piece of evidence that comprehensibility and accentedness are distinct, listener-based constructs. Type frequency, word stress (word stress appears to be especially important for comprehensibility in English; see Isaacs & Trofimovich, 2012), and grammatical accuracy were significant predictors of comprehensibility, whereas accentedness was predicted by rhythm and word stress. Each listener-based rating had a distinct set of linguistic predictors, which suggests that listeners attend to different properties of speech when evaluating ease of understanding and degree of accentedness. In another study, Saito et al. (2015) used principal components analysis to group many linguistic variables into a smaller number of factors, which were entered into regression models. Results showed that lexical and grammatical properties loaded onto one factor and pronunciation onto another. In terms of the listener-based dimensions, the two factors were significantly related to both comprehensibility and accentedness, but their weights differed: lexicogrammar predicted more variance in comprehensibility than pronunciation did, but pronunciation explained more variance in accentedness than lexicogrammar did. Whereas initial work in this area was squarely focused on L2 English, a sizable body of literature has since examined listener-based dimensions and linguistic predictors in several other L2s, including French (Bergeron & Trofimovich, 2017), German (O'Brien, 2014), Spanish (Huensch & Nagle, 2021, 2023; Nagle & Huensch, 2020), and Japanese (Akiyama & Saito, 2016).

Another important strand of work that has emerged recently focuses on understanding how comprehensibility fluctuates as the listener processes speech in real time (Nagle et al., 2019) and as speakers and listeners interact with one another (Nagle et al., 2022; Trofimovich et al., 2020). In Nagle et al. (2019), native Spanish speakers listened to approximately three minutes of L2 speech on two topics. As they listened to the recording, they used idiodynamic software (MacIntyre, 2012) to continuously evaluate the speaker's comprehensibility. Several interesting findings emerged. First, there was tremendous variation in listeners' response to speech in terms of both the number of times they rated the speaker and the magnitude of the ratings, reinforcing the view that communication is a two-way process that arises out of the interaction between speaker and listener characteristics. Simply put, each listener appeared to respond to the speech in an idiosyncratic way. At the same time, despite the variation across listeners, there were common themes and points of convergence. For instance, most listeners overlooked lapses in language use if the ideas were coherent, but even minor issues could provoke a sizable shift in comprehensibility, especially when the issue interfered with or disrupted listeners' emergent understanding of the message. Researchers have also begun to study multivariate influences on comprehensibility (Nagle et al., 2022; Tsunemoto et al., 2022) and to fill out the other side of the regression equation by including comprehensibility not as the dependent variable but as a predictor of other communicative outcomes (Nagle et al., 2023). In Nagle et al. (2022), participants rated their own and their partner's comprehensibility, collaborativeness, and anxiety seven times over a 17-minute interaction, during which dyads completed three interactive tasks. Results showed that participants' self and partner collaborativeness and anxiety ratings were significantly associated with their perception of their partner's comprehensibility, providing evidence that comprehensibility has an important behavioral and affective dimension that is co-constructed in an interactive setting.

As this summary makes evident, doing research on listener-based dimensions of speech involves several types of sampling, notably, sampling speakers, sampling speech (i.e., because the entire sample is rarely presented to the listener for rating), and sampling the listeners themselves. The rating task must also be built, and the resulting ratings must be validated. These are the methodological issues I address in this chapter, paying special attention to listener sampling procedures.

Sampling Speakers

In previous chapters, we haven't zoomed in on speakers very much, other than thinking about the broad population from which we have sampled. Traditionally, SLA research participants, including participants in L2 pronunciation research, have mostly been young adults (i.e., college-aged students) from Western, Educated, Industrialized, Rich, and Democratic (WEIRD) contexts. Research has also focused extensively on L2 English speakers to the exclusion of other L2s and L1-L2 pairings in which English is not represented at all (see, e.g., Crowther & Isbell, 2023). In and of itself, this is not especially problematic if our goal is to generalize to WEIRD populations.

For instance, if we predominantly teach and research instructed learners who are taking university-level language courses, then it's sensible to sample learners from that population. It is problematic, however, if we take those findings to be representative of L2 learning in general. That is, the problem comes from generalizing beyond the characteristics of the sample. In fact, scholars have observed that SLA knowledge has been built on overly narrow samples that do not reflect the diverse language learning contexts and realities around the globe, which means that we should take care when discussing what we "know" about SLA (Andringa & Godfroid, 2020). As a result, the same scholars have advocated for replicating prominent SLA research using more diverse samples, including non-academic ones (Andringa & Godfroid, 2019; see also https://osf.io/mp47b/).

Research priorities are complex, dictated by our interests and the contextual, logistic, and institutional realities within which we work, but there are a few simple principles that we can follow to make our samples more representative. One easy step is to describe our samples and target populations more precisely. For instance, instead of discussing "L2 learners" or "L2 Spanish learners," we could describe the sample and population as "college-aged L2 Spanish learners." Figure 5.1 is a simple graphic illustrating some of the ways in which we can conceptualize the sample and its relationship to several possible populations, displayed as nested layers. As we move from the inner core outwards, it's fair to say that the likelihood of our findings holding true for broader and broader potential populations decreases. Put another way, we can have the most confidence that our findings generalize to the most proximal population, and as we move outward, we should become more cautious in terms of claims of generalization. In describing their research on mobile gamification and elementary students' Spanish achievement and self-efficacy, Rachels and Rockinson-Szapkiw made the following observation: "The results of this study may not be generalizable

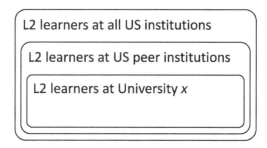

FIGURE 5.1   Illustration of How Increasingly Broad Participant Populations Can Be Conceptualized.

Researching the Production of Global Features **139**

to populations that differ significantly from the sample including those at different levels of elementary [Spanish], or more diverse populations than the sample studied" (2018, p. 85). They went on to explain the ways in which future research on the topic can enhance their findings by considering various facets of sampling. Statements of this nature would be a welcome addition to all SLA research reports, including L2 pronunciation studies.

If researchers define the target population in precise terms, then they can purposefully sample participants who meet inclusion criteria until the target sample size is reached. This option is more labor-intensive because it likely involves multiple rounds of participant recruitment and may necessitate recruiting participants beyond researchers' immediate academic sphere, but it guarantees a more representative sample. Put another way, rather than relying on convenience sampling, researchers could construct a representative sample considering the demographic characteristics of the population to which findings should generalize (see, e.g., Andringa, 2014). In Huensch and Nagle (2021), we examined how speaker proficiency affected interrelationships among intelligibility, comprehensibility, and accentedness. We screened participants using an Elicited Imitation Task (EIT; Ortega et al., 2002; Solon et al., 2019) and used EIT scores to select participants for inclusion in the study, with the goal of creating a representative sample of scores. We limited screening to EIT scores because that was a central variable in our study, but the same principle could be applied to other variables.

Several intermediate options exist. For instance, researchers can cast a wide net, recruiting a diverse sample of participants without any pre-screening and then subsequently examine whether subsamples within the larger sample systematically differ along key variables. In some cases, researchers may even opt to rerun analyses on relevant subsamples (see, e.g., Kirk et al., 2021). As multi-site collaborations become more common, teams will also be able to recruit more diverse samples, at least in terms of the educational settings and sociodemographic characteristics of the sites where data are collected.

Sampling Speech for Evaluation

In carrying out research on global features, researchers typically use a picture narration task, where the speaker receives a series of images, is given a short amount of planning time (e.g., 1 minute), and is then asked to describe what happened. One famous example is the suitcase narrative (e.g., Derwing & Munro, 2013), which depicts two individuals bumping into one another and exchanging suitcases without realizing it until they reach their destination and begin unpacking. This task has been used extensively in the literature. On the one hand, this affords maximum comparability across studies because researchers are using the exact same task. On the other, repeated use of a single task brings with it questions of generalizability because global ratings of pronunciation are likely to be at least partially task dependent. That is, task characteristics are likely to affect how the speakers perform and therefore how they are rated. Researchers have already begun to examine the extent to which ratings, relationships among the constructs, and linguistic predictors of global dimensions vary according to task characteristics (Crowther, Trofimovich, Isaacs, & Saito, 2015; Crowther, Trofimovich, Saito, & Isaacs, 2015; Crowther et al., 2018; Huensch & Nagle, 2023). Crowther et al. (2018) compared a picture narration task to the International English Language Testing System (IELTS) long-turn speaking task and the Internet-based Test of English as a Foreign Language (TOEFL iBT) integrated task, two real-world tasks used in high-stakes oral proficiency assessment. Although the general pattern of results documented in previous studies was corroborated—both lexicogrammar and pronunciation-predicted comprehensibility whereas accentedness was predominantly predicted by pronunciation—important differences emerged as a function of task. Notably, accentedness was associated with a greater range of predictors on the IELTS and TOEFL tasks, which indicates that the distinction between comprehensibility and accentedness, at least in terms of the linguistic predictors of each global dimension, was fuzzier on these tasks. Although this area of work is still in its infancy, Crowther and Isbell (2023) have signaled that there is a pressing need for comprehensibility studies to incorporate multiple speaking tasks. For instance, studies incorporating multiple tasks could shed light on the extent to which comprehensibility is a speaker-level trait generalizable across tasks (e.g., If speaker A is more comprehensible than speaker B on task 1, is speaker A also more comprehensible than speaker B on task 2?) and how task properties such as task complexity affect comprehensibility ratings. According to Crowther and Isbell, using 4–10 tasks is a good goal for work in this area. Here, it is worthwhile to distinguish between two types of task design and sampling: creating multiple versions of a single task (e.g., several versions of a picture narration task, all of which involve the same number of images and events depicted) and creating distinct tasks and/or task completion conditions (e.g., tasks that vary in terms of their complexity, which could be related to the number of elements they involve; although they did not focus on global dimensions of pronunciation, see Solon et al., 2017 for a good example of two versions of a task, one involving few elements and another involving many).

Researchers are accustomed to thinking about how speakers will complete the tasks they design, but it's also important to think about the impact the task may have on the listener at the evaluation stage. When the listener is asked to provide ratings, they are typically given the images or prompt the speakers received. This step is taken to ensure that the listener has a basic understanding of what the speaker was asked to produce, which should, in turn, mitigate any familiarity effects. However, even small differences in task design can affect the nature of the rating task. When the listener receives a set of images, they can begin to imagine what the speaker's description, so there is little ambiguity in terms of what the speaker might say. For prompts, ambiguity may vary. If the speaker is asked to describe what they study, the listener can easily imagine what the speaker might discuss. But if the speaker is asked to describe a meaningful event from the past year, the topic is much more open-ended, which means that the listener probably won't be able to predict what the speaker will produce. At issue is the potential predictability of the response, which could affect intelligibility scores and comprehensibility ratings. In short, when designing the speaking task, it's important to consider both the speaker (e.g., Given the speaker profile sampled for the research, will participants be able to complete the task successfully?) and the listener (e.g., How predictable is the response?).

Speaking is ultimately a social behavior, but until recently researchers have relied heavily on monologic tasks such as picture description. Monologic tasks were a sensible starting point for research into listener-based constructs. For one, they are easier to collect and process. Monologic tasks are also a good representation of several speech acts that have a monologic component, such as telling a story at the dinner table to a group of friends, giving a presentation in class, or describing previous work experience in a job interview. However, monologic tasks cannot capture the real-time adjustments that speakers make in response to verbal and visual cues from their interlocutor. In conversation at the dinner table, a friend might interrupt the speaker to ask for clarification or provide verbal and visual cues that they aren't following the story very well, and in an interview, the interviewer will probably stop the speaker periodically to ask for more detail or redirect conversation. Thus, there is a real need to understand how speakers and listeners interact and adapt to one another to co-construct a mutually fluent and comprehensible conversation. Recent work has begun to examine comprehensibility in an interactive setting (Nagle et al., 2022, 2023; Trofimovich et al., 2020; Tsunemoto et al., 2022). The use of a dialogic task shifts the focus away from comprehensibility as a static property of the speech and the speaker toward a more dynamic view that seeks to understand the ways in which speakers make themselves comprehensible to one another. In this more complex, multivariate world, what the interlocutor does and perceives matter and influence one another, and it is through this continuous process of co-adaptation that speakers come to understand one another. There are several possibilities for dialogic task design. Picture narration tasks can be reformulated as jigsaw tasks, where each speaker receives a unique set of

142 Researching the Production of Global Features

pictures and must work together to create a story without looking at the pictures their partner received. Another task is prompted response where partners are asked to come up with a set of recommendations or solutions to a shared issue. For example, in Nagle et al. (2021), we asked partners to discuss common problems students face when moving to a new city to attend college. In summary, then, there are several principles to consider as you select speaking tasks for global dimensions research:

- How many tasks will you include? Crowther and Isbell (2023) stated that researchers should include a minimum of two but suggested that 4–10 is a better target.
- Along what dimensions will those tasks differ? This directly relates to the research questions you have as a researcher, given that you may be interested in examining how task complexity features such as the number of elements and planning time affect speaker performance, linguistic dimensions of comprehensibility, fluency, and accentedness.
- Will you use monologic tasks, dialogic tasks, or a combination of the two? Including a range of monologic tasks can shed light on consistency in speaker performance across tasks, as Crowther and Isbell (2023) pointed out. Including a variety of dialogic tasks can afford the same perspective in an interactive setting. And using a combination can illuminate the extent to which speech ratings for monologic and dialogic tasks align. Of course, you should continue to think carefully about the amount of data you will generate and how feasible it will be to process and analyze it.

Preparing Speech for Evaluation

Once speakers have completed the tasks, speech samples need to be prepared for listener evaluation. The main goal is to ensure that speech samples are comparable. The most common approach is to sample the first 30 seconds of speech, excluding initial pauses and hesitations. This guideline is approximate because the sample should be cut at a natural break in the speech, such as at the end of a sentence or at the conclusion of an idea. Thus, in practice, speech samples may vary slightly, from, for instance, 25–35 seconds. Of course, this is not the only approach. Indeed, the appropriate approach can only be determined considering your research questions. For instance, in Nagle et al. (2019), we sampled nearly two to three minutes of speech because our objective was to understand how listeners rated comprehensibility over time, upgrading or downgrading the speaker throughout the sample.

As I was writing this book, I received an inquiry from a researcher outside of the pronunciation and speech community who was curious to know why

30 seconds was the benchmark we had adopted. They wondered why we did not sample, for instance, 60 seconds of speech, or take multiple samples from different points in the recording. The consensus in the field is that 30 seconds is long enough to provide a sample that is representative of the speaker's production on that task, but to my knowledge, this issue has not been empirically tested. Thus, in the same way that Crowther and Isbell (2023) have advocated for including multiple tasks to compute within-subjects correlations for comprehensibility across tasks, it could be profitable to consider including multiple speech samples from the same task for the same reason. Increasing the number of ratings per speaker by increasing the number of samples rated can afford more precise insight into global constructs.

Once the speech samples have been identified and extracted into individual WAV files using Praat (Boersma & Weenik, 2023) or other sound-editing software, they must be normalized to a consistent volume. Praat is useful for this step because it offers "Scale peak" and "Scale intensity" functions, both of which appear under the "Modify" tab. Scale peak sets the maximum intensity of the file to a specified value (0.98 is the default and a sensible threshold) and Scale intensity sets the average intensity of the file to a specified value, usually 70 decibels. Most of the time, the two functions produce similar audio files, but Scale intensity can result in clipping (peaks > 1) if the intensity is highly variable throughout the sample. When Scale intensity is used, Praat outputs a report on the amount of clipping that has occurred during normalization. If there is a large amount of clipping, I recommend using the Scale peak function.

Sampling Listeners

In the same way that speakers introduce variation by producing varying levels of accuracy and complexity in their oral performance on different tasks, listeners introduce variation by interpreting speech samples in light of their previous experience, training, and understanding of the rating scales. Recruiting an appropriate group of listeners to serve as raters means identifying the individuals with whom speakers are most likely to interact and collecting sufficient listener background information. In some cases, the listeners themselves may be of interest, which means ensuring adequate coverage of listener-relevant variables and/or recruiting several groups of listeners (see, e.g., Crowther et al., 2023, for a study involving students, faculty, and administrative staff as listeners).

The first question that should guide listener recruitment is "Who will speakers interact with?" To answer this question, it's useful to distinguish between two common research contexts: research involving second language learners, who are living in an environment in which the L2 is spoken,

144 Researching the Production of Global Features

and research involving classroom language learners, who typically enroll in L2 courses while living in an L1 environment (e.g., second vs. foreign language learners, naturalistic vs. instructed learners). In a second language context, the question of potential interlocutors is relatively straightforward because second language speakers interact with individuals in the local community. For instance, if second language speakers are university students, then it's sensible to sample university students to serve as listeners (e.g., Kennedy et al., 2015). On the other hand, university students might not be an appropriate listener group for other groups of second language speakers, such as L2 professionals, who should be evaluated by listeners working in a similar professional context (Derwing & Munro, 2009). Listener recruitment decisions are not trivial. Given that language and behavior are highly context-sensitive, we cannot assume that different groups of listeners would react similarly to the same speech samples. Nor would it be ecologically valid to collect ratings from a group of listeners that speakers will rarely interact with.

In my opinion, the question of how to sample listeners is more complex for classroom (i.e., instructed) learners. First, the L2 target is far more variable in the classroom setting because classroom learners have been exposed to a range of models through their instructors, and they may not have a clear sense of who their future interlocutors might be. Even if classroom learners have an idea of who they might interact with, their working concept of that imagined group is likely to change as their language learning goals evolve. And in some cases, instructed learners may not see themselves interacting with native speakers of the L2 at all. These dynamics make it challenging to select an appropriate listener group for classroom learners. Three approaches are possible: (1) recruiting listeners based on the L2 varieties to which learners have been exposed, (2) recruiting listeners based on the listeners with whom learners currently interact or with whom they imagine themselves interacting in the future, or (3) recruiting a diverse group of L2 listeners, with the goal of understanding the ways in which speakers are comprehensible to a broad range of potential interlocutors.

The appropriate approach depends on the speaker sample and research context. Thus, there is no one-size-fits-all method in this regard. What is important, however, is to remember that listener sampling strategies affect the listener population to which results generalize and may alter the construct definition of listener-based ratings. For example, Derwing and Munro (2013) described accentedness as "how different the speakers' accents are from a standard Canadian English accent" (p. 185), but a broader definition of accentedness (e.g., degree of foreign accent, the presence of pronunciation features that would not occur in any native variety of the L2) would be necessary for classroom learners when listeners from a range of dialects are recruited. Likewise, comprehensibility is not as easily defined for raters who are drawn from diverse dialects. What is comprehensible in one variety of English or Spanish or any other language may not be equally comprehensible in another. Ultimately, then, the key is to take a principled approach to listener recruitment, reporting recruitment decisions transparently and taking care to interpret findings in light of the listener sample. The latter point is especially important. Recruitment strategies are not problematic in and of themselves, but rather become problematic when results are overgeneralized beyond the scope of the sample. For example, if listeners from a specific L2 dialect are recruited, it would not be appropriate to extrapolate to listeners of other L2 dialects. In research on second language speakers, it may be profitable to recruit other L2 speakers to serve as listeners because the reality is that many L2 speakers end up interacting with one another. This is also true of instructed learners, whose primary contact with other L2 speakers is in conversation with one another in the language classroom (O'Brien, 2014).

Once an appropriate listener population has been defined, researchers face the practical issue of actually locating and recruiting listeners. In a second language context, this means turning to the local community of university students, working professionals, etc. For classroom learners, listener recruitment can present a logistical challenge. In many locations, there may not be any L1 listeners to recruit (if L1 listeners are the target listener group), especially for researchers working on less-commonly-taught languages. Even if L1 listeners are available, they may not match the target listener profile. One solution is to recruit listeners through online platforms such as Amazon Mechanical Turk and Prolific. Online recruitment is advantageous because it grants access to a large pool of potential listeners, while allowing researchers to target certain subgroups through filters. The primary concern with online ratings is that researchers cannot directly oversee data collection and thus have limited insight into how listeners interact with the rating task. Several validation studies have been conducted and together demonstrate that online data can be as reliable as data collected in person (e.g., Nagle & Rehman, 2021).

The exigencies of the COVID-19 pandemic necessitated a shift toward online methodologies. Though not appropriate for all studies, the research community has grown comfortable with these methods, which no longer spark concerns over data quality if appropriate measures are taken and reporting is transparent. In fact, online data collection may be more reliable than in-person protocols in some research areas (Patterson & Nicklin, 2023), so even if online data collection is not strictly necessary, researchers should consider it both a viable and desirable possibility for their work. Importantly, when working with online samples, care must be taken to ensure

146 Researching the Production of Global Features

equitable and fair treatment of participants. Online participants have the same human subjects protections as in-person participants, but guaranteeing participant rights in online, remote data collection may require special design considerations (for discussion, see Nagle & Rehman, 2021). In some cases, in-person data collection may be more appropriate (Shepperd, 2022). Thus, internet-based data collection should not be seen as a quick and easy panacea (e.g., to address sample diversity), but rather should be treated as a method with its own advantages and disadvantages that should be considered in light of the goals of the study.

Last but certainly not least, there is the issue of how many listeners to recruit. The basic goal is to recruit enough listeners to establish a sufficiently high level of reliability. There is no one-size-fits-all response because the answer depends on other aspects of study design, such as the number of samples rated, the constructs targeted, and scale length. Hirschi and Kang (2023) analyzed several data sets, applying G theory to determine the number of raters that would be required to achieve a reliability of 0.90 taking into account the design features associated with each study. Critically, including too few raters could compromise the reliability of the study, and including too many could lead to inefficient use of time and resources. Results suggested cutoffs of 15 trained and 50 untrained listeners for comprehensibility and 60 and 80 trained and untrained listeners, respectively, for accentedness. These benchmarks point to the need to recruit larger listener samples than in previous work, but as Hirschi and Kang pointed out, more research involving other study designs, languages, and so on is required before definitive conclusion can be reached. Further, these general recommendations should be interpreted as such. To make an informed decision, researchers need to consider the features of their study and, ideally, run a G-theory-inspired analysis on pilot data.

Designing the Rating Task

Designing the rating task involves making decisions related to how many times the listener is allowed to play the sample, how many points the rating scale includes, and if listeners should rate the sample for all constructs simultaneously or if they should rate each construct separately. Fortunately, these questions have been addressed in several methodological studies. The number of points included in rating scales, or scale length, has been a topic of debate. There are two types of scales: ordinal scales and interval scales. Both imply ranking (e.g., a score of 4 is higher than a score of 3), but only interval scales imply equidistant steps. Put another way, the distance from 3 to 4 and 4 to 5 on an interval scale should be equal, but on an ordinal scale, that may not be true.

Most speech researchers have treated ratings as interval scales, which means that the goal is to create a scale with enough steps to capture differences among participants but not so many steps that distinctions become blurry. Scholars have generally settled on a minimum scale length of nine points (Southwood & Flege, 1999), but the reality is that appropriate scale length can only be determined by considering other aspects of research design, such as the expected range of speaker performance. For example, Isaacs and Thomson (2013) found significant overlap in scale steps for the nine-point rating condition, but the five-point condition showed much better separation (more distinct steps along the scale), which they attributed to the fact that the L2 speakers in their study were relatively homogenous in terms of their ability. Likewise, although Munro (2017) found that nine-point scales could adequately capture differences in comprehensibility and accentedness, listeners in his study used an average of 15 steps when rating comprehensibility through direct magnitude estimation (direct magnitude estimation is a technique where a reference is presented and stimuli are assigned a number according to how different the stimulus is from the referent; for instance, a stimulus that is twice as accented as the referent could be given a rating of 2, a stimulus ten times as accented a rating of 10, and so on). While it can be tempting to adopt a certain scale length (e.g., 9 points) based on previous research, it is important to consider whether that length will yield valid results in light of other study features.

Some researchers have begun to employ continuous 100- or 1000-point sliders. In that case, the researchers are not assuming that there are 100 or 1,000 potentially distinct levels of comprehensibility. Instead, the goal is to adopt a scale that can be modeled as a continuous outcome measure rather than an ordinal one. Regardless of scale length, researchers can take assurance in the fact that effects are generally consistent across studies (e.g., if an effect in study A is significant, it also tends to be significant in study B, even if the two studies used different rating scales). At the same time, because studies use different scale lengths, and because listener groups interpret construct definitions and scales slightly differently, direct comparisons related to the magnitude of effects cannot be made across studies (Isaacs & Thomson, 2013; Munro, 2017). Put another way, it's not appropriate to discuss the scores that experienced raters assigned in two different studies, but it is appropriate to compare the effect of rater experience on scoring decisions. When comparing rating studies, the focus is on effects rather than the magnitude of differences.

Another topic that has received attention is simultaneous versus sequential ratings. In a simultaneous design, listeners hear each sample only once before evaluating it along all relevant scales. Conversely, in a sequential design, listeners hear each sample multiple times, evaluating all samples along a given dimension before moving onto the next one, until all samples have been rated on all dimensions. From a methodological perspective, research suggests that the two procedures are comparable, though listeners may be harsher when rating certain features in a sequential paradigm (O'Brien, 2016). Practically speaking, because researchers are oftentimes interested in listeners' first impression, and because rater fatigue can affect data quality, in my view simultaneous ratings seem preferable for most studies.

As studies become larger, in terms of both the number of speakers sampled and the number of speaking tasks they complete, it becomes increasingly necessary to consider rating designs that are not fully crossed. In a fully crossed design, all listeners evaluate all samples. In studies involving a small number of samples (e.g., a set of samples that could be rated in an hour or less), a single session can be held in which all raters evaluate all items. However, when the study includes more samples than can be rated in an hour, the researcher must either hold multiple sessions, breaking the total number of files to be evaluated into a reasonable number (e.g., 60 per session) or adopt an alternative, sparse-rating design in which all files are evaluated by a subset of raters (i.e., all files are rated by k raters), but the set of raters that evaluates each file is different.

There are many potential rating designs, but two designs that have been used successfully are a semi-crossed design and a random-raters design. In a semi-crossed design, the researcher creates blocks of files that are then assigned to raters. For instance, if 600 files are to be rated, 10 blocks of 60 files could be created, and each of these blocks could be assigned to 10 raters. This design ensures sufficient connectivity in the data because each block essentially represents a fully-crossed design. In that case, inter-rater reliability, a measure of how consistent raters are and/or how much they agree in their ratings, can be estimated for each block. In this design, a unique group of raters evaluates each block. Another approach is to subdivide files in the same way but assign one of the blocks to all raters (or embed shared files across blocks so that some files appear in all blocks). This allows the researcher to compute inter-rater reliability for the files that were evaluated by all raters. In a truly random-raters design, each file is evaluated by a unique group of raters. That is, the researcher does not prearrange the files into blocks in any way. This approach has not been employed very much in the speech research literature but would be suitable for very large studies involving thousands of files to be rated (e.g., Peabody, 2011).

Each option comes with advantages and disadvantages. For blocked designs, care must be taken to balance the various elements of the study within each block. For example, in a longitudinal training study involving an experimental and a control group, it would be important to ensure that an equal number of samples from each group at each data point are included in each block. This can be a challenge when there are many facets of the design that need to be taken into consideration. For a random-raters design, there can be concerns with rater severity. Perhaps the group of raters that evaluated one file were far harsher than the group of raters that evaluated another file, such that the score the speaker receives reflects individual differences among the raters rather than the speaker's performance on the speaking task. When different sets of raters are employed, one option is to run a Rasch model, which can output fair scores after accounting for differences in rater severity (Isbell & Lee, 2022). When mixed-effects models are involved, raters can also be modeled as a random effect, which is another means of accounting for differences among raters.

Validating L2 Speech Ratings Data

Validating scalar ratings data means ensuring that listeners have understood and implemented ratings scales properly and that ratings are reliable. With respect to the former, researchers frequently include L1 samples (or very high proficiency L2 samples) among rated items to check listeners' understanding of rating scales and descriptors. Ratings for these control samples should be heavily skewed toward the upper end of the scale. If listeners consistently assign lower scores to control samples, then they may have misunderstood the scales or instructions. In that case, researchers may need to decide whether data from those listeners should be excluded from analysis. For example, Munro and Derwing (2001) reported removing outlier data from a listener who "assigned several ratings of 3 and 4 to the native speakers" (p. 458) on nine-point comprehensibility and accentedness scales. Cases like this one, where listeners assign L1 speakers very low values, are clear-cut, but what about borderline cases where listeners rate L1 speakers moderately lower than expected? Would a listener who assigned native speakers scores of 6 and 7 (or 7 and 8) be considered an outlier, and what would the cutoff be for 1,000-point sliding scales? Unless there is very clear evidence that the listener has grossly misinterpreted the scale, I recommend against eliminating any listeners. Instead, I suggest two approaches. First, it's a good idea to compute reliability when questionable listener cases are included versus removed from the data. If the reliability coefficients suggest that removing those listeners would substantially enhance reliability, then removing them might be a good option. A second more comprehensive approach would be a sensitivity analysis by running analyses with and without potentially problematic listeners.

A reliability coefficient should also be computed. The most common reliability index is Cronbach's alpha, a measure of the degree of intercorrelation among raters when raters are treated as fixed items. The intraclass

150 Researching the Production of Global Features

correlation coefficient (ICC) is an alternative measure that offers greater flexibility in terms of whether raters should be treated as random, whether reliability should be based on absolute agreement or consistency, and whether reliability is meant to generalize to an average score pooled over a group of raters or to a score provided by a single rater. When the ICC is used, it's important to report complete information on the ICC variant. For shorter five- and seven-point scales, absolute agreement may be of interest, especially if specific rating criteria and instructions are given, whereas for longer scales, such as the 1,000-point sliders that have become increasingly common in L2 speech research, absolute agreement among raters is highly unlikely (in fact, in my experience, absolute agreement is highly unlikely even when using short scales). Rather, consistency, or raters' tendency to rank samples similarly irrespective of the exact scores assigned, is often more appropriate. Likewise, in most L2 speaking research, reliability indices are not meant to represent the reliability of a score provided by a single individual, but rather a group average, making an average-measure ICC appropriate. It has been common practice to compute and report a single reliability measure, but in many studies, it would be helpful to have more than one estimate, such as estimates of absolute agreement and consistency (Hallgren, 2012; Isbell, 2017).

Statistical Analysis

Ratings data can be ordinal or continuous, which means we can model it using an ordinal or a linear mixed-effects model. Ordinal models are uncommon in the field and conceptually and statistically more challenging to fit (because you are modeling the probability of observing each step on the rating scale), so rather than going into this advanced topic, I focus on linear models, assuming that the dependent variable is a rating given on a 100-point sliding scale.

Example 1: Development of Comprehensibility, Fluency, and Accentedness

For this example, we're interested in tracking L2 speakers' comprehensibility, fluency, and accentedness over time (Derwing & Munro, 2013; Huensch & Tracy-Ventura, 2017). We'll assume that we're dealing with classroom learners of L2 Spanish. Students enrolled in intermediate Spanish courses at our institution recorded themselves responding to a prompt at various points throughout the semester, at approximately monthly intervals. We select data points corresponding to the beginning, middle, and end of intermediate 1 and the middle and end of intermediate 2, giving us a total

TABLE 5.1 Summary of Missing Data Structure for the Global Dimensions Data

	Intermediate 1			Intermediate 2	
Session	0	1	2	3	4
Subject n	200	200	200	143	143
Sample n	156	154	170	114	109

of five data points. Our primary goal is to understand how students' oral communicative competence, defined in terms of students' comprehensibility, fluency, and accentedness, develops during intensive communicative language instruction. We ask students to give us permission to use their class data for research purposes, and many consent, giving us an initial sample of 200 individuals. In theory, we could have a maximum of 1,000 samples (200 participants × 5 data points) if the data sets were complete. We'll assume, however, that (1) not all participants continue from intermediate Spanish 1 to intermediate Spanish 2 and (2) some of the data at each wave is missing at random (e.g., because participants did not upload a recording for that assignment). Table 5.1 summarizes these sources of missingness (in the data, I recorded the first session as 0 so that the intercept can be estimated). Normally, with this number of files, a pseudo-random raters design would be adopted. However, we'll assume a fully crossed design where the same ten listeners evaluated all speech samples.

Our independent, or predictor, variables in this data set are:

- Session, which we treat as a continuous variable because the intervals are equally spaced.
- Rating, a categorical variable that has three levels (comp, accent, and fluency) referring to the construct rated
- Session × Rating, an interaction term. This variable tests if the rate of change varied by construct, that is, if each construct showed a distinct rate of change over time.

Our dependent variable is Score, which we will treat as a continuous dependent measure.

First, we summarize the data numerically and graphically. Descriptive statistics, pooled over listeners and organized by rating and session, are given in Table 5.2. These averages show that all three ratings improved over time, but comprehensibility and fluency improved far more than accentedness. Furthermore, the fact that standard deviations (*SDs*) increased over time suggests a fanning out pattern, and the fact that *SDs* for accentedness grew substantially larger over time suggests that this fanning out pattern was more pronounced for accentedness than for the other two constructs.

The group trajectory plot, shown in Figure 5.2, confirms that comprehensibility and fluency improved more than accentedness. The group plot also shows that development (at least at the group level) was linear for all rated dimensions and that comprehensibility and fluency developed at approximately the same rate.

This is a relatively large data set, so rather than plotting a subset of individual cases (e.g., $n = 10$), we will use a spaghetti plot to get a sense of

TABLE 5.2 Descriptive Statistics for Comprehensibility, Fluency, and Accentedness over Time

Session	Comprehensibility	Fluency	Accentedness
0	47.00 (14.94)	41.75 (14.17)	35.89 (15.65)
1	52.86 (14.39)	47.77 (13.43)	37.51 (16.52)
2	58.85 (15.34)	55.66 (14.37)	39.43 (18.53)
3	65.24 (17.36)	60.73 (16.46)	41.89 (21.00)
4	69.79 (18.57)	68.24 (18.88)	45.03 (25.01)

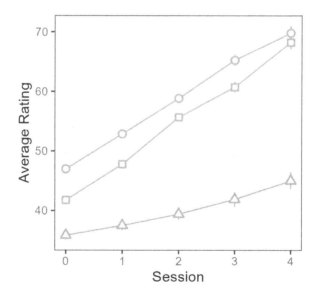

FIGURE 5.2 Group Changes in Comprehensibility, Fluency, and Accentedness.

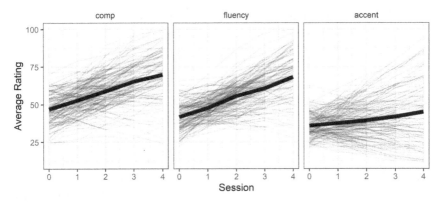

FIGURE 5.3   Spaghetti Plot of Changes in Comprehensibility, Fluency, and Accentedness.

how all participants changed over time on each dimension, which can help us understand the total amount of heterogeneity in starting points and trajectories. In Figure 5.3, the thick black line represents the group trajectory (the same one shown in the group plot), and the thin, transparent black lines show individual trajectories. From the spaghetti plot, we can see that our intuition about variability in change over time was correct: For all rated constructs, there is about the same amount of variability in the intercept, or starting point, but variability in rate of change is not the same for the three constructs. Instead, comprehensibility and fluency show similar patterns, whereas accentedness shows a much more pronounced fan shape. Although we cannot easily make out individual cases in this plot, we can see that individual trajectories are mostly linear, which means that we probably don't need to test any higher-order growth terms (e.g., quadratic). Put another way, representing change as linear seems like a reasonable approach for the data.

At this point, we could generate a range of diagnostic plots, such as histograms of the outcome variable for each dimension, Q-Q plots, and box or violin plots for each dimension at each wave. We've seen this step in previous chapters, so for this chapter, I'm going to skip it, jumping straight into the analysis. We're going to use a mixed-effects model to analyze the data. After we fit the model, we'll inspect model assumptions (normality of residuals, linearity, etc.) and deal with and report any violations that arise.

Our principal interest is understanding (1) how participants change on each dimension over time (i.e., as a function of Session) and (2) the amount of individual variability in starting points and rates of change. To examine (1), we focus on the fixed effects portion of the model, and to examine (2) we focus on random effects. We start by fitting the maximal fixed effects

154 Researching the Production of Global Features

model of interest, which includes an interaction between Rating and Session to allow for different rates of change (i.e., variable effects of Session) on each listener-based construct.

```
fm.cfa <- lmer (score ~ rating * session +
        (1 | participant) +
        (1 | listener), data = data.cfa)
```

When we call for a summary of the model, we see that all effects are statistically significant (as anticipated based on the plots we generated). This model includes by-participant and by-listener random intercepts, but these intercepts do not tell us anything about individual differences in rate of change, so before we begin interpreting the model, we need to fit by-participant random slopes for Session. As a reminder, mixed-effects modeling experts agree that the following random effects should be modeled whenever possible: (1) random intercepts, (2) random slopes for within-unit effects, and (3) random slopes for within-unit interaction terms (Brauer & Curtin, 2018). We'll try by-participant random slopes for Session first. The code for this model is given below.

```
fm.cfa.rs1 <- lmer (score ~ rating * session +
            (1 + session | participant) +
            (1 | listener), data = data.cfa)
```

The only change we have made to the code from the fixed effects model is to include Session in the by-participant random effect term: (1 + session | participant). This model didn't converge. Instead, we received the following convergence error:

Warning: Model failed to converge with max|grad| = 0.00758284 (tol = 0.002, component 1)

We can try one of Brauer and Curtin's (2018) "nonintrusive remedies" for resolving convergence issues: increasing the number of iterations. The default for *lme4* is 10,000, so I'll double it, increasing to 20,000, by adding a new argument to the code. In general, when we're manipulating how the model gets fit, we need the lmerControl argument. In this case, we need a chunk of code that tells R to increase the number of model iterations to 20,000.

```
fm.cfa.rs1 <- lmer (score ~ rating * session +
            (1 + session | participant) +
            (1 | listener),
```

Researching the Production of Global Features **155**

```
data = data.cfa, REML = T, lmerControl(optCtrl = list(maxfun
= 20000)))
```

Even after increasing the number of iterations, the model didn't converge. Another simple technique we can try is changing the optimizer. We'll keep the increased number of iterations but add another chunk of code to change the optimizer.

```
fm.cfa.rs1 <- lmer (score ~  rating * session +
                    (1 + session | participant) +
                    (1 | listener),
                  data = data.cfa, REML = T,
                  lmerControl(optimizer = "bobyqa",
                    optCtrl = list(maxfun = 20000)))
```

This time, the model converged. Comparing the random slopes model to the model without random slopes shows that adding by-participant random slopes for Session significantly improved fit: $\chi^2(2) = 751.28$, $p < 0.001$. We'll try fitting the within-subjects interaction term. This model is much more complicated because Rating is a factor with three levels. Therefore, more parameters are estimated, one for each additional level of the factor and one for each additional level of the interaction as well as the full set of covariances. If this doesn't make a lot of sense, don't worry. The point is, in total, 18 new parameters are estimated. This model also proved to be a significant improvement over its predecessor model (fm.cfa.rs1, shown above).

I used plots to check the assumptions of the model: normality, linearity, and homogeneity of variance. Residuals were normally distributed, but the plots for linearity and homogeneity of variance suggested that those assumptions may not be upheld, so results should be interpreted cautiously.

We can summarize the model using the summary() function, but that won't be very informative. Rating is a factor with three levels: comprehensibility, fluency, and accentedness. One of our goals is to examine the extent to which the rate of change differs by Rating. Put another way, do all three constructs develop at approximately the same rate, or do they show different rates of change? The default for factors in R is to use treatment coding where one level (the first level in alphabetical order) is set as the baseline against which the other levels are compared. Our baseline is Construct = comprehensibility. Because of treatment coding, when we summarize our model, we get a rather complicated output that includes interactions between Session and Rating for fluency and accentedness. These interaction terms indicate the extent to which the rate of change on each construct differs from the rate of change in comprehensibility. Simply put, these are difference estimates. Notice, however, that we probably want two additional pieces

156 Researching the Production of Global Features

of information: (1) we want to know what the rate of change on each construct was and (2) we want to compare rates of change for fluency and accentedness, a comparison not given in the current model. We can do both using the *emmeans* package (Lenth, 2023). To get the desired data, we use the emtrends() function because we are interested in the interaction between a categorical predictor (Rating) and a continuous one (Session).

emtrends(fm.cfa.rs2, pairwise ~ rating, var = "session")

The syntax for this function is simple: we specify the model object first (fm. cfa.rs2), tell the function that we want pairwise contrasts by Rating, and we define the target variable as Session. The first part of the output, $emtrends, gives the estimated trend for Session for each level of Rating, and the second part, $contrasts, gives pairwise contrasts for Session between all levels of Rating. In both cases, degrees of freedom are shown as infinite because the default number of observations that the package takes is 3,000. We can expand this to the number of observations in the data set to get an accurate estimate of degrees of freedom for our data, but this computation is intensive and may take a long time to run or crash R altogether. The data set is simply too large to estimate the degrees of freedom, so I would skip that step and simply report as much in the manuscript. The output tells us that the estimated rates of change and 95% confidence intervals (*CIs*) for comprehensibility, fluency, and accentedness are 5.64 [4.87, 6.40], 6.58 [5.90, 7.25], and 1.85 [1.05, 2.65], respectively. The pairwise contrasts show statistically significant differences in rates of change for comprehensibility and accentedness and for fluency and accentedness but not for comprehensibility and fluency (Table 5.3).

The sign of the estimate is derived by the order of the levels of Rating. Fluency and accentedness are subtracted from comprehensibility and accentedness is subtracted from fluency. Thus, the negative estimate for the comparison between comprehensibility and fluency indicates that fluency showed a greater rate of change than comprehensibility, whereas the positive estimates for the other two comparisons demonstrate that comprehensibility and fluency showed a greater rate of change than accentedness.

TABLE 5.3 Pairwise Estimated Differences in Rates of Change across Listener-based Constructs

	Estimate	95% CI	SE	z	p
Comp vs. Fluency	−0.94	[−2.17, 0.29]	0.52	−1.80	0.171
Comp vs. Accent	3.77	[2.39, 5.18]	0.60	6.37	<0.001
Fluency vs. Accent	4.73	[3.44, 6.02]	0.55	8.59	<0.001

Researching the Production of Global Features **157**

We should discuss another analytical option: fitting three separate models. This approach would have allowed us to estimate the intercept and rate of change for each construct, so why not take that approach? Two reasons. First, following that approach, even though we would have been able to generate estimates of the developmental slopes for each rating and compare them descriptively, we would not have been able to make any inferential comparisons about differences in rate of change. That is, we would not have had statistical evidence that the rate of change on one construct was significantly different from the other, nor would we have been able to estimate the magnitude of that difference because we would have fit separate models without the interaction term. Second, running a single multivariate model that corresponds to the research goals is better than running several univariate models because the multivariate model controls for Type 1 error rates better and leads to better statistical power.

In summary, from this analysis, we can conclude that (1) participants improved on all three listener-based constructs over the yearlong (i.e., two semester) window of observation, (2) there were statistically significant differences in the rates of change, such that fluency = comprehensibility > accentedness, and (3) there were between-participant differences in the intercept and the rate of change on each construct.

Example 2: The Effect of Study Abroad on Comprehensibility Development

For this example, we're interested in examining comprehensibility development in a sample of university-level learners of L2 Spanish. To examine their development over time, across the university language curriculum, we run a study in which we ask an initial sample of 100 participants to narrate a picture description several times throughout their university language studies. We begin collecting data in participants' third semester of university Spanish studies, and we continue collecting data through graduation, or participants' eighth semester. As shown in Table 5.4, we collect data at mostly

TABLE 5.4 Summary of Total Number of Participants and Number of Participants Who Have Studied Abroad

Chronological Time	Fall 1	Fall 1	Spring 1	Fall 2	Spring 2	Spring 3
Session	0	1	2	3	4	5
Semesters of Spanish	2	3	4	5	6	8
Total *n*	100	100	92	80	60	42
n study abroad	0	0	15	14	19	0
Total *n* study abroad	0	0	15	29	48	48

158 Researching the Production of Global Features

equal intervals, but toward the end of the study, we space data collection out. Over time, some participants drop out of the study (e.g., because they decide to stop studying Spanish, because they are no longer interested in participating in our study), reducing our sample size at each data point. As with the first example, we'll assume a fully crossed design where the same group of ten listeners evaluated all speech samples.

We know that many students choose to study abroad in a Spanish-speaking country during the summer or during an academic semester. To capture that information, at each session, we ask participants if they studied abroad in a Spanish-speaking country since our last meeting. We record this information simply as a categorical variable, either "yes" they studied abroad or "no" they did not (*n* study abroad in Table 5.4). We're interested in understanding the effect of study abroad on development, but we're especially interested in how the timing of the study abroad experience affects the gains that participants achieve and their development in the following semesters. We'll assume that in our context learners study abroad during their fourth, fifth, or sixth semester. Because learners study abroad at different times, we can treat the timing of study abroad as a categorical grouping variable. In our data set, we therefore have the following independent variables:

- Session, which is categorical because sessions were not spaced at equal intervals.
- Semester, a continuous variable we have created based on the categorical Session variable. This variable maps Session into Semesters.
- SA.Sem, a categorical variable that indexes the semester when the participant studied abroad.
- SA, a categorical variable that indexes whether the participant has studied abroad. If the participant has not studied abroad, this is coded as "no," and if they have, it is coded as "yes." For instance, in our data set, a participant who studied abroad in their fourth semester would have a set of entries as follows:

id	session	semester	sa.sem	sa
s01	0	2	4	no
s01	1	3	4	no
s01	2	4	4	yes
s01	3	5	4	yes
s01	4	6	4	yes
s01	5	8	4	yes

Our outcome variable is comprehensibility, which we will assume we measured on a 100-point slider and can therefore treat as continuous.

Researching the Production of Global Features **159**

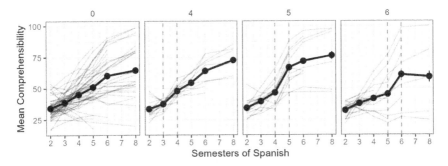

FIGURE 5.4 Group Changes in Comprehensibility over Time as a Function of the Timing of Study Abroad.

First, we plot the data, making sure we map sa.sem into the plot as a grouping factor so that we can get a sense of how the timing of study abroad affects comprehensibility development. This plot is given in Figure 5.4. The study abroad period is indicated by the vertical dashed lines. The thick black line represents the group trajectory, and the thin, transparent black lines individual trajectories. Note that some of these trajectories do not extend across the entire study because we simulated missing data for some participants. From this plot, we can immediately see that studying abroad is beneficial; compared to the group that did not study abroad (0), the groups that studied abroad showed greater gains in comprehensibility over time (on average, for the group). The plot also suggests that studying abroad approximately halfway through university language training (SA = 5) is more beneficial than studying abroad earlier (SA = 4) or later (SA = 6), which suggests a window of opportunity during which studying abroad is maximally beneficial for development.

Descriptive statistics by study abroad group and semester are given in Table 5.5. These statistics show that all groups improved, but SA = 5 improved the most, confirming what is visually displayed in Figure 5.4. Furthermore, *SD*s tended to increase for all groups over time, indicating a fanning out in trajectories, which means that homogeneity of variance is unlikely to hold for the data set. We could generate a range of diagnostic plots by semester and study abroad group, as we have in previous chapters, but for the sake of space, I won't include that information here. You can try making these plots following the examples I have given for other data sets.

Our goal is to understand the effect of the timing of studying abroad on comprehensibility development. This suggests a model with an interaction between Semester and SA Group (the sa.sem variable in the data set). This defines our fixed effects structure. Semester is a within-subjects variable, but sa.sem is not, which means that the only by-participant random slope we can fit is semester (we cannot fit the interaction term as a by-participant

160 Researching the Production of Global Features

random slope because sa.sem is a between-subjects variable). This defines the random effects structure of the model. The target model is given in the following chunk of code.

```
fm.compsa <- lmer (score ~ session * sa.sem +
                (1 | listener) +
                (1 + session | participant),
                data = data.compsa)
```

This model converged. In the first example in this chapter, we didn't summarize the model at all because we wanted to compare rates of change for all three constructs. In other words, there was not a sensible baseline for comparison. For these data, it makes sense to summarize the model, comparing the groups that studied abroad to the group that did not (sa.sem = 0), which has been set as the baseline. This model will compare (1) the intercepts for the study abroad groups to the intercept for the group that did not study abroad and (2) the rates of change for the study abroad groups to the rate of change for the group that did not. To help you understand how to interpret this model, I have provided a list of model terms and what they mean in Table 5.6. Effects are shown in the exact order and

TABLE 5.5 Means and Standard Deviations by Semester and Study Abroad Group

Semester	No SA	Study Abroad Groups		
		SA = 4	SA = 5	SA = 6
2	34.28 (12.40)	33.62 (11.28)	34.40 (11.30)	32.44 (10.61)
3	38.86 (11.85)	37.59 (9.91)	39.63 (11.01)	37.88 (11.03)
4	45.19 (14.76)	48.07 (11.24)	46.58 (14.67)	41.70 (13.51)
5	51.12 (17.66)	54.55 (11.85)	66.74 (16.08)	45.24 (18.75)
6	60.19 (20.42)	63.99 (15.42)	71.70 (19.19)	60.83 (25.71)
8	64.57 (22.63)	72.60 (14.98)	76.22 (23.56)	59.14 (29.90)

TABLE 5.6 Model Terms and Their Meaning

Fixed Effect	Meaning
(Intercept)	Intercept for sa.sem0
Semester	Effect of semester for sa.sem0
sa.sem4	Difference between sa.sem0 intercept and sa.sem4 intercept
sa.sem5	Difference between sa.sem0 intercept and sa.sem5 intercept
sa.sem6	Difference between sa.sem0 intercept and sa.sem6 intercept
semester:sa.sem4	Difference between effect of semester for sa.sem0 and sa.sem4
semester:sa.sem5	Difference between effect of semester for sa.sem0 and sa.sem5
semester:sa.sem6	Difference between effect of semester for sa.sem0 and sa.sem6

with the exact label given in the model. As shown, the effects in this model are treatment coded, which means they refer to differences relative to the baseline sa.sem = 0 group.

To help you understand how you could report the model, I have provided a summary in Table 5.7. I have renamed some of the fixed effect terms to make them easier to interpret for readers. For instance, I have indented the difference measures for the study abroad groups so that it's clear that comparisons were made between the group that did not study abroad and the three groups that did. One other thing that is important for model interpretation is the way we have coded semester. Remember that we began collecting data in participants' second semester, so the first data point is semester = 2. The intercept that gets estimated in the model is semester = 0, which means that the model is estimating an intercept that was not observed. We can solve this issue by centering semester on 2: 2, 3, 4, 5, 6, and 8 become 0, 1, 2, 3, 4, and 6.

As reported, there was no difference in the intercepts for the groups, which suggests that they began the study with approximately the same mean comprehensibility. The positive coefficient for the effect of semester shows that the group that did not study abroad improved their comprehensibility over time, and the non-significant differences with the SA 4 and 6 groups suggest that those groups showed a similar rate of positive change over

TABLE 5.7 Summary of Linear Mixed-Effects Model Fit to Comprehensibility Data

Fixed effects	Estimate	SE	t	95% CI	p
Intercept No SA	34.80	2.10	16.54	[30.67, 38.92]	<0.001
vs. SA = 4	−0.90	2.04	−0.44	[−4.91, 3.10]	0.659
vs. SA = 5	−1.95	2.09	−0.93	[−6.05, 2.15]	0.354
vs. SA = 6	−2.54	1.95	−1.36	[−6.20, 1.31]	0.179
Semester No SA	4.70	0.72	6.50	[3.28, 6.12]	<0.001
vs. SA = 4	1.05	1.55	0.68	[−1.98, 4.09]	0.498
vs. SA = 5	4.68	1.57	2.99	[1.61, 7.75]	0.004
vs. SA = 6	0.69	1.41	0.49	[−2.08, 3.47]	0.625

Random effects	SD	Correlation
Speakers		
Intercepts	6.62	
Slopes: Session	5.06	−0.55
Items		
Intercepts	5.92	

Note. Model syntax: lmer(score ~ session * sa.sem + (1 + session | participant) + (1 | listener). The baseline for sa.sem was sa.sem = 0, which represents students who did not study abroad. P values have been generated using the Satterthwaite approximation included in the lmerTest package (Kuznetsova et al., 2017). 95% CIs were generated using the Wald method.

162 Researching the Production of Global Features

time. The significant positive coefficient for SA 5, combined with its confidence interval, suggests that the SA 5 group showed a stronger positive trend than the group that did not study abroad, a difference that could have been as small as approximately 2 units per semester or as large as approximately 8 units per semester.

Beyond comparing the study abroad groups to the group that did not study abroad, we're probably interested in comparing the study abroad groups to one another. We can use the emtrends() function of the *emmeans* (Lenth, 2023) package to generate pairwise comparisons like we did before.

emtrends(fm.compsa, pairwise ~ sa.sem, var = "semester")

Table 5.8 shows the result of this step. Notice first that all slopes are positive, suggesting a rate of change ranging from 3 units per semester (the lower limit of the confidence interval for SA 4) to 12 units per semester (the upper limit of the confidence interval for SA 5). In terms of pairwise comparisons, we have strong evidence that the SA 5 group is different from the others. In the case of No SA versus SA 5, the comparison reached statistical significance. Although the comparisons between SA 5 and SA 4 and SA 6 did not reach significance, the confidence intervals suggest a difference that could be as large as 8 units per semester, a difference that should not be discounted simply because $p > 0.05$ and 0 was included in the confidence interval (Amrhein et al., 2019). The estimates for the comparisons between No SA and the SA groups are the same as those given

TABLE 5.8 Estimated Slopes and Pairwise Comparisons for All Groups

	Estimate	*95% CI*	*SE*	*z*	*p*
Slopes					
No SA	4.70	[3.28, 6.12]	0.72		
SA 4	5.75	[3.07, 8.44]	1.37		
SA 5	9.38	[6.66, 12.11]	1.39		
SA 6	5.40	[3.01, 7.78]	1.22		
Pairwise Comparisons					
No SA vs. SA 4	−1.05	[−5.03, 2.93]	1.55	−0.68	0.905
No SA vs. SA 5	−4.68	[−8.71, −0.66]	1.57	−2.99	0.015
No SA vs. SA 6	−0.69	[−4.33, 2.94]	1.41	−0.49	0.961
SA 4 vs. SA 5	−3.63	[−8.64, 1.39]	1.95	−1.86	0.246
SA 4 vs. SA 6	0.36	[−4.35, 5.07]	1.83	0.20	0.997
SA 5 vs. SA 6	3.99	[−0.76, 8.73]	1.85	2.16	0.135

Note. The emmeans package (Lenth, 2023) was used to compute estimated slopes and estimated pairwise differences. For pairwise comparisons, p values were adjusted for multiple comparisons using the Tukey method.

in the model summary reported in Table 5.7. The p values, however, have changed because the *emmeans* package adjusts for multiple comparisons using the Tukey method.

In summary, from this analysis, we know that all groups improved their comprehensibility over time. Descriptively, all of the study abroad groups seemed to improve more than the group that did not study abroad, but that improvement was only reliably different for students studying abroad midway through their language studies (i.e., for SA 5). That group also appeared to achieve greater gains relative to the other study abroad groups.

Summary and Recommendations

- Sample at least 20–30 seconds of speech per speaker and task. The sample should be cut at a natural pause or break. Avoid clipping the sample in the middle of a thought group.
- Whenever feasible, collect multiple samples of speech, either using different versions of the same spontaneous production task or different spontaneous production tasks altogether. Collecting multiple samples from each speaker (at each session) will lay the groundwork for understanding within-speaker variability in comprehensibility (Crowther & Isbell, 2023).
- Think carefully about the rating scale that listeners will use and what it implies, especially with respect to the number of rating option (e.g., 5, 9, 100). Different scales are amenable to different types of analyses, and the way reliability is assessed may also depend on scale length (e.g., agreement cannot be expected for 100-point scales).
- Remember that listeners are randomly sampled from a population of potential listeners. Take care to define the relevant listener population, to collect listener background data, and to interpret findings in light of the target listener population included in the study. Also consider how listeners will be recruited. Use recruitment practices (in-person, online) that will allow you to build a listener sample that is maximally representative of the target listener profile.

Chapter Questions

1. In this chapter, we have predominantly discussed measuring comprehensibility using a Likert rating scale. What are the advantages and limitations of this method? What other methods could be used to measure comprehensibility? What are their advantages and limitations?
2. Think about measuring comprehensibility or another listener-based construct longitudinally in the research setting and language in which

you work. How often will you collect data? What listeners will you recruit for the rating task? If you use a Likert scale, how many steps will it have?
3. The data sets in this chapter contained missing data. In what ways might this missing data affect the results? In other words, is it possible that certain participant characteristics are associated with missingness? For instance, could the participants who participated throughout the study be highly motivated? Based on your response, what can we say about the participant population to which our findings should generalize?
4. Pick one of the data sets and subset it so that you have complete cases for participants (i.e., all participants are observed at all sessions). Rerun the analysis. How do the results change? Revisit your answer to the previous question in light of the updated results.

References

Akiyama, Y., & Saito, K. (2016). Development of comprehensibility and its linguistic correlates: A longitudinal study of video-mediated telecollaboration. *The Modern Language Journal, 100*(3), 585–609. https://doi.org/10.1111/modl.12338

Amrhein, V., Greenland, S., & McShane, B. (2019). Scientists rise up against statistical significance. *Nature, 567*, 305–307. https://doi.org/10.1038/d41586-019-00857-9

Andringa, S. (2014). The use of native speaker norms in critical period hypothesis research. *Studies in Second Language Acquisition, 36*(3), 565–596. https://doi.org/10.1017/s0272263113000600

Andringa, S., & Godfroid, A. (2019). Call for participation. *Language Learning, 69*(1), 5–10. https://doi.org/10.1111/lang.12338

Andringa, S., & Godfroid, A. (2020). Sampling bias and the problem of generalizability in applied linguistics. *Annual Review of Applied Linguistics, 40*, 134–142. https://doi.org/10.1017/s0267190520000033

Bergeron, A., & Trofimovich, P. (2017). Linguistic dimensions of accentedness and comprehensibility: Exploring task and listener effects in second language French. *Foreign Language Annals, 50*(3), 547–566. https://doi.org/10.1111/flan.12285

Boersma, P., & Weenik, D. (2023). *Praat: doing phonetics by computer* (Version 6.3.17) [Computer program]. http://www.praat.org/

Brauer, M., & Curtin, J. J. (2018). Linear mixed-effects models and the analysis of nonindependent data: A unified framework to analyze categorical and continuous independent variables that vary within-subjects and/or within-items. *Psychological Methods, 23*(3), 389–411. https://doi.org/10.1037/met0000159

Crowther, D., & Isbell, D. R. (2023). Second language speech comprehensibility: A research agenda. *Language Teaching*, 1–17. https://doi.org/10.1017/S026144482300037X

Crowther, D., Isbell, D. R., & Nishizawa, H. (2023). Second language speech comprehensibility and acceptability in academic settings: Listener perceptions and speech stream influences. *Applied Psycholinguistics, 44*(5), 858–888. https://doi.org/10.1017/S0142716423000346

Crowther, D., Trofimovich, P., Isaacs, T., & Saito, K. (2015). Does a speaking task affect second language comprehensibility? *The Modern Language Journal, 99*(1), 80–95. https://doi.org/10.1111/modl.12185

Crowther, D., Trofimovich, P., Saito, K., & Isaacs, T. (2015). Second language comprehensibility revisited: Investigating the effects of learner background. *TESOL Quarterly, 49*(4), 814–837. https://doi.org/10.1002/tesq.203

Crowther, D., Trofimovich, P., Saito, K., & Isaacs, T. (2018). Linguistic dimensions of L2 accentedness and comprehensibility vary across speaking tasks. *Studies in Second Language Acquisition, 40*(2), 443–457. https://doi.org/10.1017/s027226311700016x

Derwing, T. M., & Munro, M. J. (1997). Accent, intelligibility, and comprehensibility: Evidence from four L1s. *Studies in Second Language Acquisition, 19*(1), 1–16.

Derwing, T. M., & Munro, M. J. (2009). Comprehensibility as a factor in listener interaction preferences: Implications for the workplace. *The Canadian Modern Language Review, 66*(2), 181–202. https://doi.org/10.3138/cmlr.66.2.181

Derwing, T. M., & Munro, M. J. (2013). The development of L2 oral language skills in two L1 groups: A 7-year study. *Language Learning, 63*(2), 163–185. https://doi.org/10.1111/lang.12000

Dragojevic, M., & Giles, H. (2016). I don't like you because you're hard to understand: The role of processing fluency in the language attitudes process. *Human Communication Research, 42*(3), 396–420. https://doi.org/10.1111/hcre.12079

Dragojevic, M., Giles, H., Beck, A.-C., & Tatum, N. T. (2017). The fluency principle: Why foreign accent strength negatively biases language attitudes. *Communication Monographs, 84*(3), 385–405. https://doi.org/10.1080/03637751.2017.1322213

Fuertes, J. N., Gottdiener, W. H., Martin, H., Gilbert, T. C., & Giles, H. (2012). A meta-analysis of the effects of speakers' accents on interpersonal evaluations. *European Journal of Social Psychology, 42*(1), 120–133. https://doi.org/10.1002/ejsp.862

Gass, S., & Varonis, E. M. (1984). The effect of familiarity on the comprehensibility of nonnative speech. *Language Learning, 34*(1), 65–87. https://doi.org/10.1111/j.1467-1770.1984.tb00996.x

Hallgren, K. A. (2012). Computing inter-rater reliability for observational data: An overview and tutorial. *Tutorials in Quantitative Methods in Psychology, 8*(1), 23–34. https://doi.org/10.20982/tqmp.08.1.p023

Hirschi, K., & Kang, O. (2023). How many raters can be enough? G Theory applied to assessment and measurement of L2 speech perception. *Language Teaching Research Quarterly, 37*, 213–230. https://doi.org/10.32038/ltrq.2023.37.12

Huensch, A., & Nagle, C. (2021). The effect of speaker proficiency on intelligibility, comprehensibility, and accentedness in L2 Spanish: A conceptual replication and extension of Munro and Derwing (1995a). *Language Learning, 71*(3), 626–668. https://doi.org/10.1111/lang.12451

Huensch, A., & Nagle, C. (2023). Revisiting the moderating effect of speaker proficiency on the relationships among intelligibility, comprehensibility, and accentedness in L2 Spanish. *Studies in Second Language Acquisition*, 45(2), 571–585. https://doi.org/10.1017/S0272263122000213

Huensch, A., & Tracy-Ventura, N. (2017). L2 utterance fluency development before, during, and after residence abroad: A multidimensional investigation. *The Modern Language Journal*, 101(2), 275–293. https://doi.org/10.1111/modl.12395

Isaacs, T., & Thomson, R. I. (2013). Rater experience, rating scale length, and judgments of L2 pronunciation: Revisiting research conventions. *Language Assessment Quarterly*, 10(2), 135–159. https://doi.org/10.1080/15434303.2013.769545

Isaacs, T., & Trofimovich, P. (2012). Deconstructing comprehensibility. *Studies in Second Language Acquisition*, 34(3), 475–505. https://doi.org/10.1017/s0272263112000150

Isbell, D. R. (2017). Assessing pronunciation for research purposes with listener-based numerical scales. In O. Kang & A. Ginther (Eds.), *Assessment in second language pronunciation* (pp. 89–111). Routledge.

Isbell, D. R., & Lee, J. (2022). Self-assessment of comprehensibility and accentedness in second language Korean. *Language Learning*, 72(3), 806–852. https://doi.org/https://doi.org/10.1111/lang.12497

Kennedy, S., Foote, J. A., & Santos Buss, L. K. D. (2015). Second language speakers at university: Longitudinal development and rater behaviour. *TESOL Quarterly*, 49(1), 199–209. https://doi.org/10.1002/tesq.212

Kirk, S., Grinstead, J., & Nibert, H. J. (2021). Anxiety, lexicon, and morphosyntax in instructed L2 Spanish. *Foreign Language Annals*, 55(1), 309–323. https://doi.org/10.1111/flan.12576

Kuznetsova, A., Brockhoff, P. B., & Christensen, R. H. B. (2017). lmerTest Package: Tests in linear mixed-effects models. *Journal of Statistical Software*, 82(13), 1–26. https://doi.org/10.18637/jss.v082.i13

Lenth R (2023). _emmeans: Estimated Marginal Means, aka Least-Squares Means_. R package version 1.8.4-1, <https://CRAN.R-project.org/package=emmeans>.

Levis, J. (2020). Revisting the intelligibility and nativeness principles. *Journal of Second Language Pronunciation*, 6(3), 310–328. https://doi.org/10.1075/jslp.20050.lev

Levis, J. M. (2005). Changing contexts and shifting paradigms in pronunciation teaching. *TESOL Quarterly*, 39(3), 369–377. https://doi.org/10.2307/3588485

MacIntyre, P. D. (2012). The idiodynamic method: A closer look at the dynamics of communication traits. *Communication Research Reports*, 29, 361–367.

Munro, M. J. (2017). Dimensions of pronunciation. In O. Kang, R. I. Thomson, & J. M. Murphy (Eds.), *The Routledge handbook of contemporary English pronunciation* (pp. 413–431). Taylor & Francis.

Munro, M. J., & Derwing, T. M. (1995). Foreign accent, comprehensibility, and intelligibility in the speech of second language learners. *Language Learning*, 45(1), 73–97. https://doi.org/10.1111/j.1467-1770.1995.tb00963.x

Munro, M. J., & Derwing, T. M. (2001). Modeling perceptions of the accentedness and comprehensibility of L2 speech: The role of speaking rate. *Studies in Second Language Acquisition*, 23, 451–468. https://doi.org/10.1017/S0272263101004016

Munro, M. J., & Derwing, T. M. (2020). Foreign accent, comprehensibility and intelligibility, redux. *Journal of Second Language Pronunciation, 6*(3), 283–309. https://doi.org/10.1075/jslp.20038.mun

Nagle, C., Trofimovich, P., & Bergeron, A. (2019). Toward a dynamic view of second language comprehensibility. *Studies in Second Language Acquisition, 41*(04), 647–672. https://doi.org/10.1017/s0272263119000044

Nagle, C., Trofimovich, P., Tekin, O., & McDonough, K. (2023). Framing second language comprehensibility: Do interlocutors' ratings predict their perceived communicative experience? *Applied Psycholinguistics, 44*(1), 131–156. https://doi.org/10.1017/S0142716423000073

Nagle, C. L., & Huensch, A. (2020). Expanding the scope of L2 intelligibility research. *Journal of Second Language Pronunciation, 6*(3), 329–351. https://doi.org/10.1075/jslp.20009.nag

Nagle, C. L., & Rehman, I. (2021). Doing L2 speech research online: Why and how to collect online ratings data. *Studies in Second Language Acquisition, 43*(4), 916–939. https://doi.org/10.1017/S0272263121000292

Nagle, C. L., Trofimovich, P., O'Brien, M. G., & Kennedy, S. (2022). Beyond linguistic features: Exploring behavioral and affective correlates of comprehensible second language speech. *Studies in Second Language Acquisition, 44*(1), 255–270. https://doi.org/10.1017/S0272263121000073

O'Brien, M. G. (2016). Methodological choices in rating speech samples. *Studies in Second Language Acquisition, 38*(3), 587–605. https://doi.org/10.1017/s0272263115000418

O'Brien, M. G. (2014). L2 learners' assessments of accentedness, fluency, and comprehensibility of native and nonnative German speech. *Language Learning, 64*(4), 715–748. https://doi.org/10.1111/lang.12082

Ortega, L., Iwashita, N., Norris, J. M., & Rabie, S. (2002). *An investigation of elicited imitation tasks in crosslinguistic SLA research.* Second Language Research Forum, Toronto, Canada.

Patterson, A. S., & Nicklin, C. (2023). L2 self-paced reading data collection across three contexts: In-person, online, and crowdsourcing. *Research Methods in Applied Linguistics, 2*(1), 100045. https://doi.org/10.1016/j.rmal.2023.100045

Peabody, M. A. (2011). *Methods for pronunciation assessment in computer aided language learning.* [Doctoral dissertation, Massachusetts Institute of Technology].

Rachels, J. R., & Rockinson-Szapkiw, A J. (2018). The effects of a mobile gamification app on elementary students' Spanish achievement and self-efficacy. *Computer Assisted Language Learning, 31*(1), 72–89. https://doi.org/10.1080/09588221.2017.1382536

Saito, K., Trofimovich, P., & Isaacs, T. (2015). Using listener judgments to investigate linguistic influences on L2 comprehensibility and accentedness: A validation and generalization study. *Applied Linguistics, 38*(4), 439–462. https://doi.org/10.1093/applin/amv047

Shepperd, L. (2022). Including underrepresented language learners in SLA research: A case study and considerations for internet-based methods. *Research Methods in Applied Linguistics, 1*(3), 100031. https://doi.org/10.1016/j.rmal.2022.100031

Solon, M., Long, A. Y., & Gurzynski-Weiss, L. (2017). Task complexity, language-related episodes, and production of L2 Spanish vowels. *Studies in Second Language Acquisition*, *39*(2), 347–380. https://doi.org/10.1017/s0272263116000425

Solon, M., Park, H. I., Henderson, C., & Dehghan-Chaleshtori, M. (2019). Revisiting the Spanish elicited imitation task: A tool for assessing advanced language learners? *Studies in Second Language Acquisition*, *41*(5), 1027–1053. https://doi.org/10.1017/S0272263119000342

Southwood, M. H., & Flege, J. E. (1999). Scaling foreign accent: direct magnitude estimation versus interval scaling. *Clinical Linguistics & Phonetics*, *13*(5), 335–349. https://doi.org/10.1080/026992099299013

Trofimovich, P., & Isaacs, T. (2012). Disentangling accent from comprehensibility. *Bilingualism: Language and Cognition*, *15*(4), 905–916. https://doi.org/10.1017/s1366728912000168

Trofimovich, P., Nagle, C. L., O'Brien, M. G., Kennedy, S., Taylor Reid, K., & Strachan, L. (2020). Second language comprehensibility as a dynamic construct. *Journal of Second Language Pronunciation*, *6*(3), 430–457. https://doi.org/10.1075/jslp.20003.tro

Tsunemoto, A., Lindberg, R., Trofimovich, P., & McDonough, K. (2022). Visual cues and rater perceptions of second language comprehensibility, accentedness, and fluency. *Studies in Second Language Acquisition*, *44*(3), 659–684. https://doi.org/10.1017/S0272263121000425

6

RESEARCHING PRONUNCIATION TRAINING AND INSTRUCTION

Introduction

I titled this chapter "Pronunciation training and instruction" because my sense is that the terms have a slightly different usage. "Training" tends to evoke perception training, especially high variability phonetic training (HVPT) where learners are presented with a large number of examples of target sounds and contrasts and asked to identify them (Barriuso & Hayes-Harb, 2018; Thomson, 2018), whereas "instruction" tends to evoke production-oriented instruction, which can involve drawing learners' attention to pronunciation using techniques such as form-focused instruction (Saito & Lyster, 2012). Production-oriented instruction can also include providing learners with information about the way sounds are physically articulated and how L2 sounds differ from sounds in the L1 (Kissling, 2013).

A large body of literature has emerged on both perception training and production instruction, and this body of literature has been synthesized in several meta-analyses. As displayed in Table 6.1, these meta-analyses have shown that perception training leads to medium gains in segmental perception and small gains in segmental production (Sakai & Moorman, 2018) and pronunciation instruction leads to medium gains in the production of segmental and suprasegmental features (Lee et al., 2015) and medium gains in learners' ability to perceive suprasegmental features (McAndrews, 2019). Drilling down into the perception training literature, Zhang et al. (2021) compared multi-talker and single-talker conditions and found that multi-talker conditions are more beneficial for perception learning but do not appear to have the same benefit for production. These meta-analyses

DOI: 10.4324/9781003279266-6

170 Researching Pronunciation Training and Instruction

TABLE 6.1 Summary of Meta-Analytic Findings on Perception Training and Pronunciation Instruction

Study & Analysis	Between-Subjects	Within-Subjects
Sakai & Moorman (2018): 18 studies		
• Effect of perception training on immediate gains in segmental perception	0.93	0.92 [0.51, 1.33]
• Effect of perception training on immediate gains segmental production	0.89	0.54 [0.36, 0.72]
Zhang et al. (2021): 18 studies		
• Benefit of multi-talker perception training relative to single-talker training on immediate gains in segmental perception	0.56 [0.13, 1.00]	
• Benefit of multi-talker perception training relative to single-talker training on immediate gains in segmental production	−0.04 [−0.57, 0.49]	
Lee et al. (2015): 86 studies		
• Global effect of pronunciation instruction on immediate gains	0.80 [0.77, 0.81]	0.89 [0.85, 0.94]
• Effect of pronunciation instruction on immediate gains in segmental production	0.87 [0.84, 0.93]	0.89 [0.84, 0.95]
• Effect of pronunciation instruction on immediate gains in suprasegmental production	1.05 [0.99, 1.11]	1.03 [0.95, 1.11]
McAndrews (2019): 17 studies		
• Effect of suprasegmental instruction on immediate gains in suprasegmental perception	0.94	

Note. All meta-analyses reported many effect sizes, taking into account several moderator variables. Representative effect sizes are given here. All meta-analyses reported Cohen's d, but Zhang et al. (2021) reported Hedge's g, which is a bias-corrected form of Cohen's d. In the Sakai and Moorman (2018) meta-analysis, the authors computed gains for experimental groups (within-subjects) and gains for experimental groups relative to control groups (between-subjects) for studies that included a control group. In McAndrews (2019), the effect size refers to immediate gains in categorization accuracy. For full details, please refer to the original studies.

leave little doubt that training and instruction work, which means that the relevant question is no longer, "Are training and instruction effective?" but rather "What make training and instruction most effective?" or "How can training and instruction be optimized?" (Nagle & Hiver, 2023).

The meta-analyses cited above also point to a multitude of variables that moderate the efficacy of training/instruction. Some of these variables are what the learner brings to the table. For instance, Perrachione et al. (2011) examined how well participants learned tonal contrasts using HVPT. They gave learners a pitch perception aptitude test to measure individual differences in learners' ability to perceive pitch. High aptitude learners—learners who performed well on the pitch perception test—showed robust gains in learning over time, but low aptitude learners did not. A critical component of HVPT is the inclusion of stimuli produced by many talkers in many phonetic contexts. Thus, the authors reasoned that the extensive variability in the stimuli may have overwhelmed participants with lower aptitude for pitch perception. To mitigate the effects of cognitive overload, the authors created a new training condition with the same number of talkers, but they presented talkers one at a time. Put another way, overall variability was the same, but trial-by-trial variability was minimized because the presentation of talkers was blocked (i.e., stimuli from talker A, then stimuli from talker B). In this condition, all learners performed well and showed evidence of learning. Thus, individual differences in aptitude were effectively neutralized by restructuring the nature of the training, leading to a training paradigm that was beneficial for all learners. This is an excellent example of how training characteristics can be altered to optimize gains for all. To organize this chapter, I break it into two larger units: researching perception training and researching production training (i.e., pronunciation instruction). Within each of these areas, I examine the current state of the art and relevant methodological decisions. As in other chapters, I include two worked data examples, one dealing with perception training and another on production training. I end with information on testing long-term learning and what I see as an important avenue of future research: integrated training paradigms involving both perception and production training and complex/adaptive paradigms that change as the participant moves through them (i.e., as participants learn).

Researching Perception Training

Picking a Topic

There are several questions that guide contemporary perception training research. One deeply rooted research topic is the extent to which training helps learners encode L2 sounds and contrasts accurately. This research has its origin in early work using HVPT to help L1 Japanese learners of English perceive and produce the English /l/-/r/ contrast, which does not exist in Japanese and is challenging for Japanese speakers to perceive and produce accurately (Bradlow et al., 1997, 1999; Lively et al., 1993; Logan et al., 1991). As its name suggests, the conceptual keystone of the training paradigm was variability. The idea was that by exposing learners to the target contrast in a range of phonetic environments using stimuli spoken by many different talkers, learners would encode the contrast more robustly (for a detailed explanation of design choices, see Logan et al., 1991). Because HVPT is the most researched perception training paradigm, I will focus on it in this section. Even though I use HVPT as an example, many, if not all, of the considerations I discuss in this section apply generally to other types of perception training.

Since those initial studies, work on HVPT has grown exponentially. The key question that has driven this work is related to talker variability, that is, whether multi-talker training is always more beneficial than single-talker training. Zhang et al.'s (2021) meta-analysis suggests that it is, but the findings are not quite as robust as might be expected because results for multi-talker and single-talker conditions show considerable heterogeneity. Part of this heterogeneity can be linked to diversity in study design. Researchers have targeted different sounds and contrasts, in distinct learner populations and contexts, using diverse experimental procedures. Even a cursory comparison of studies reveals that there is little consistency with respect to the number of training sessions, length of the intersession interval, and number of trials per session. Zhang et al. (2021) analyzed some of these study characteristics to determine how they moderated the efficacy of single- and multi-talker training. Their results are informative and point to several interesting avenues for research, but we have not yet reached the critical threshold of studies needed for robust moderator analyses in this area. We are beginning to get a sense of the average effect we can expect as a result of HVPT, but far more research is needed to understand how experimental design choices affect learning during training, and performance and generalization after it (Thomson, 2018). As Perrachione et al. (2011) showed in their study, how variability is structured and delivered throughout training can impact learning, leading to marked gains for some learners and far more muted results for others.

Another prominent strand of research in this area is related to input enhancement, that is, how the contrastiveness of stimuli can be augmented to help learners attend to relevant phonetic cues and, simultaneously, disregard irrelevant or minimally relevant phonetic cues. This enhancement may be integrated into an HVPT-based approach, or it may be implemented in a different type of paradigm altogether. For instance, English vowel contrasts are predominantly cued by spectral differences, that is, by differences in vowel quality, but many L2 listeners rely on vowel duration, which is not an especially reliable cue in most varieties of English. To help learners attend to spectrum and deprioritize duration, researchers may create a synthetic continuum, where spectral differences are heightened and duration differences are dampened. Over time, as the learners become more sensitive to spectrum and less sensitive to duration, they may transition to more and more natural stimuli, until they are working with completely natural stimuli that have not been acoustically manipulated in any way (Kondaurova & Francis, 2010). Other researchers have examined whether providing visual information, such as showing a video of the target sound being produced, helps learners encode the target sounds more accurately than audio-only conditions (Zhang et al., 2021). While methodologically distinct, these studies are conceptually linked by their goal of enhancing the contrastiveness of L2 sounds and making their acoustic correlates more available to learners who are not accustomed to attending to those acoustic dimensions.

There are many perceptual training variables that could be manipulated, so the challenge of developing a research program in this area is doing so in a systematic way that allows for maximum comparability with previous work. The key is to think not about one study but rather about a series of studies, conducted in sequence, in which one or two variables are altered while maintaining all other variables constant. Such an approach has the best potential to shed light on the variables that are the most important regulators of learning. Once those variables are determined, their levels of measurement must also be set in a meaningful way. Consider, for instance, a research program centered on the number of talkers, number of sessions, and spacing of sessions. Each of these variables has many potential levels of measurement. At the most granular level, researchers could compare a single-talker condition to conditions with 2, 3, 4, 5 talkers, and so on, but this approach would be too granular and would not be a prudent use of resources. Some levels have theoretical importance and should certainly be included in nearly all studies. For example, including a single-talker condition is sensible given the current interest in quantifying single-talker versus multi-talker conditions (Zhang et al., 2021). The single-talker condition can also serve as a meaningful baseline against which multi-talker conditions can be compared. What about the multi-talker conditions? In my view, it makes sense to increase the amount of variability by a multiplier. For example, variability could be scaled exponentially, such that a single-talker condition is compared to conditions with 2, 4, and 8 talkers. Alternatively, a study could be set up to compare conditions with 1, 3, and 9 talkers.

Going beyond 3 or 4 comparison conditions is probably not warranted in most cases. For one, as the number of levels increases, the number of potential comparisons grows exponentially (with two levels, 1 vs. 2; with three levels, 1 vs. 2, 2 vs. 3, and 1 vs. 3; with four levels, 6 comparisons and with five levels, 10; given by the formula $n(n-1)/2$ where n refers to the number of levels), and this problem is compounded if the target variable is crossed with any other variable. There are other meaningful multipliers that could be considered, such as 1, 5, and 25 talkers. The latter example also brings into focus the issue of practicality. Creating stimuli based on 5 talkers should not be very difficult, but building a stimulus set based on 25 talkers would require a considerable amount of work. Sampling an excessively large number of talkers may not be an efficient use of resources. At the same time, if the sole focus of the study is to determine the optimal number of talkers, then it might be completely reasonable to create an array of talker conditions differing by one talker. In this case, the only variable would be the number of talkers, and the goal would be to optimize that facet of study design. In short, there are two potential approaches to any variable that could be manipulated: (1) to adopt a more granular focus, increasing the number of levels of that variable, with the goal of determining an optimal cut-off point or (2) to adopt a broader approach, sampling fewer levels of the variable, with the goal of examining potentially meaningful breakpoints, possibly in combination with other variables.

We can take a similar approach to the number of sessions and their spacing. The number of sessions determines the amount of total input and practice that participants receive (assuming the number of trials per session is held constant), and the intersession interval determines how the input and practice are distributed over time. Currently, we have little information on how these variables shape learning because there has been "no consistency across studies with regard to length of individual sessions, nor how they are distributed over time" (Thomson, 2018, p. 213). The logic we applied to the number of talkers also applies to the number of sessions. Namely, we should strike a balance between creating conceptually and practically meaningful comparisons while ensuring feasibility. For their moderator analyses, Sakai and Moorman (2018) set a cutoff of 6 sessions to categorize studies as consisting of long or short interventions. Longer interventions were slightly more effective than shorter interventions, but we should not put too much stock in that finding because the confidence intervals for the two study lengths overlapped considerably. Nevertheless, we could adopt their cutoff as a reference point, creating comparisons based on that point, such as 3 sessions, 6 sessions, and 9 sessions. We could also consider including 12 sessions, for the purpose of halving (3) and doubling (12) the baseline condition of 6 sessions. Unfortunately, we have no information on spacing, but we can take some guidance from two related areas of work: the science of sleep and the practice optimization literature.

With respect to the science of sleep, the memory consolidation that occurs during sleep appears to contribute significantly to L2 sound learning. When training sessions occur before and after sleep, participants perform far better than when sessions occur within the same day (Earle & Myers, 2015a, 2015b). Furthermore, the more sleep, the better (Earle et al., 2017).

These findings indicate that (1) we should not hold more than one training session per day and (2) we should ask participants about the amount of sleep they get on average, especially before and after training days as sleep duration could be a meaningful covariate in our analysis. With respect to practice optimization, drawing upon cognitive psychology research, Suzuki (2017) linked the intersession interval to the retention interval, that is, to the timing of the posttests. Two intersession intervals were included in the study, each representing a specific ratio of the retention interval: 3.3 days and 7 days. The 3.3-day intersession interval represented an optimal ratio, whereas the 7-day interval did not, and results showed that the 3.3-day group outperformed the 7-day group across the board on both posttests. Adopting this study as a benchmark, we could structure our intersession intervals similarly, or we could anchor them to a different retention interval (Suzuki, 2017 tested retention after 7 and 21 days). We also have to think about the context of the study. On one hand, if we run our study in the lab, then we can ask participants to come in whenever we want. On the other hand, if we run our study in the classroom, then we have to conform to the class schedule.

Up to this point, we have discussed building blocks, including how researchers can generate interesting research questions, map those questions onto variables, and then select meaningful levels of comparison. Most of the time, however, contemporary research does not target a single variable but rather two or more variables, examining how those variables affect learning when considered independently and in interaction with one another. Once we begin combining variables, we have to reevaluate the conceptual merit of the study and its feasibility, focusing specifically on the number of comparisons. Imagine that we wanted to examine the number of talkers and the number of sessions. With four levels for number of talkers (e.g., 1, 3, 6, 9) and three levels for number of sessions (e.g., 3, 6, 9), we could have up to 12 experimental groups, which would mean up to 66 comparisons if we compared all groups to one another. This clearly isn't feasible, nor is it conceptually sound to simply cross everything with everything else and compare it. Instead, we would need to be more selective, and to do that, we might return to the notion of variability. For example, we might consider training for fewer sessions (e.g., 3, 6) with more talkers (e.g., 6, 9) and training for more sessions (e.g., 6, 9) with fewer talkers (e.g., 1, 3). In other words, we could scale the intensity of the training depending on the number of talkers: more talkers with fewer sessions and fewer talkers with more sessions. Alternatively, we might argue that more sessions are necessary when there are more talkers because learners might need more time to sort out the higher variability multi-talker conditions. Regardless of the predictions we make and the approach we take, the main takeaway is that we need to think carefully about the approach, linking concept to method, and report on the concept and method as clearly as possible.

We're assuming that we should combine variables like number of sessions and number of talkers. However, it may not make sense to do so at this point in the trajectory of HVPT research. The field has probably not yet reached a state of knowledge where both variables are well understood, so as a first step, we might conduct initial studies targeting each of the variables independently. These studies would give us insight into how each variable can be optimized. Then, based on these results, we could design a more complex multivariate study in which we combine the two variables in conceptually and empirically meaningful ways. For example, we could ask how the number of talkers or the number of sessions interacts with one another or with the length of the intersession interval, with the goal of decreasing the number of sessions while maintaining a high level of learning. Put another way, perhaps we can decrease the number of sessions without compromising learning by either manipulating the number of talkers or altering the intersession interval. Crucially, in setting up these comparisons, we must hold all other elements of methodology constant, including: the population from which we sample, the target structure, the number of trials per session, and our testing instruments. Otherwise, it's impossible to determine whether differences in learning are due to the variables we have manipulated or to differences in other elements of methodology that we didn't control. Once we have carried out this work, we can then proceed to replication studies to build a body of evidence for the effects observed in the initial studies and their boundary conditions.

To be clear, this is not the only way to develop a systematic and meaningful research program, nor are these the only variables that could be manipulated. Rather, these hypothetical studies should be taken as examples of how a sound research program can be developed. Many factors go into designing a study and crafting a research program, both conceptual and practical, and the best research programs take both dimensions into consideration. One especially important consideration is the research-practice divide. An effective intervention that is impractical to put into practice in the language classroom or curriculum may be practically useless. If the goal is to bridge the research-practice divide, then researchers must consult and collaborate with language teachers about what would be possible to implement (Sato & Loewen, 2022).

Measuring Learning

One challenge of doing experimental work is developing a robust test of learning. A robust test of learning has two components: testing the durability of learning and testing generalization to novel targets, which for perception training means generalization to new talkers and new items. Nearly all intervention work involves a pretest-posttest design, but it has been surprisingly uncommon to include one or more delayed posttests to examine the retention of learning over time (Nagle, 2022). Perhaps for this very reason, meta-analyses have focused on quantifying the average effect size at posttest and, as such, we have little meta-analytic information on the average amount of retention that can be expected after training (but see Rato & Oliveira, 2023). This issue is not trivial. Some backsliding between the immediate and delayed posttest is to be expected, but it's easy to imagine that in some cases the amount of backsliding observed could be substantial. In the most extreme case, there could be no statistically significant difference between performance on the pretest and performance on the delayed posttest, which would suggest that the training was not effective at promoting durable, long-term learning. More likely, performance at the delayed posttest will fall somewhere between the pretest and immediate posttest. Thus, it is up to the researcher to determine a cutoff for meaningful learning. In other words, beyond what amount of backsliding is the training no longer worthwhile? To give a concrete example, if scores improve by 30% from the pretest to immediate posttest but the difference between the pretest and delayed posttest is only 12%, then is the training still effective enough to warrant implementation? The training has catalyzed learning, but has it catalyzed enough learning? The answer to this question depends on several factors, including anticipated effect sizes for similar training paradigms (though we do not yet have meta-analytic indices that would provide an anchor for interpreting retention data), contextual factors such as local resources, and the nature of the training itself, including how time- and labor-intensive it is to implement. To put a point on it, as a field, we have not yet had a conversation about how much is enough, nor do we at present have the data to make any definitive determinations, but as researchers, we can and should still consider what is meaningful within the context of our study. For instance, in a study on optimizing fluency training, Suzuki observed that "although it was difficult to establish a meaningful effect size for the ANCOVA results, the medium effect size of 0.0588 [based on education research] was selected as the minimum effect size for a *meaningful main effect* [emphasis added], which can be regarded as not too liberal, or at least not too conservative" (2021, pp. 299–300). Ignore the specific number that Suzuki selected and focus instead on the argumentation used to establish a minimally meaningful effect size for the study. This is the type of critical thinking that is crucial for training-based research (and Suzuki's study is an excellent example of clear and comprehensive reporting in many other aspects, so certainly worth the read).

Another important consideration is the extent to which learning generalizes to new talkers and new items, that is, to talkers and items that were not included in the training. The logic applied to delayed posttesting also applies here. If the training is only effective at promoting better performance on trained talkers and items, then the training is not very effective at all. There are several ways to test different levels of generalization. Testing new talkers is common because one of the central goals of HVPT and, indeed, other perceptual training paradigms, is to help learners process speaker-to-speaker variability. Related, learners should be able to generalize their ability to identify the sound or contrast in previously unencountered words. Testing generalization to new items can involve (1) testing the target feature in the same phonetic context using new items, (2) testing the target feature in a new but similar phonetic context, or (3) testing the target feature in an entirely new phonetic context that is not very similar to the contexts learners were trained on. For example, in Thomson (2012), participants were trained on vowels after bilabial stops (/b/ and /p/) and tested on vowels after velar stops (/g/ and /k/, a new but similar phonetic context) and vowels after fricatives (/s/ and /z/, a new phonetic context). There was evidence for generalization to the novel stop context but not the novel fricative context. This finding is not surprising because phonetic cues show context-sensitive properties. Thus, understanding the extent to which training promotes generalization to diverse talkers, items, and phonetic environments is a central criterion for determining the efficacy of a particular program.

Finally, researchers sometimes test if perception training leads to gains in production (e.g., Huensch, 2016). That is, they test for cross-modality effects. If a perception training paradigm is shown to improve both perception and production, then it could be considered especially impactful. In their meta-analysis, Sakai and Moorman (2018) found that perception training leads to small but significant gains in production, on average. Thus, there is a precedent for testing production, which could be considered another form of generalization.

In summary, researchers should include at least one delayed posttest that occurs after the closure of the training period. The exact timing of the delayed posttest depends on other elements of study design and anticipated retention intervals. It's also worthwhile to consider including multiple delayed tests to understand the shape of learning after training (Nagle, 2022). The focus of current research has been on learning curves before, during, and immediately after training, but we rarely think about the fact that development continues to unfold well after the training has concluded. Likewise, multiple generalization tests should be included. Minimally, researchers should test generalization to new talkers, holding the items or phonetic context constant, as well as generalization to new items or contexts, holding the talkers constant. The most rigorous test of generalization crosses these two conditions: novel items produced by novel talkers. That condition could be considered the "holy grail" of training, but if that level of generalization is not achieved, researchers should not be discouraged.

Developing the Training Procedure

Picking a topic and determining what and when to test are important conceptual decisions, but attending to the configuration of the training is equally important. The general approach is to give a pretest, administer the training, and then give the immediate and delayed posttests. During training, participants hear a large number of aural stimuli, make perceptual judgments (e.g., identify them, discriminate them), and receive feedback. For instance, on a given trial, a participant might hear a stimulus, see several orthographic options, and identify what they heard from among those options. Within this general structure, detailed decisions must be made about the structure of the training (i.e., how the stimuli are blocked and presented to the participant), response options, and feedback. These are the decisions I focus on in this section.

There are several approaches to blocking stimuli. One approach is to randomize everything, so that the stimuli are presented in a completely random order to each participant. This means that from one trial to the next, the participant might hear stimuli produced by different talkers and might work with the target contrast presented in distinct phonetic environments. In other words, complete randomization leads to a high amount of trial-by-trial variability. In some cases, high trial-by-trial variability may be desirable, but several studies suggest that blocking by talker is beneficial for learning (Perrachione et al., 2011; Zhang et al., 2021). In this way, overall variability remains high, but trial-by-trial variability is reduced. Consider a paradigm with six trained talkers, each of whom produced five stimuli (for information on how to build a stimulus set, see Chapter 2 on researching perception). Table 6.2 shows what the first ten trials of this training paradigm could look like under the two conditions. As shown in the first column, in a completely random paradigm, the listener could receive a stimulus produced by any talker on any trial. In the second and third columns, however, trials are blocked by talker. For a given talker, the listener could receive any stimulus produced by that talker, but within that talker block, the listener would not receive a stimulus produced by another talker. Further, the second and third columns illustrate two potential blocked orders, reinforcing the idea that the order of talkers is randomized, as well as the order of trials within talkers.

What about blocking by context? If speakers are trained on items produced in multiple phonetic contexts, should stimuli be blocked by context as well? There is not yet empirical evidence on this topic, but if reducing trial-by-trial variability is beneficial for learning, then blocking by context could be beneficial. The goal of any HVPT is to balance consistency and variability. There needs to be enough variability to catalyze robust learning but not so much variability that it overwhelms the learner. In some

180 Researching Pronunciation Training and Instruction

TABLE 6.2 Examples of Possible Randomization and Blocking Formats

Trial	Completely Random	Blocked by Talker Order 1	Blocked by Talker Order 2
1	Talker 1, Stimulus 1	Talker 1, Stimulus 5	Talker 3, Stimulus 1
2	Talker 4, Stimulus 5	Talker 1, Stimulus 2	Talker 3, Stimulus 3
3	Talker 3, Stimulus 2	Talker 1, Stimulus 1	Talker 3, Stimulus 4
4	Talker 3, Stimulus 5	Talker 1, Stimulus 4	Talker 3, Stimulus 2
5	Talker 6, Stimulus 4	Talker 1, Stimulus 3	Talker 3, Stimulus 5
6	Talker 2, Stimulus 2	Talker 4, Stimulus 2	Talker 1, Stimulus 5
7	Talker 1, Stimulus 2	Talker 4, Stimulus 4	Talker 1, Stimulus 4
8	Talker 5, Stimulus 4	Talker 4, Stimulus 5	Talker 1, Stimulus 1
9	Talker 4, Stimulus 4	Talker 4, Stimulus 1	Talker 1, Stimulus 2
10	Talker 4, Stimulus 1	Talker 4, Stimulus 3	Talker 1, Stimulus 3

cases, blocking by talker and by context could be the right choice, whereas in other cases, it may be better to block by talker but not by context. For instance, perhaps for novice learners, more consistency would be beneficial, whereas more advanced learners might benefit from blocking by talker but randomizing contexts. These questions remain open and are ripe for more research, but the key takeaway here is to take a principled approach, explain it, and acknowledge limitations.

Response options must also be considered. There is an abundance of options: actual images, representative images, actual words, keywords, or phonetic symbols. Images avoid orthography, but not all words are image-able, and it may be impossible to select imageable words while controlling for other criteria such as the number of syllables, stress pattern, and phonetic context in which the sounds appear. Using representative images, such as nautical flags (Thomson, 2012) or fictitious characters (Nagle, 2018), is another option, but then familiarization must be included to ensure that participants learn the association between the image and what it represents. Orthographic options are simpler, especially for instructed learners who are exposed to the written and aural forms of words from the very onset of learning, but then inaccurate responses could be due to an incomplete or inaccurate understanding of L2 sound-symbol correspondences. In L2s with a transparent orthography, the use of orthographic response options is less problematic, and the effect of orthography can be minimized by using high-frequency words or keywords that learners are likely to know. In a study comparing HVPT with two response options, keywords and phonetic symbols, Fouz–González and Mompeán (2021) found that both experimental groups improved their perception of L2 English vowels compared to a control group that did not receive HVPT. Furthermore, there were no significant differences between the experimental groups, which suggests that both options were equally effective at promoting learning. Interestingly, because the authors blocked stimuli by phonetic context rather than by talker, the results also provide evidence that blocking by context is an effective means of structuring variability to promote learning. It's also important to bear in mind that the use of phonetic symbols was possible in the study because participants were enrolled in an English Phonetics and Phonology course that included instruction on the International Phonetic Alphabet (IPA). In short, the choice of what response options to use is dictated both by experimental and by contextual constraints. For researchers interested in tightly controlling the phonological form of the stimuli, learned images or orthographic choices (in standard orthography, keywords, or IPA) are good options. For researchers who are less concerned about the form of the word and thus willing to train learners using a range of possible stimuli, real images may be a viable option. And, if helping learners map sound-spelling correspondences is a goal of the research, then orthographic options could be desirable. Researchers must be clear about the goal of the work and must consider participant characteristics to set up an appropriate training format.

Last, but certainly not least, several other aspects of the training must be configured. First, feedback must be provided. Typically, right/wrong feedback is given, and if the listener responds incorrectly, the trial repeats so that they can select the correct option (or the correct option is shown and the audio is automatically replayed). Second, the timing of trials must be set. One important question to consider is when response options will become available. Response options can be made available from the onset of the trial or presented after the audio stimulus has played. If the audio plays first, then the amount of time that elapses between presentation of the stimulus and presentation of the response options must be set. Thinking about how word recognition works, it seems sensible to present the stimulus before the response options become available. That way, the listener must process, encode, and retrieve the target before identifying it. In this case, an inter-stimulus interval of 1.5 seconds is probably sufficient to encourage phonological processing and retrieval, but the length of the inter-stimulus interval has also been a topic of considerable debate in the speech processing literature (for discussion, see Chapter 2 on researching perception).

Perception Summary

In this section, we have discussed how to select a perception training topic, attending both to the current state of the art and to researcher interests, which are dictated by individual preferences and goals as well as contextual affordances. The perception training literature, especially the HVPT literature, has reached a relatively mature state, which means that now is an ideal time to begin to delve into the variables that could regulate the efficacy of HVPT (and other training paradigms). Variables such as the number of trained talkers and contexts, number of sessions and trials per sessions, and intersession interval can be combined in meaningful ways to shed light on how training can be optimized by adjusting several variables at once. All training studies must have two key features to achieve maximal impact: inclusion of at least one delayed posttest and at least one generalization condition, which together provide information on how durable and robust learning is. Simply put, HVPT is known to be effective, so now research questions should center on what configuration of HVPT leads to the best retention and generalization for most learners. It bears repeating that contemporary training research should seek the best outcome for the greatest number of learners. To do so, researchers will likely need to broaden the contexts in which they train learners and the types of learners that receive training. Expanding beyond laboratory studies to the classroom, and from the classroom to online, self-guided training, and training learners who are not the college-aged samples typically recruited in experimental research will be essential features of future work.

We have also discussed how to set up the training with respect to the order in which stimuli are presented, the response options, and what happens on a given trial. There is no one-size-fits-all model for these decisions, so researchers must take care to consider their research goals, and once decisions are made, they must report on them transparently. All methodological decisions involve tradeoffs but picking the "right" tradeoffs is not always easy. Researchers should carefully consider whether the decisions they make will allow them to answer their research questions or, alternatively, if making certain methodological choices could undermine the design of the study.

Statistical Analysis: The Shape of Learning during HVPT

As Thomson (2018) pointed out, we still know relatively little about the shape of learning during training. This is because training data are rarely analyzed, even though such data could illuminate important information on the rate and end state of learning at the conclusion of training. As a result, and because training data are time series data characterized by many measurements at equally spaced intervals, I have chosen to model and analyze training data for this example.

We'll assume that learners completed ten sessions of HVPT training focusing on a challenging L2 vowel contrast, a design that broadly mirrors Thomson (2012). Normally, in HVPT, participants would work with more than one vowel contrast, but for the sake of simplifying the analysis, I focus on just one here. As a reminder, in an HVPT paradigm, the participant would hear a word with one of the target vowels, identify it, and then receive correct/incorrect feedback. For this example, we'll also assume that we manipulated two variables: the number of talkers presented during training (five or ten) and the intersession interval (3 days or 7 days; that is, training twice per week or once per week). The variables we have held constant are the number of sessions (both intersession interval groups completed ten sessions, but the 3-day group necessarily completed the training over a shorter window) and the number of stimuli trained per session (n = 100). Crossing these two variables, each with two levels, yields four experimental groups, as shown in Table 6.3. Finally, we'll assume that we had ten participants per group.

Our primary goal is to understand how the number of talkers and the length of the intersession interval, independently and in interaction, affect the rate and shape of learning during training. Our variables are shown in Table 6.4.

As in previous chapters, the first step is data inspection. Given that, we have ten training sessions, rather than inspecting means and standard deviations at each session for each group (i.e., 4 groups × 10 sessions = 40 point estimates), it's easier to visualize performance over time. As shown in Figure 6.1, all groups improved over time, but some groups seem to have improved more than others, with the 5-talker, 3-day (5t3d) group improving the most and the 10-talker, 3-day (10t3d) group improving the least. Thus, combining a high number of talkers with a short intersession interval

TABLE 6.3 Summary of Variables and Experimental Groups in Simulated HVPT Data

	5-talker condition	*10-talker condition*
3-day intersession interval	5t3d	10t3d
7-day intersession interval	5t7d	10t7d

TABLE 6.4 Summary of Study Variables

Variable	*Type*	*Description and Levels/Range*
subject (n = 40)	Factor	An index variable that refers to the subjects
item (n = 100)	Factor	An index variable that refers to the items/ trials
Group	Factor	Experimental group, with four levels: 5t3d = 5 talkers, 3-day intersession interval 5t7d = 5 talkers, 7-day intersession interval 10t3d = 10 talkers, 3-day intersession interval 10t7d = 10 talkers, 7-day intersession interval
Talker	Factor	5t, 10t
intersession	Factor	3d, 7d
Session	Continuous	0–9
Correct	Binary	0 (incorrect), 1 (correct)

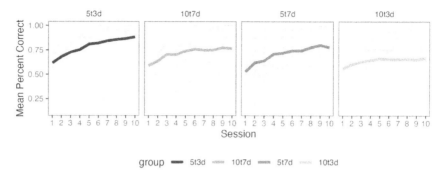

FIGURE 6.1 Performance over Training by Group.

seems to slow learning, at least relative to the other combinations in the study.

Now, we can fit a model to the data. Here, analysis of variance (ANOVA) doesn't make sense due to the large number of sessions, so we will proceed straight to the mixed-effects model. We could try to fit curved trajectories by incorporating polynomial terms for session (e.g., linear session, quadratic session) to approximate the curvature we see in the plots. However, the group-level trajectories don't seem to show much curvature, so fitting a linear trajectory seems like a good approach for this data. If we wanted to be certain, we could build and compare models with complex trajectories (e.g., linear vs. linear + quadratic), but again, that doesn't seem necessary here.

We designed this study with a specific model in mind: We wanted to test the interaction between Talker and Intersession. Following the literature, we're assuming that including more talkers is beneficial (10t > 5t group). We're also assuming that training more frequently is more beneficial (3d > 7d). Finally, we're making one final conceptual leap, a leap yet to be investigated, assuming that training frequently with many talkers may result in a slower rate of learning over time (10t3d performs worse than the others). In real data, these hypotheses may prove true or false, but in this example, I simulated the data with these effects in mind. In this case, because we're interested in testing a specific set of effects, it makes sense to fit the maximal fixed effects model of interest, which would include those terms and their interaction, as well as by-participant and by-item random intercepts. As a reminder, we fit a logistic model with a binomial distribution because our outcome variable is binary (0/1, which corresponds to incorrect/correct).

```
fm.hvpt <- glmer(correct ~ session * talker * intersession +
          (1 | participant) +
          (1 | item),
        data = data.hvpt, family = "binomial")
```

We could contrast-code the effects of Talker and Intersession (e.g., assign a value of –0.5 to Talker = 5 and a value of 0.5 to Talker = 10; Linck & Cunnings, 2015), but in this case, I prefer not to do that for two reasons. First, following the logic of this simulation, we have specific beliefs about how each of these variables may affect learning. Put another way, we have a baseline condition against which we want to compare the other condition. For Talker, we expect the higher variability condition—the condition with more talkers—to potentially outperform the lower variability condition. For Intersession, we expect the shorter interval to outperform the longer interval. In other words, we expect more frequent training to perform better. For these reasons, we can set the 5-talker and 7-day conditions as the baselines against which the other levels are compared. The other reason I prefer not to contrast code for this data set is because in my experience contrast-coding multiple variables in a glmer model makes the directionality and strength of coefficients much more difficult to interpret. Importantly, because we are not contrast-coding, we need to remember that the intercept of the model and the estimate for Session refer to the intercept and rate of change for the baseline group, which is Talker = 5 and Intersession = 7, so the 5t7d group. If we contrast-coded, the estimates would refer to the grand mean, pooling over groups.

The next model we fit is the model with by-participant random slopes for Session. We could also fit by-item random slopes for Session because Session is a within-items variable. More specifically, we have assumed that participants worked with the same set of items at each Session, so we can include Session as an item-level random effect. Remember that we need to fit an appropriate random effects structure, integrating random slopes whenever possible (random intercepts, then random slopes for within-unit effects, then random slopes for within-unit interactions), to build an accurate model of the data (i.e., to appropriately capture within-unit variability in effects; Brauer & Curtin, 2018), which is why we include by-item random slopes in addition to the by-participant random effects.

```
fm.hvpt.rs2 <- glmer(correct ~ session * talker * intersession +
              (1 + session | participant) +
              (1 + session | item),
          data = data.hvpt, family = "binomial")
```

Comparing the random slopes models to simpler models shows that both models were a significantly better fit to the data than their predecessor model. I used the *DHARMa* package (Hartig, 2022) to simulate and inspect model residuals for assumption checking. The simulated residuals

186 Researching Pronunciation Training and Instruction

did not reveal any problems with model fit. We're ready to summarize the model and extract comparison information for the four groups.

The way we fit the model allows us to estimate the unique effects of Talker and Intersession, as well as their interaction. We could have integrated Group (four levels) and its interaction with Session, but had we done that, we would not have been able to recover estimates for the independent effects of increasing talker variability and manipulating the length of the intersession interval. Model fm.hvpt.rs2 is summarized in Table 6.5. It's important to remember that the interaction terms refer to the difference between estimates for the baseline group and the estimates for the other groups. For example, the estimated rate of change for the 5t7d group is the estimate for Session ($OR = 1.31$). The estimate for Session × Talker (10) refers to the difference between the rate of change for the 5t7d group and the 10t7d group, the estimate for Session × Inter. (3) refers to the difference between the 5t7d group and the 5t3d group, and the estimate for Session × Talker (10) × Inter. (3) refers to the difference between the 5t7d group and the 10t3d group. We didn't contrast-code Talker and Intersession, so we can't use this model to recover the grand mean intercept and rate of change, pooling over the groups. To give you an idea of the overall rate of change, I refit the model with contrast-coded effects. In that model, the estimate for Session was $OR = 1.26$ ($SE = 0.05$, 95% CI = $[1.16, 1.36]$, $p < .001$).

TABLE 6.5 Summary of Logistic Mixed-Effects Model Fit to the HVPT Training Data

Fixed Effects	OR	SE	z	95% CI	p
Intercept	0.91	0.15	−0.59	[0.66, 1.25]	0.557
Session	1.31	0.10	3.60	[1.13, 1.52]	<0.001
Talker (10)	1.26	0.29	1.01	[0.81, 1.97]	0.310
Inter. (3)	1.35	0.31	1.33	[0.87, 2.12]	0.185
Talker (10) × Inter. (3)	0.83	0.27	−0.58	[0.44, 1.56]	0.565
Session × Talker (10)	0.98	0.10	−0.18	[0.80, 1.20]	0.858
Session × Inter. (3)	1.02	0.11	0.18	[0.83, 1.25]	0.855
Session × Talker (10) × Inter. (3)	0.84	0.12	−1.15	[0.63, 1.13]	0.250

Random Effects	SD	Correlation			
Subjects					
Intercepts	0.48				
Slopes: Session	0.22	−0.47			
Items					
Intercepts	0.33				
Slopes: Session	0.14	−0.25			

Researching Pronunciation Training and Instruction **187**

TABLE 6.6 Estimated Rate of Change in Probability of Responding Correctly and Pairwise Comparisons by Group

	OR	95% CI
Estimated Effect of Session		
5t7d	1.31	[1.13, 1.52]
5t3d	1.33	[1.15, 1.55]
10t7d	1.29	[1.11, 1.49]
10t3d	1.11	[0.95, 1.28]
Pairwise Contrasts for Session		
5t7d vs. 10t7d	1.02	[0.78, 1.33]
5t7d vs. 5t3d	0.98	[0.75, 1.28]
5t7d vs. 10t3d	1.18	[0.91, 1.55]
10t7d vs. 5t3d	0.96	[0.74, 1.26]
10t7d vs. 10t3d	1.16	[0.89, 1.52]
5t3d vs. 10t3d	1.21	[0.92, 1.58]

Note. Based on model syntax: glmer(correct ~ Session * Talker * Intersession + (1 + Session | participant) + (1 + Session | item), family = binomial).

We'll use this model to extract estimated rates of change (i.e., estimates for Session) for each group and compare the groups to one another. We can do that with the **emtrends()** function of the *emmeans* package (Lenth, 2023). The estimated slopes and pairwise comparisons between all groups are given in Table 6.6. As we discussed in previous chapters, it may not make sense to compare all groups to one another. In that case, if we had specific groups we wanted to compare, we could set a priori contrasts to get those comparisons.

In summary, from this analysis, we can conclude that all groups improved over time throughout the training. We also know that the number of talkers and the length of the intersession interval did not significantly moderate the rate of change. Furthermore, although the three-way interaction did not reach statistical significance, based on the model estimates and the pairwise comparisons extracted from the final model, it appears that the 10t3d group experienced the slowest rate of change. Admittedly, that rate was not significantly different from the rates observed for the other groups, but the estimates and confidence intervals suggest that the 10t3d group was indeed different from the others.

Researching Production Training

Picking a Topic

There is tremendous diversity in the production training literature. Production training may focus on the production of specific features, or it may be oriented toward global dimensions of pronunciation such as comprehensibility. Researchers have drawn upon a range of approaches to help learners improve their production of specific features, including form-focused instruction with corrective feedback (Saito & Lyster, 2012), task-based pronunciation instruction (McKinnon, 2017; Solon et al., 2017; for a review, see Mora & Levkina, 2017), explicit phonetics instruction (Kissling, 2013), and visual feedback training (González López & Counselman, 2013; Offerman & Olson, 2016; Olson, 2014a, 2019; Olson & Offerman, 2021). There has also been a tradition of assessing the efficacy of pronunciation, speaking, and listening courses to determine the extent to which the targeted nature of those courses helps learners improve their pronunciation beyond what they would achieve in another more general communicative language course (Lord, 2005; Sturm, 2013). These courses often make use of activities such as journaling (Kennedy et al., 2014) and podcasting (Lord, 2008), which encourage students to reflect on their pronunciation and take notice of individual problem areas. Compared to research on specific features, research examining the effect of training on global dimensions of pronunciation is somewhat rare. Nevertheless, studies suggest that shadowing (Foote & McDonough, 2017) and drama-based activities (Galante & Thomson, 2017) can help learners improve their fluency and comprehensibility.

Researchers interested in examining production training must think carefully about the developmental timeline of the target feature, that is, how much training would be required to catalyze meaningful change in the production of the feature. For example, a shorter intervention may lead to appreciable gains in specific features, whereas a far longer and more intensive intervention might be necessary to stimulate gains in global dimensions of pronunciation such as comprehensibility. Thus, just like for perception training, for production training, it's important to consider not just what goes into the training, but how it will be structured over time. For example, how many training sessions will participants complete and how often will they complete them? Manipulating these variables could have a dramatic effect on the amount of learning observed and, crucially, the extent to which learning is retained over time and generalizes to untrained words, contexts, and so on. In fact, one increasingly central question in production research is how controlled pronunciation knowledge (i.e., what learners are able to produce under tightly controlled conditions where they can focus their attention on their pronunciation) and spontaneous pronunciation knowledge (i.e., what learners produce on meaning-oriented tasks that demand greater cognitive engagement) are related to one another and develop over time (Saito & Plonsky, 2019). It may be the case that controlled pronunciation knowledge can be trained over a short window using relatively simple, controlled tasks such as reading and picture naming. Training spontaneous pronunciation knowledge, which would enable learners to produce intelligible and comprehensible variants fluently in communicative scenarios, might require a far more extensive training regimen with respect to both the tasks included and the length of the intervention. In fact, to train spontaneous knowledge, or to help learners automatize their controlled knowledge, it may be necessary to scaffold the intervention from simple to more complex tasks, such that learners are able to consolidate their knowledge under controlled conditions before engaging in more complex, meaning-oriented practice. The fact that longer interventions lead to greater gains on average than shorter interventions is not surprising (Lee et al., 2015), but such meta-analytic findings should not be taken as evidence that longer is always necessary and better. Indeed, if the primary goal of intervention research is to understand how it can be optimized, then researchers must consider the interplay among the functional load of the target structure, the anticipated effect size of the training, and logistics and resource allocation. These considerations often form trading relationships.

Consider a few different scenarios. If the target structure has a high functional load (e.g., English vowel contrasts like /i/-/ɪ/, liquids like /l/-/ɹ/), it may be worthwhile to invest considerable resources to help learners improve their production of that feature. Here, resources refer mostly to time: the time needed to develop materials for the intervention, to implement the intervention, and to assess training outcomes. Eventually, provided the training has a positive result, resources might also include the time needed to train teachers to implement the intervention themselves. Even for a high functional load structure, however, we will need to determine the minimum effect size we accept as practically significant, irrespective of its statistical significance. Put another way, statistically meaningful improvement is not always practically meaningful. If the target structure is quite important for effective (i.e., intelligible and comprehensible) oral communication, then we may accept a small-to-medium effect (see Lee et al., 2015 for effect size benchmarks) as acceptable, even if the training is relatively resource intensive. In this case, the importance of the structure itself drives decision-making.

Next, consider a target structure that has lower functional load. In this case, it seems clear that to train this feature we would search for an intervention that is (1) relatively quick and easy to implement and/or (2) leads to medium-to-large production gains. Perhaps we would accept a more logistically complex intervention if the gains were large, but the point is that without a sizable improvement, the resources used to train a low functional load structure could probably be used more efficiently for other purposes. As a third and final example, consider the intervention itself rather than the target structure. Perhaps we have a sound theoretical rationale for using a particular intervention to target a particular feature. In this case, our goal is not resource optimization, but rather understanding the strengths and limitations of a particular training paradigm. In other words, researchers may select a particular training paradigm and target structure for practical, pedagogical purposes, for theoretical reasons (e.g., understanding the type of learning that occurs under different exposure conditions), or both. Researchers are guided by diverse needs and interests, some of which are certainly tied to the context in which they work, so the answers to these questions must also be context-specific. The important takeaway is that these and similar questions are the types of questions we must ask ourselves before engaging in empirical work, and there are countless examples of research that fit into each of these broad categories.

Saito (2015) examined Japanese speakers' production of the English /l/-/ɪ/ contrast, a notoriously difficult contrast for some L2 English speakers which also has a high functional load. The experimental groups participated in four one-hour sessions in which they received form-focused instruction. They were additionally divided into a group that received only the instruction and a group that received instruction and corrective feedback on their production. Participants completed several warm-up activities, which were identification tasks designed to draw learners' attention to their perception and production of English /l/ and /ɪ/. Instruction was carried out over a two-week period. The experimental groups showed a significant improvement in their listening ability from the pretest to the posttest with a medium effect size. Their production, which was rated by their teachers, also showed significant improvement, with a small effect size for the instruction-only group and a medium-to-large effect size for the instruction and corrective feedback group. In terms of the scenarios laid out previously, then, we could characterize this study as involving (1) a high functional load feature, (2) an efficient intervention, in the sense that it could easily be integrated into the curriculum without displacing other topics, and (3) a medium effect for listening and a medium, on average, effect for speaking. Although this study did not include a delayed posttest, it did include several production tasks to elicit production under both controlled and spontaneous conditions. Thus, Saito's (2015) results speak to the extent to which participants improved their production of the target feature on a meaning-oriented task that approximates realistic speaking conditions.

In another study focusing on a specific segmental feature, Olson (2019) examined the effect of visual feedback training on English speakers' production of word-initial Spanish stops consonants. While crosslinguistic functional load comparisons are tricky, it seems reasonable to say that the functional load of Spanish stops is probably slightly lower than the functional load of English /l/-/ɪ/ but certainly not negligible. In other words, word-initial stops could be considered a medium-to-high functional load segment in Spanish. In Olson's (2019) study, participants recorded themselves and printed and labeled visual representations of their speech at home, analyzed the representations and compared them to a L1 speaker in class, and then re-recorded themselves. Thus, the intervention was conducted within a single hour-long class period, in addition to the small amount of preparatory work and homework that participants completed outside of class. Results showed a small but significant improvement in the acoustic accuracy of participant's production from the pretest to the posttest, and there was no significant difference in results from the immediate posttest to the delayed posttest, suggesting that learning was retained. Furthermore, learning generalized to untrained phonemes (participants were trained on a stop consonant at one place of articulation, such as /p/, but tested on all places of articulation, /p, t, k/). Returning to our scenarios, we could characterize this study as involving (1) a medium functional load segment, (2) an intervention that is short and simple but requires some technical expertise to implement, and (3) modest learning that is retained and generalizable.

Finally, consider a study targeting global comprehensibility. Derwing et al. (2014) developed a comprehensive pronunciation course to help highly skilled workers at a window factory improve their intelligibility and comprehensibility. This course included evaluating and training the partici-pants' perception and production of a range of problematic segmental and suprasegmental features. Listener-based ratings of participants' comprehen-sibility on two speaking tasks, a suitcase narrative and a job-specific safety talk, showed a small but statistically significant gain from the pretest to the posttest. Compared to other studies where interventions tend to last a few hours on average, in Derwing et al. (2014), participants took part in a far more intensive and comprehensive pronunciation intervention. Nonethe-less, the authors characterized the intervention as relatively modest in scope: "Despite receiving only 17 hours of pronunciation instruction over a period of 3 months, augmented by listening and speaking homework assignments, [the participants] showed evidence of improvement in both targeted skills" (p. 542). This characterization, combined with the fact that comprehen-sibility gains were small according to field-specific benchmarks for inter-preting within-subjects comparisons (Lee et al., 2015; Plonsky & Oswald, 2014; Saito & Plonsky, 2019), reinforces the view that considerable time and effort are needed to bring about change in global constructs like com-prehensibility. In terms of our scenarios, this study would represent (1) an important global construct in a high-stakes professional setting, (2) an in-tensive intervention, and (3) demonstrable gains in the perception and pro-duction of specific features and modest gains in global comprehensibility.

In summary, historically, pronunciation training research has been cen-tered on quantifying the extent to which training is effective. There is no question that it is. Thus, the field has shifted away from asking the simple question of whether pronunciation training works toward a more nuanced set of questions related to how it can be optimized. Optimization demands consideration of both the impact (e.g., quantified via effect sizes) and efficiency (e.g., the number of sessions administered, their length, and complexity) of the intervention. Researchers should consider answering the following questions before engaging in training research:

With respect to the target structure, why is it worth training? Here, two answers are possible but not mutually exclusive. The target structure may be practically important if it has a medium-to-high functional load in the target language. In that case, training that target structure stems from the need to help learners produce more intelligible and comprehensible speech. Another reason may be rooted in theory. The target structure itself may not have high practical relevance but training that structure could allow the researcher to address key theoretical issues. To give one example, recall that Olson (2019) used visual feedback training to help English speakers improve their production of Spanish voiceless stops, /p, t, k/. However, in his study, he assigned learners to work with stops at one place of articulation, later testing the extent to which learners improved their production at the other, untrained places of articulation. Using this design, Olson was therefore able to gain insight into precisely what the participants were learning. This study bears resemblance to Thomson (2012), who administered perception training for English vowels in one stop consonant context (/p/ and /b/), testing generalization to a new stop consonant context (/k/ and /g/) and to a new fricative context (/s/ and /z/). In short, in some cases, the target structure is trained for its intrinsic value, whereas in other cases, the rationale rests on the target structure as a vehicle that allows the researcher to ask and answer theoretical questions.

With respect to the intervention, why is a particular training schedule and set of activities appropriate? As noted elsewhere, until recently, pronunciation instruction was heavily focused on demonstrating that it worked, without considering the conditions under which it can be made to work optimally. Thus, in many studies, it has been common to compare one experimental group to a control group, or to compare two qualitatively different experimental groups (e.g., groups that receive different types of instruction altogether, cf. Derwing et al., 1998; groups that do or do not receive corrective feedback, cf. Saito, 2015). In these studies, it is impossible to derive one experimental group from another because the experimental groups are composed of different elements. Certainly, comparing different types of instruction remains an important dimension of pronunciation research. At the same time, there is increasing interest in delving into quantitative differences with respect to how the training is configured. Here, groups could be derived from one another by manipulating the quantity of one of the variables. For instance, experimental groups could receive the exact same type of training but differ with respect to the number of sessions or the intersession interval.

With respect to gains, what is the minimum amount of learning that can be considered practically meaningful, irrespective of statistical significance? This point is quite important because given a large enough sample size, even small differences between groups can be reliably detected. Thus, as statisticians have pointed out time and time again, statistical significance is a coarse-grained and, in some cases, meaningless metric for assessing the impact of an intervention. Though at present rare, some researchers have begun to specify minimally meaningful effect sizes, drawing upon meta-analytic literature inside and outside of the field and precursor studies (e.g., Suzuki, 2021). Having a clear understanding of the effect size that can be anticipated for a given intervention enables researchers to design and implement more impactful studies, and it also allows them to provide clearer insight into the practical significance of their findings. To be clear, the goal of research is not necessarily to find large, statistically significant effects. Rather, the principle that underlies research design is to align method and analysis with research questions, irrespective of the outcome or results. In short, all findings, be they null or statistically significant and small, medium, or large in terms of effect size, are valuable and should be reported and interpreted.

Designing the Intervention

There can be a lot of decision-making involved in the way production training can be implemented, which means researchers must take care to select or develop a training paradigm that is informed by their research goals. Sometimes, researchers are interested in incorporating pronunciation instruction into the language classroom. In that case, they may opt for communicatively-oriented pronunciation instruction, such as form-focused instruction (Saito, 2015) or task-based pronunciation teaching (Gurzynski-Weiss et al., 2017). Thus, pronunciation instruction is designed following the principles of the general approach into which it is incorporated: communicative language teaching or task-based language teaching. In the case of Saito (2015), the implementation of corrective feedback for one of the experimental groups was also informed by the state of the art in that area.

Technology-enhanced interventions are becoming increasingly common. For instance, researchers (and teachers) may use automatic speech recognition systems to provide learners with instant feedback (for an overview, see Cucchiarini & Strik, 2017). Speech analysis programs like Praat, which are not designed for pedagogical purposes, have also been used to train pronunciation targets with a straightforward visual component that can be easily identified, such as prosodic contours (Hardison, 2004) and stop consonants (Olson, 2014a, 2014b). Specialized programs are also being developed for specific learner populations, target languages, and sounds. For example, researchers have developed and tested a "golden speaker" application that allows learners to hear the L2 produced in a nativelike way in their own voice (Ding et al., 2019).

The most important aspect of selecting a training paradigm and designing the intervention is thinking carefully about the mechanism through which the paradigm might catalyze pronunciation learning. Corrective feedback may help learners instantly notice the gap between their pronunciation and the target pronunciation (Saito, 2015), and if learners are themselves feedback providers, then they may also develop greater phonological awareness, which could in turn help them improve their own pronunciation even if they do not receive feedback (Martin & Sippel, 2021, 2023). Similarly, visual feedback training gives learners an important tool for seeing the difference between their pronunciation and the target pronunciation. For target structures with a clear visual signature, learners can use visual cues to monitor their learning over time. In short, when designing an intervention, researchers need to provide a plausible explanation for why and how the intervention might work to bring about changes in pronunciation.

Selecting Variables for Experimental Manipulation

There are many quantitative variables that can be targeted in research designs, far more than I can address in this chapter, so here I focus on variables that are directly related to how the training is administered over time. Olson and Offerman (2021) compared three experimental groups, all of whom participated in a visual feedback training paradigm designed to help English speakers improve their production of voiceless stop consonants in Spanish. One group received a one-shot intervention, whereas the other two groups participated in three sessions. The simultaneous three-session group worked with all three places of articulation (/p/, /t/, /k/) at each session, whereas the sequential three-session group worked with one place of articulation per session (e.g., /p/ in session 1, /t/ in session 2, and /k/ in session 3). All three groups improved, but the sequential training group appeared to outpace the other two, which suggests that the blocked nature of the sequential training, with one stop consonant phoneme per session, rather than the number of sessions, was the primary regulator of the amount of learning over time. However, Olson and Offerman (2021) was a reanalysis of data reported in several studies, studies with comparable but not identical methods. To gain accurate insight into how the number and

Researching Pronunciation Training and Instruction **195**

blocking of sessions affect learning, it would be important to control other aspects of methodology in a close replication study (Nagle & Hiver, 2023).

Replication is important, but it's not our focus here, so we should think about what studies would be logical extensions of this paradigm, that is, logical extensions into the effects of number of sessions and blocking. To start, researchers could increase the number of sessions, comparing three and six sessions (i.e., doubling the number of sessions to create two multi-session groups). This variable could also be fully crossed with the blocking variable, leading to a symmetrical design with four experimental groups, as shown in Table 6.7. For the three-session sequential condition, there is only one order, at least in terms of the frequency of training each phoneme (i.e., each phoneme would get trained at one session), but for the six-session sequential condition, there are two options. In option 1, the same phoneme is trained back-to-back, whereas in option 2, the full set of phonemes is trained sequentially before repeating the full set a second time. If we believe that blocking facilitates learning, then it seems like option 1 might be a more advantageous blocking condition, giving learners additional time to practice and master the target phoneme before moving to the next phoneme, but we could test both options if we had a strong theoretical rationale for how the two options might lead to different results. In that case, we would likely need to draw upon studies comparing blocked versus interleaved practice.

In this experimental design, we have another important variable to consider: the total number of practice items to be completed during the course of training. If we equate practice items across sessions so that learners work with the exact same number of items at each session, then the six-session conditions will work with twice as many items as the three-session conditions. In this design, the number of sessions represents the total amount of practice. Another option would be to equate the total number of practice items across the conditions, in which case, across the entire training, the three- and six-session conditions would work with the same number

TABLE 6.7 Possible Experimental Groups in Follow-Up Visual Feedback Training Study

Session	Three/ Simultaneous	Three/ Sequential	Six/ Simultaneous	Six/ Sequential1	Six/ Sequential2	Six/ Combined
1	/p, t, k/	/p/	/p, t, k/	/p/	/p/	/p/
2	/p, t, k/	/t/	/p, t, k/	/p/	/t/	/t/
3	/p, t, k/	/k/	/p, t, k/	/t/	/k/	/k/
4	N/A	N/A	/p, t, k/	/t/	/p/	/p, t, k/
5	N/A	N/A	/p, t, k/	/k/	/t/	/p, t, k/
6	N/A	N/A	/p, t, k/	/k/	/k/	/p, t, k/

of items, but the six-session conditions would work with fewer items at each session. In this design, the number of items is held constant and the intensity of the training session (i.e., the number of items per session) is manipulated. Each of these designs is viable but responds to a different research question.

When the total number of items is equated, then comparing the three- and six-session conditions is rooted in the notion of massed (more items over a shorter window) versus distributed (fewer items over a longer window) practice. That is, the relevant underlying variable is practice type or schedule. When the number of items is equated at each session, the comparison is about the total amount of practice, that is, whether more practice is beneficial. One could easily imagine several outcomes: (1) three- and six-session conditions lead to comparable gains, in which case, more training is not advantageous at all, (2) the six-session condition leads to additional gains, but those gains are not as pronounced as, for instance, the gains achieved when moving from a single session to three sessions (e.g., comparing one-session, three-session, and six-session simultaneous models), or (3) the six-session condition produces clear and robust gains above the three-session condition. Importantly, the number of phonemes trained also partially determines the number of sessions necessary; with three phonemes, the number of sessions must be a multiple of three. If, on the other hand, we limited trained phonemes to /p/ and /t/, then we could compare two- and four-session (and six-session, were we interested) conditions to one another. We would also be able to test generalization to /k/, an untrained phoneme.

Other training characteristics that would need to be specified are the words and contexts included in the training. Participants could work with the same set of words each session, or they could work with different words whose phonetic properties have been controlled (i.e., a different but phonetically comparable set of words). They could also work with words in isolation, words in utterances, or both. These variables could have an impact on learning, so holding them constant across experimental groups is critical. What this example brings to light, then, is that care must be taken to equate experimental groups across a range of variables to be controlled, such that findings can be uniquely attributed to the experimental manipulation (e.g., the number of sessions, blocking).

All the options discussed to this point involve strict separation between the simultaneous and sequential models, but this need not be the case. A combined model, in which participants begin with sequential training before moving to simultaneous training, could also be developed and tested. The rationale behind this condition might rest upon beginning with a paradigm that is less cognitively complex, in which participants can focus their attention on a single phoneme, before scaffolding into the simultaneous training, which is arguably more cognitively complex. To be clear, we would not necessarily attempt to compare all groups to one another in a single study. Doing so would require a large sample size that could be difficult to achieve, and study logistics would be complicated. Instead, a subset of the groups would be compared at each stage of the research, and this rationale would be laid out in each research product (e.g., in study 1, three/simultaneous, three/sequential, six/simultaneous, and six/sequential/1; in study 2, six/sequential/1, six/sequential/2, and six/combined). Of course, in this design, advancing from one stage of the research to the next is predicated on a positive result in the previous stage. If there were no clear benefit to the six-session condition relative to its three-session counterpart, then it might not make much sense to continue testing it. Manipulating the number of sessions and the blocking of items is possible with many training paradigms beyond visual feedback training, and the effect of these variables may (i.e., is likely to) depend on the nature of the training itself. Thus, to develop a comprehensive understanding of how these manipulations work, it would be necessary to expand the scope of research to include a variety of target structures, training paradigms, and learner populations.

Another variable that could be meaningfully manipulated would be the intersession interval, or the amount of time that elapses between sessions. To manipulate this variable, the number of sessions and the number of items per session would be held constant (assuming the intersession interval were the only variable of interest). Creating meaningful comparisons for the length of the intersession interval depends on other study design features. For instance, if we carry out the training in an instructed, classroom setting, where learners attend a certain number of class meetings per week on fixed days, then we must consider the class meeting schedule. This is precisely what Suzuki (2021) did in a study on the optimal distribution of L2 grammar practice. In that study, both experimental groups participated in four training sessions, but the intersession interval differed. For one group, the intersession interval was 3.3 days, and for the other group, it was 7 days. Importantly, it was impossible to create equal intervals in the shorter intersession interval condition. For the 3.3-day group, session 2 took place three days after session 1, session 3 four days after session 2, and session 4 three days after session 3, creating a 3-4-3 schedule. Laboratory-based or online studies could train learners on any schedule, but if the goal is to develop findings that are applicable to the classroom, then the training schedule that is adopted should closely mirror the practices of a typical class, including the assignment or activity structure. The intersession interval could also be crossed with, for instance, the number of sessions. When crossing variables, however, I recommend limiting the complexity of the design to two variables with two levels. With two target variables, each with two levels, there

198 Researching Pronunciation Training and Instruction

are four experimental groups. Increasing the number of variables and/or the number of levels tested beyond this threshold would quickly lead to an unwieldy design, assuming variables are fully crossed. Furthermore, as I laid out for perception research, as the number of experimental groups increases, decisions must be made about which groups should be compared to one another because it's not sensible to compare all groups to one another. Thus, as the experimental design complexity increases, so does the complexity of the decision-making and the analysis.

Measuring Learning

Measuring learning principally involves thinking about how durable and generalizable learning is. I discussed this issue extensively in relation to testing learning in perception, so rather than repeat that information here, I will briefly summarize key points and discuss one of the key features of measuring the generalizability of production training: generalization from controlled to spontaneous production.

As with measuring perception learning, measuring production learning requires researchers to consider how learning might fade over time. Put another way, it is nearly a foregone conclusion that there will be some backsliding in learning, but determining the time course and shape of that backsliding is essential for understanding the long-term impact of production training. For trained items and contexts, we would expect to see robust learning on the posttest, and this learning should be retained relatively well over time, with little backsliding on delayed posttests. Put another way, it's reasonable to expect the strongest and most durable learning for what was trained.

Imagine we compare three experimental approaches, all using the same paradigm but manipulating factors related to the intensity and spacing of sessions. Groups A and B show a similar amount of learning on the posttest, whereas Group C shows slightly better performance than the other groups. On the delayed posttest, all three groups show some evidence of backsliding. For Group A, this backsliding is not statistically significant, but for Groups B and C, it is. Furthermore, for Group C, who showed the most pronounced learning from the pretest to the posttest, the amount of backsliding is greater than for the other groups. If we only looked at the posttest, we would assume that all three groups showed similar amounts of learning, perhaps with a slightly larger effect for Group C compared to the other two groups. Looking further down the road, however, suggests qualitative differences in the learning that occurred: moderate and sustained learning for one Group A, moderate but somewhat fragile learning for Group B, and substantial but ephemeral learning for Group C.

Imagine including a second delayed posttest. Perhaps by that time, Group C has reverted to near-pretest levels of performance, Group B has performance that is partway between pretest and posttest scores, and Group A continues to show evidence of sustained learning with a small, but statistically insignificant, amount of backsliding. Now imagine that the training for Group A is difficult to set up and administer, whereas the training paradigms for Groups B and C are far simpler. In this case, despite the positive trajectory for Group A, it could be more efficient and sensible to move forward with the training for Group B, on the assumption that a "booster" training could be given to shore up learning and prevent significant backsliding. All of this is purely hypothetical, but this example illustrates how the inclusion of one or more delayed posttests is critical for understanding the longer-term efficacy of an intervention.

Another important criterion for establishing the efficacy of a training paradigm is generalization beyond what was trained. Generalization can take many forms: to novel items, to novel contexts, or to novel tasks. Often, it is impossible to test all possible forms of generalization, and even if it were possible, it would not be advisable to do so without a strong rationale for the decision (after all, participants can't spend hours in testing). Thus, for instance, researchers may test trained items in novel contexts or on a novel task, untrained items in a similar context and under similar task characteristics, or fully novel items on a fully novel task. Olson and Offerman (2021) described testing the same set of stop-consonant-initial words over time, but the utterances in which the target words appeared varied. They could have also tested novel words or tested the extent to which the controlled production training generalized to a more spontaneous task, such as timed picture description. The latter, testing the extent to which training promotes the development of spontaneous production knowledge, as opposed to controlled production knowledge (Saito & Plonsky, 2019), is a central concern of contemporary production research. One challenge in this area is equating items across controlled and spontaneous tasks. If items are concrete and imageable, then they can be included in both sets (e.g., reading the items and generating an image in which they appear). In some cases, however, generating a set of items suitable for use on both controlled and spontaneous tasks may prove difficult, if not impossible. If learners show evidence of learning on a controlled task with trained items but not on the spontaneous task with novel items, then it's impossible to know if lack of learning stems from the use of different items or task differences. Whenever possible, then, at least a subset of trained items should be embedded into a spontaneous task.

Part of measuring production learning is deciding how to quantify it. Quantification can involve acoustic measurements, but it can also

200 Researching Pronunciation Training and Instruction

involve listener-based assessments of intelligibility, comprehensibility, and accentedness. For research conducted in a pedagogical context for the purpose of helping learners improve their pronunciation, listener-based assessments are a sensible and necessary measure of learning. After all, the basic question underlying any intervention is if it will help learners communicate more successfully (i.e., if it will make their pronunciation easier to understand). At the same time, listener-based assessments introduce a constellation of listener-level variables that, if not controlled, can influence results. On the one hand, this influence is not problematic because communication is fundamentally a two-way street. Thus, any listener-based influence evident in the assessment would almost certainly reflect the reality of communication, where such an influence would also be at play. On the other hand, on purely methodological and statistical grounds, uncontrolled listener-based influences can introduce noise into the data, obscuring true intervention effects. Thus, for listener-based assessments, researchers must take care to construct a relevant and representative listener group and to collect sufficient demographic information from that group (for a discussion on sampling listeners, see Chapter 4 on researching the production of global features).

Listener-based assessments can be relatively coarse-grained, in the sense that they may not be sensitive enough to show evidence of learning even when some learning has occurred. It is open to debate whether learning that is not evident in listener-based measures is practically meaningful, but for the purpose of determining whether an intervention is effective, it may be worthwhile to include acoustic measures. These measures may show evidence of learning that has not yet risen to a level at which it could be detected by listeners. If possible, including both listener-based assessments and acoustic measurements offers another advantage: examining the relationship between (changes in) the acoustic measures and (changes in) the listener-based measures. The mapping between acoustics and listener perception is multidimensional and quantal. Large changes in acoustic dimensions may produce small changes in listener perception or may not drive listener perception at all. Likewise, small changes in acoustic features may sometimes trigger precipitous changes in listener assessments. Thus, much work remains to be done on the relationship between the acoustic characteristics of speech and its intelligibility and comprehensibility.

Production Summary

Like perception training research, production training research has rapidly reached a point of methodological maturity. As such, simple pretest-posttest studies comparing one experimental group to a control group for the most part are no longer positioned to advance the state of the art. A robust approach to production training research would therefore include: (1) multiple experimental groups that compare several distinct approaches to training; (2) at least one but ideally multiple delayed posttests to shed light on how learning changes after training; and (3) relevant generalization tests, especially tests of whether learning generalizes from controlled to spontaneous tasks. With respect to (1), at this stage in the research trajectory, it would be sensible to compare novel experimental groups to a comparison group that receives some form of pronunciation training known to be effective. In this way, research can continue to advance the state of the art by probing whether the novel approach promotes learning above and beyond an established approach. In this chapter, I have advocated for a quantitative, incremental approach to optimizing production training by taking the same paradigm and manipulating training characteristics. Researchers could certainly test training paradigms that are altogether different. Yet, it is my view that rather than generating and testing new paradigms, it would be more advantageous at present to work with the diverse paradigms we currently have at our disposal, testing how they can be optimized.

Statistical Analysis: Visual Feedback Training: Retention Over Time

Throughout the section on production training, I have referred to Olson and Offerman's (2021) work comparing several approaches to visual feedback training. In their study, they drew upon data from their previous work to compare groups differing in the number of sessions they completed and the way the sessions were structured. As a reminder, one group participated in a single session, whereas the other two groups participated in three sessions. For the three-session groups, one participated in simultaneous training, working with all places of articulation at each session, and the other in sequential training, working with one place of articulation per session. Because the data were compiled from different studies and repurposed for the comparative analysis, there were minor, but not insignificant, differences in how the training was implemented. I have advocated elsewhere (Nagle & Hiver, 2023) that this study is an ideal candidate for replication for two reasons. First, it's positioned to advance the state of the art in pronunciation training by illuminating some of the variables that contribute to optimal production learning outcomes. Second, by aligning the method across experimental groups, which was not possible for the repurposed data, we can gain more precise insight into the true effect of the target variables. For these reasons, I have chosen to simulate a data set based on the original study, altering the effects slightly in ways that could be expected once methodological differences are addressed.

We'll assume that we replicated Olson and Offerman (2021), following the methodological suggestions given in Nagle and Hiver (2023). In our replication proposal, we highlighted the following points:

1 Replicating the study at a single site, assigning two intact classes to each paradigm
2 Aligning the test items across the groups, such that each group is tested using the exact same set of items
3 Training the one-session group on all three places of articulation, which would make it directly comparable to the three-session simultaneous group
4 Ensuring consistency with respect to the items the groups work with during training, including the units into which the items are embedded (e.g., individual words, utterances)
5 Testing generalization to production on a more spontaneous task

Imagine that we have addressed 1–4. Thus, for the purpose of simulation, what has changed is the number of intact classes included in the study and, as a result, the sample size. We could also simulate (5), but the design of the study is already relatively complex, so I have chosen not to add a generalization condition into the simulation. We'll also assume that we included a comparison group that received pronunciation instruction on the properties of Spanish stops and their differences with English without visual feedback. This comparison group will serve as a control group to test whether visual feedback boosts learning above and beyond traditional pronunciation instruction. A summary of the groups and the structure of the training is given in Table 6.8.

We give participants a list of 30 words to read (10 each for /p/, /t/, and /k/) before, immediately after, and four weeks after training. We measure voice onset time (VOT) in each word. The variables we have for this study are shown in Table 6.9.

TABLE 6.8 Summary of Study Groups and Procedure

Session	Traditional	Short	Long Simultaneous	Long Sequential
1	Phonetic description	Visual feedback (VF)	VF /p, t, k/	VF /p/
2	N/A	N/A	VF /p, t, k/	VF /t/
3	N/A	N/A	VF /p, t, k/	VF /k/

TABLE 6.9 Summary of Study Variables

Variable	Type	Levels/Range
Class ($n = 8$)	Factor	An index variable that refers to the intact classes. For this example, we will assume that class sizes are unequal, such that the number of students per class and therefore the number of students per group varies somewhat.
Subject ($n = 154$)	Factor	An index variable that refers to the subjects
Item ($n = 30$)	Factor	An index variable that refers to the items
Group	Factor	traditional, short, longsim (long simultaneous), longseq (long sequential)
Test	Factor	pretest, posttest, delayed
Phone	Factor	p, t, k
VOT	Continuous	18–87

Our research questions and predictions are:

- What is the effect of the training paradigm on the production of Spanish stops? In line with Olson and Offerman (2021), we predict that all visual feedback groups will outperform the traditional group. Additionally, we predict that the long sequential group will show the greatest gains (i.e., the greatest reduction in VOT) on the posttest.
- To what extent are the gains made as a result of visual feedback training retained over time? We predict some backsliding for the visual feedback groups, but we hypothesize that the long sequential group will show less backsliding than the other two visual feedback groups. Put another way, the long sequential group should show the greatest retention over time, evidenced by VOT on the delayed posttest that is comparable to VOT on the immediate posttest.

As a first data exploration step, we might want to visualize how the two classes assigned to each group performed over time, which will give us a sense of whether or not the classes performed similarly. We could generate a basic plot focusing exclusively on the class variable, but I think it's advantageous to create a data-rich plot that allows us to see how the classes in each experimental condition performed on each phone over time. In other words, we want to create a plot that includes four variables: Group, Phone, Time, and Class. There are many ways to do this, but the approach I took was to generate a violin plot to visualize distributions, mapping Group and Phone to columns and rows, Time to the x-axis, and Class to color, as shown in Figure 6.2.

204 Researching Pronunciation Training and Instruction

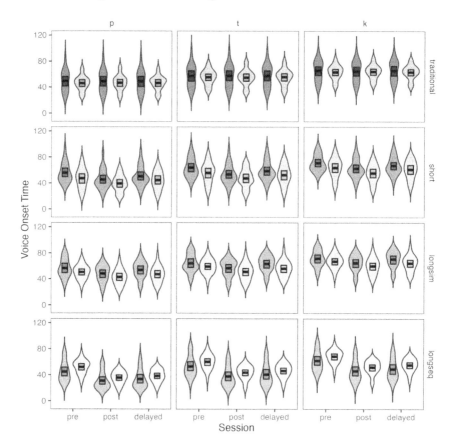

FIGURE 6.2 Plot Showing Performance of the Classes within Each Group over Time by Phone.

Note. The boxes represent the mean and 95% confidence interval.

If we focus on the potential effect of class, comparing the two colors in each column of the figure, we can see that the distributions are similar, which suggests that the two classes assigned to each condition performed similarly. From the plot, we can also see that the short, longsim, and longseq groups improved over time, at least descriptively, insofar as they produced shorter VOT on the posttest. We can also see that the longseq group seems to have achieved the greatest improvement and retained that improvement over time. The descriptive statistics given in Table 6.10 paint a similar picture.

Having inspected the data, we're now ready to analyze it. By this point, I hope you feel more comfortable with mixed-effects modeling. I also hope to have convinced you that it's a superior analytical tool to ANOVA most of the time, especially when we have repeated and/or nested observations.

Researching Pronunciation Training and Instruction **205**

TABLE 6.10 Descriptive Statistics for VOT Production over Time by Group and Phone

Group	Phone	Session		
		Pre	Post	Delayed
Traditional (n = 37)	/p/	47 (16)	48 (16)	47 (16)
	/t/	56 (16)	56 (17)	56 (17)
	/k/	64 (19)	64 (19)	64 (19)
Short (n = 40)	/p/	52 (17)	42 (16)	48 (16)
	/t/	60 (17)	51 (17)	56 (17)
	/k/	68 (20)	59 (20)	64 (20)
Long Sim. (n = 36)	/p/	53 (14)	45 (14)	50 (15)
	/t/	61 (15)	54 (15)	59 (15)
	/k/	69 (18)	62 (19)	67 (19)
Long Seq. (n = 41)	/p/	48 (15)	33 (13)	36 (14)
	/t/	56 (16)	41 (15)	43 (16)
	/k/	65 (19)	49 (19)	52 (20)

Note. Two intact classes were assigned to each group. Because these classes had different numbers of students, the number of participants per group varied.

Nonetheless, I will quickly provide an overview of the ANOVA approach so that we can compare it to the mixed-effects model because the use of ANOVA to analyze factorial designs remains common in the field.

As in previous chapters, we will use the aov_car() function from the *afex* package (Singmann et al., 2023) to run the ANOVA. This package requires us to write a formula, specifying the within-subjects effects of Session, Phone, and their interaction in the error term.

```
fm.anova <- aov_car(vot ~ group * session * phone +
Error(participant/session * phone),
data = data.vf)
```

In previous chapters, we aggregated the data first before passing it to aov_car() so that each participant had a single observation at each level of the within-subjects factors. In this data set, we have three levels each for Phone and Session, so participants should have nine observed means. Aggregating before passing to aov_car() can be advantageous because it reminds us that we cannot run an ANOVA on the trial-level data. However, this aggregation is not strictly necessary because aov_car() automatically aggregates data if it detects more than one observation per cell. If it aggregates data, it returns a warning indicating that the data has been aggregated: "Warning: More than one observation per design cell, aggregating data using 'fun_aggregate = mean.'"

206 Researching Pronunciation Training and Instruction

If we call the model object, then we can see that there are significant main effects for Group, Session, and Phone, and a significant Group × Session interaction. The interactions involving Phone are not statistically significant. These effects are summarized in Table 6.11.

Among these effects, we are interested in the Group × Session interaction, which indicates that at least two of the groups showed different amounts of learning over time. However, Group is a variable with four levels, and Session is a variable with three, so we do not yet know which groups are different from one another and at what time points they're different. We'll use the emmeans() function from the *emmeans* package (Lenth, 2023) to get that information. Given the design of our study, we likely want two sets of comparisons: one examining the performance of each group by session and another comparing the performance of various groups within sessions. We can request pairwise comparisons by session within groups and by groups within sessions using the following code.

```
emmeans(fm.anova, pairwise ~ session | group) # by session within group
emmeans(fm.anova, pairwise ~ group | session) # by group within session
```

The estimated marginal means that the first function (by session, within group) outputs are given in Table 6.12. Summarizing this data, we can see that the traditional group did not improve at all because there are no

TABLE 6.11 Summary of ANOVA Fit to Visual Feedback Training Data

Effect	F	df	η^2G	p
Group	4.78	3,150	0.085	0.003
Session	476.20	1,192	0.055	<0.001
Phone	7602.76	2,265	0.193	<0.001
Group × Session	97.51	4,192	0.034	<0.001
Group × Phone	1.89	5,265	<0.001	0.092
Session × Phone	0.95	4,563	<0.001	0.428
Group × Session × Phone	1.95	11,563	<0.001	0.030

Note. A Greenhouse-Geisser adjustment has been applied to within-subjects effects, and df has been rounded to the nearest whole number.

TABLE 6.12 By Session Comparisons within Groups Based on ANOVA

Comparison	Traditional	Short	Long Sim.	Long Seq.
Pre vs. Post	−0.03	9.06***	7.58***	15.73***
Post vs. Delayed	−0.16	−5.15***	−5.30***	−2.91***
Pre vs. Delayed	−0.19	3.91***	2.29**	12.82***

Note. * $p < 0.05$, ** $p < 0.01$, *** $p < 0.001$.

significant differences between any time points. In contrast, all three visual feedback groups improved from the pretest to the posttest and experienced some backsliding from the posttest to the delayed posttest. Despite this backsliding, all visual feedback groups maintained a significant difference between the pretest and the delayed posttest, indicating that at least some learning was retained. The coefficients also reveal important information about the magnitude of change. The long sequential group showed the greatest change over time and the least amount of backsliding, followed by the short group and then the long simultaneous group.

Table 6.13 shows the between-group comparisons at each time point. There were no significant differences on the pretest, as expected. On the posttest, only the long sequential group was significantly different from the traditional group. The long sequential group was also significantly different from the other two visual feedback groups. This same pattern of results was evident on the delayed posttest, where the long sequential group was significantly different from all other groups. Thus, the long sequential paradigm was much more effective than the short and long simultaneous paradigms.

Up to this point, we have assumed that we want to compare all groups to one another. However, this may not be the case. For instance, we may want to compare the traditional group to pooled data for all three visual feedback groups, which would give us a sense of the extent to which visual feedback training, irrespective of how it is implemented, is superior to traditional pronunciation instruction. We may also want to compare the short paradigm to pooled data for the long paradigms, which would respond to whether more training is better. Finally, we could compare the two long groups, ignoring all other groups. If we want these comparisons, we need to build our own contrasts. The first step to setting contrasts is generating a reference grid of objects using emmeans().

rgrid <- emmeans(fm.anova, ~ group * session)

Calling the grid returns a list of 12 estimated marginal means, one for each group at each session. Then, we use this grid to generate a set of contrasts.

TABLE 6.13 By Group Comparisons within Sessions Based on ANOVA

Comparison	Pre	Post	Delayed
Traditional vs. Short	−3.93	5.16	0.17
Traditional vs. Long Sim.	−5.21	2.40	−2.74
Traditional vs. Long Seq.	−0.72	15.04***	12.29***
Short vs. Long Sim.	−1.28	−2.75	−2.90
Short vs. Long Seq.	3.22	9.89**	12.12***
Long Sim. vs. Long Seq.	4.49	12.64***	15.02***

Note. * $p < 0.05$, ** $p < 0.01$, *** $p < 0.001$.

208 Researching Pronunciation Training and Instruction

For the sake of simplicity (and because we know there are no significant differences at pretest), we will make these contrasts only for the posttests.

```
contrasts <- list(trad_all_post     = c(0,0,0,0,-1,1/3,1/3,1/3,0,0,0,0),
                   trad_all_del      = c(0,0,0,0,0,0,0,0,-1,1/3,1/3,1/3),
                   short_long_post   = c(0,0,0,0,0,-1,1/2,1/2,0,0,0,0),
                   short_long_del    = c(0,0,0,0,0,0,0,0,0,-1,1/2,1/2),
                   sim_seq_post      = c(0,0,0,0,0,0,-1,1,0,0,0,0),
                   sim_seq_del       = c(0,0,0,0,0,0,0,0,0,0,-1,1))
```

What we are doing is assigning 0 to entries we do not want included in the comparison, a negative value to the baseline group, and positive values to the comparison groups. The baseline and comparison groups must sum to 0, so we assign the baseline group a value of 1 and comparison groups a values of $1/k$ where k is the number of comparison groups. The sign of the number, positive or negative, determines what gets subtracted from what. For instance, if we assign a negative value to the traditional group, as shown in the first two entries of the preceding contrast code, then the traditional group is subtracted from the mean of the other groups. Once we have configured the contrasts, we then use the list with the reference grid object in the contrast() function. We also call for a p value adjustment for multiple comparisons using the adjust argument.

```
contrast(rgrid, contrasts, adjust = "mvt")
```

This will produce a list of 6 estimated mean differences instead of the 18 comparisons included in the complete list. The results of this analysis are given in Table 6.14. According to this analysis, any type of visual feedback training, regardless of its implementation, leads to an improvement over traditional training. Although this improvement persists at the delayed posttest, it is no longer statistically significant. The long training does not appear to lead to statistically robust gains over the short training, at least when both the long simultaneous and long sequential trainings are considered as

TABLE 6.14 Planned Group Comparisons within Sessions Based on ANOVA

	Post	*Delayed*
Traditional vs. All	−7.53*	−3.24
Short vs. Long	−3.57	−4.61
Long Sim. vs. Long Seq.	−12.64***	−15.02***

Note: * $p < 0.05$, ** $p < 0.01$, *** $p < 0.001$. p values have been adjusted for multiple comparisons.

a group, but the long sequential is significantly more effective than the long simultaneous training. From this analysis, we can tentatively conclude that visual feedback training is effective overall, but it is most effective when it is blocked by place of articulation. Without blocking, even more training may not promote durable gains.

Now, we'll build the mixed-effects model and compare it to the ANOVA results. We'll treat participants and items as random effects. Class could also be a random effect, but I didn't simulate any class-level random effects, so I have decided to leave it out of the model for the sake of model fitting. First, we fit the full fixed effects model, including the three-way Group × Session × Phone, mirroring the ANOVA.

```
fm.vf <- lmer(vot ~ group * session * phone +
              (1 | participant) +
              (1 | item), data = data.vf)
```

Then we integrate by-subject random slopes for Session, Phone, and Session × Phone and by-item random slopes for Session (Phone is a between-items factor, so we can't fit by-item random slopes for that term). If this were real data, we would attempt it, but for this data set, given our interest in the effect of Session, I focus on fitting those random effects. The model with by-subject random slopes for Session converged, but the model with by-subject and by-item random slopes for Session was singular. Thus, the best-fitting model for this data set is as follows.

```
fm.vf.rs <- lmer(vot ~ group * session * phone +
                 (1 + session | participant) +
                 (1 | item), data = data.vf)
```

When I checked model assumptions (normality, linearity, and homogeneity of variance), there were a few problems, likely arising due to some extreme residuals. I could prune those observations from the model and refit it, but the problem with pruning cases with large residuals is that in the refitted model there may be a new set of observations with extreme values. This can, in turn, lead to a cycle of pruning and refitting that, in my view, is ill-advised. Thus, here I report the full model, noting that assumptions do not appear to be fully upheld. If I wanted to prune the data, I would follow a sensitivity-based approach, fitting the full and pruned models and examining how estimates change when observations are removed.

Remember that in our model we have a three-way interaction involving three factors. Thus, the model will output a large number of estimates corresponding to every possible combination of the three factors. R interprets

210 Researching Pronunciation Training and Instruction

factors in alphabetical order, so normally it would set Group = longseq and Session = delayed as the baseline against which the other levels of each factor are compared. Before we fit our model, I reordered the levels, setting Group = traditional and Session = pre as the baselines. The intercept in our model therefore refers to performance of the traditional group, and the estimate for Session refers to the rate of change for that group. If our primary interest was in comparing the other groups to the traditional group, then we could summarize the model, interpreting estimates. However, as we laid out for the ANOVA, our goal is to extract a more complete set of comparisons: at each time point, comparing the groups to one another, and for each group, comparing the time points to one another. We need the emmeans() function again.

```
emmeans(fm.vf.rs, pairwise ~ session | group) # by session within group
emmeans(fm.vf.rs, pairwise ~ group | session) # by group within session
```

When we run this analysis, we get a message indicating that the degrees of freedom calculation has been disabled. By default, the emmeans() function uses the Kenward-Roger method to estimate the variance-covariance matrix for the model object and the denominator degrees of freedom for the t-test. In data sets with a large number of observations, this estimation method can be computationally intensive and exceedingly slow, as the note indicates. When degree of freedom calculations are disabled, emmeans() assumes an asymptotic distribution, returning z values instead of t values. In the output, to indicate an asymptotic distribution, degrees of freedom are shown as infinite. If we want to enable degree of freedom calculations, we can change the test limit by setting the pbkrtest.limit argument to a value higher than the number of observations in the data, but it has been my experience that with large data sets consisting of (tens of) thousands of observations, R crashes when pbkrtest.limit is increased. I don't think the t-to-z method is necessarily problematic as long as we report it in the manuscript.

These comparisons, as well as the planned comparisons, return the exact same values as ANOVA (to reproduce the tables, see the R markdown) for two reasons; first, because there is no missing data. If we had missing data, ANOVA would remove entire cases, whereas the mixed-effects model would retain all data points, weighting estimates depending on the number of observations available. Second, I minimized the random effect variance in the data, especially item-level random effects. Although in this case the results were similar, don't take this result as indicative that ANOVA is functionally equivalent to the mixed-effects model. Mixed-effects models are the appropriate analysis for hierarchical data structures.

In summary, based on the results of these analyses, we can say with confidence that the three visual feedback groups improved significantly from the pretest to the posttest and experienced minor but statistically significant backsliding from the immediate posttest to the delayed posttest. Based on the size of the coefficients, the long sequential group improved the most and retained what they learned the best. Turning to the group-wise analysis at each session, visual feedback, considered collectively, appears to be more effective than traditional pronunciation instruction, but the gains associated with visual feedback don't necessarily lead to an advantage in the long term based on a non-significant difference between the visual feedback groups and the traditional group on the delayed posttest. Likewise, there doesn't seem to be an advantage for more visual feedback training sessions as opposed to fewer. Thus, for this simulated data, the most advantageous paradigm seems to be the sequential one, in which training was blocked by place of articulation.

Integrated and Complex Designs

Throughout this chapter, I have advocated for testing paradigms that differ by degree along 1–2 key variables. This approach makes the most sense to me because it allows us as a field to isolate and understand the effect of a given variable on learning. Once we have documented the strength of an effect and constructed a plausible range within which it may vary, then we could move onto more complex, integrated training paradigms. I want to acknowledge that this approach is predicated on a modular, experimental view of training research. Other approaches are also possible, so I would like to briefly outline the ways in which researchers have set about designing and testing more complex paradigms, including adaptive paradigms. My definition of a "complex" paradigm is one in which (1) the structure of the training changes over time and/or (2) perception and production are trained together. My definition of "adaptive" is a training paradigm in which the nature of the training is not fixed but rather is calibrated based on participants' performance. Adaptive paradigms are typically technologically enhanced because participant performance must be tracked in real time to determine how the training should proceed (e.g., whether it should become more or less difficult, whether it should progress to a new block or to the next phase).

In my reading of this literature, most studies using complex, adaptive paradigms aim to maximize learning by combining several techniques known to be effective. Thus, the research is not designed with the intention of evaluating individual elements of the training paradigm. Instead, the efficacy of the entire paradigm is assessed so that a recommendation can be made about whether the set of training features that have been assembled works well. Although conceptually distinct from the approach I have laid out in this chapter, the same types of design guidelines apply.

Delving into the specifics of adaptive training is beyond the scope of this chapter. For researchers interested in considering developing an adaptive paradigm, one critical concern is how performance is tracked and what thresholds are used to determine how the training progresses. Simply put, how well do participants have to perform and for how long (e.g., correct responses on three consecutive trials? On five?) before adaptation begins? Likewise, how does difficulty scale over the training and why is that adaptation or scaling likely to be beneficial?

Learning beyond Training

In intervention research, it's common and sensible to adopt a relatively narrow assessment of learning, evaluating the learning of trained material and its generalization. However, an overlooked, yet important, dimension of learning is the impact training might have on learner psychology. Put another way, if one of the goals of an intervention is to lay the groundwork for, if not stimulate, long-term pronunciation learning, then as researchers we should be concerned with how learners respond to the intervention itself. Chances are, if they find it engaging, they may continue to reflect upon and practice their pronunciation on their own, well after the training has concluded. And, if the training equips them with the knowledge and tools to examine and improve their pronunciation, then they may continue to leverage what they learned about pronunciation learning to their long-term benefit. On the most practical level, if the training is boring and monotonous, then during training, learners' attention may wane relatively quickly, leading to lackluster gains not because the training paradigm itself is ineffective but because it does not sufficiently encourage learners to attend to the training and invest effort. That is, the paradigm may be effective, but the user experience, if abysmal, may attenuate gains.

In my view, assessing learner (i.e., user) satisfaction should be a baseline component of any research design, on par with assessing learning itself. Yet, barring a handful of examples (e.g., Olson, 2014b), such assessments are rare. To put this example into more concrete terms, imagine a learner participates in a pronunciation intervention that they find interesting. After the training, they start to notice the way words are pronounced and to imitate the pronunciation of those words more often in class. They also search for pronunciation resources, finding videos and explanations online, exploring different target language accents, and so on. All of this supports their development. Thus, far beyond what any training posttest would show, it's not the training, but rather the interests and behaviors that the training potentially catalyzes that are the long-term levers of development. To test this, we can include an assessment of the training itself, asking learners to provide insight into how interesting, engaging, and user-friendly it was. This information can be collected via a Likert-type survey, through open-ended questions, interviews, and focus groups. There are models in the pronunciation literature that can serve as a guide (Olson, 2014b), but we can also draw upon user experience research to inform methodology in this area. We can also begin studying learner interest and behavior alongside the intervention. Put another way, rather than viewing the intervention as an isolated, stand-alone event, we can place it into a much broader developmental trajectory. In this approach, we could administer surveys designed (1) to tap into learners' motivation to improve their pronunciation and (2) to take stock of the range of pronunciation learning behaviors in which they engage (see, e.g., Sardegna et al., 2018). We could administer the survey before training, at the pretest, and at each posttest. We could also administer the surveys over a longer window. For instance, if the training and testing take place within a single semester of language instruction (assuming we're working with instructed language learners), then we might consider administering the surveys the following semester, so that we capture potential attitudinal and behavioral changes over the academic year. One challenge we will face is what Al-Hoorie et al. (2020) have characterized as "the questionnaire curse," which refers to an overreliance on self-report metrics. I will return to this point in the next chapter, but for now, suffice it to say that it would be important to collect behavioral data to supplement self-report data. At present, this research would be quite novel for the field, and thus, the methods suggested here are tentative and would need to be tested and refined. The important takeaway is that we should seriously consider measuring learner engagement, enjoyment, and the attitudinal and behavioral changes that may come about through training.

Summary and Recommendations

We have covered a lot of conceptual ground in this chapter. Figure 6.3 summarizes some of the most important decisions to be made when carrying out intervention research.

214 Researching Pronunciation Training and Instruction

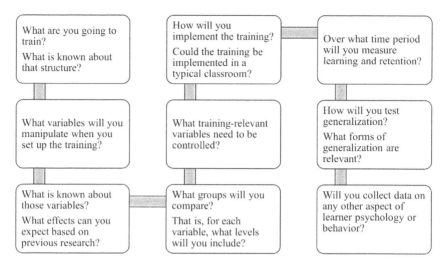

FIGURE 6.3 Decision Roadmap for Experimental Design in Training Research.

Chapter Questions

1. Find a perception or production training study published in the last two years. What variables did the authors manipulate? What groups did they compare? What rationale did they give for selecting the variables they did?
2. For the same study that you found, did the authors test generalization and retention? If so, how?
3. Pick one of the data sets analyzed in this chapter and write up a results section for it. What information should you include? Compare your write-up to your classmates'.

References

Al-Hoorie, A. H., Hiver, P., Kim, T.-Y., & De Costa, P. I. (2020). The identity crisis in language motivation research. *Journal of Language and Social Psychology*, *40*(1), 136–153. https://doi.org/10.1177/0261927x20964507

Barriuso, T. A., & Hayes-Harb, R. (2018). High variability phonetic training as a bridge from research to practice. *The CATESOL Journal*, *30*(1), 177–194.

Bradlow, A. R., Akahane-Yamada, R., Pisoni, D. B., & Tohkura, Y. (1999). Training Japanese listeners to identify English /r/ and /l/: Long-term retention of learning in perception and production. *Perception & Psychophysics*, *61*(5), 977–985.

Bradlow, A. R., Pisoni, D. B., Akahane-Yamada, R., & Tohkura, Y. (1997). Training Japanese listeners to identify English /r/ and /l/: IV. Some effects of perceptual learning on speech production. *Journal of the Acoustical Society of America*, *101*(4), 2299–2310.

Brauer, M., & Curtin, J. J. (2018). Linear mixed-effects models and the analysis of nonindependent data: A unified framework to analyze categorical and continuous independent variables that vary within-subjects and/or within-items. *Psychological Methods*, *23*(3), 389–411. https://doi.org/10.1037/met0000159

Cucchiarini, C., & Strik, H. (2017). Automatic speech recognition for second language pronunciation training. In O. Kang, R. I. Thomson, & J. M. Murphy (Eds.), *The Routledge handbook of contemporary English pronunciation* (pp. 556–569). Routledge.

Derwing, T. M., Munro, M. J., Foote, J. A., Waugh, E., & Fleming, J. (2014). Opening the window on comprehensible pronunciation after 19 years: A workplace training study. *Language Learning*, *64*(3), 526–548. https://doi.org/10.1111/lang.12053

Derwing, T. M., Munro, M. J., & Wiebe, G. (1998). Evidence in favor of a broad framework for pronunciation instruction. *Language Learning*, *48*(3), 393–410. https://doi.org/10.1111/0023-8333.00047

Ding, S., Liberatore, C., Sonsaat, S., Lučić, I., Silpachai, A., Zhao, G., Chukharev-Hudilainen, E., Levis, J., & Gutierrez-Osuna, R. (2019). Golden speaker builder – An interactive tool for pronunciation training. *Speech Communication*, *115*, 51–66. https://doi.org/10.1016/j.specom.2019.10.005

Earle, F. S., Landi, N., & Myers, E. B. (2017). Sleep duration predicts behavioral and neural differences in adult speech sound learning. *Neuroscience Letters*, *636*, 77–82. https://doi.org/10.1016/j.neulet.2016.10.044

Earle, F. S., & Myers, E. B. (2015a). Sleep and native language interference affect nonnative speech sound learning. *Journal of Experimental Psychology: Human Perception & Performance*, *41*(6), 1680–1695. https://doi.org/10.1037/xhp0000113

Earle, F. S., & Myers, E. B. (2015b). Overnight consolidation promotes generalization across talkers in the identification of nonnative speech sounds. *Journal of the Acoustical Society of America*, *137*(1), EL91–EL97. https://doi.org/10.1121/1.4903918

Foote, J. A., & McDonough, K. (2017). Using shadowing with mobile technology to improve L2 pronunciation. *Journal of Second Language Pronunciation*, *3*(1), 34–56. https://doi.org/10.1075/jslp.3.1.02foo

Fouz-González, J., & Mompeán, J. A. (2021). Exploring the potential of phonetic symbols and keywords as labels for perceptual training. *Studies in Second Language Acquisition*, *43*(2), 297–328. https://doi.org/10.1017/s0272263120000455

Galante, A., & Thomson, R. I. (2017). The effectiveness of drama as an instructional approach for the development of second language oral fluency, comprehensibility, and accentedness. *TESOL Quarterly*, *51*(1), 115–142. https://doi.org/10.1002/tesq.290

González López, V., & Counselman, D. (2013). L2 acquisition and category formation of Spanish voiceless stops by monolingual English novice learners. In J. Cabrelli Amaro, G. Lord, A. de Prada Pérez, & J. E. Aaron (Eds.), *Selected Proceedings of the 16th Hispanic Linguistics Symposium* (pp. 118–127). Cascadilla Proceedings Project.

Gurzynski-Weiss, L., Long, A. Y., & Solon, M. (2017). TBLT and L2 pronunciation: Do the benefits of tasks extend beyond grammar and lexis? *Studies in Second Language Acquisition*, *39*(2), 213–224. https://doi.org/10.1017/S0272263117000080

Hardison, D. M. (2004). Generalization of computer-assisted prosody training: Quantitative and qualitative findings. *Language Learning & Technology*, *8*(1), 34–52. http://llt.msu.edu/vol8num1/hardison/

Hartig, F. (2022). DHARMa: Residual Diagnostics for Hierarchical (Multi-Level / Mixed) Regression Models. R package version 0.1.5. <http://florianhartig.github.io/DHARMa>.

Huensch, A. (2016). Perceptual phonetic training improves production in larger discourse contexts. *Journal of Second Language Pronunciation*, 2(2), 183–207. https://doi.org/10.1075/jslp.2.2.03hue

Kennedy, S., Blanchet, J., & Trofimovich, P. (2014). Learner pronunciation, awareness, and instruction in French as a second language. *Foreign Language Annals*, 47(1), 79–96. https://doi.org/10.1111/flan.12066

Kissling, E. M. (2013). Teaching pronunciation: Is explicit phonetics instruction beneficial for FL learners? *The Modern Language Journal*, 97(3), 720–744. https://doi.org/10.1111/j.1540-4781.2013.12029.x

Kondaurova, M. V., & Francis, A. L. (2010). The role of selective attention in the acquisition of English tense and lax vowels by native Spanish listeners: comparison of three training methods. *Journal of Phonetics*, 38(4), 569–587. https://doi.org/10.1016/j.wocn.2010.08.003

Lee, J., Jang, J., & Plonsky, L. (2015). The effectiveness of second language pronunciation instruction: A meta-analysis. *Applied Linguistics*, 36(3), 345–366. https://doi.org/10.1093/applin/amu040

Lenth R (2023). _emmeans: Estimated Marginal Means, aka Least-Squares Means_. R package version 1.8.4-1, <https://CRAN.R-project.org/package=emmeans>.

Linck, J. A., & Cunnings, I. (2015). The utility and application of mixed-effects models in second language research. *Language Learning*, 65(S1), 185–207. https://doi.org/10.1111/lang.12117

Lively, S. E., Logan, J. S., & Pisoni, D. B. (1993). Training Japanese listeners to identify English /r/ and /l/. II: The role of phonetic environment and talker variability in learning new perceptual categories. *Journal of the Acoustical Society of America*, 94(3), 1242–1255. https://doi.org/10.1121/1.408177

Logan, J. S., Lively, S. E., & Pisoni, D. B. (1991). Training Japanese listeners to identify English /r/ and /l/: A first report. *Journal of the Acoustical Society of America*, 89(2), 874–886. https://doi.org/10.1121/1.1894649

Lord, G. (2005). (How) Can we teach foreign language pronunciation? On the effects of a Spanish phonetics course. *Hispania*, 88(3), 557–567. https://doi.org/10.2307/20063159

Lord, G. (2008). Podcasting communities and second language pronunciation. *Foreign Language Annals*, 41(2), 364–379. https://doi.org/10.1111/j.1944-9720.2008.tb03297.x

Martin, I. A., & Sippel, L. (2021). Is giving better than receiving? *Journal of Second Language Pronunciation*, 7(1), 62–88. https://doi.org/10.1075/jslp.20001.mar

Martin, I. A., & Sippel, L. (2023). Long-term effects of peer and teacher feedback on L2 pronunciation. *Journal of Second Language Pronunciation*, 9(1), 20–46. https://doi.org/10.1075/jslp.22041.mar

McAndrews, M. (2019). Short periods of instruction improve learners' phonological categories for L2 suprasegmental features. *System*, 82, 151–160. https://doi.org/10.1016/j.system.2019.04.007

McKinnon, S. (2017). TBLT instructional effects on tonal alignment and pitch range in L2 Spanish imperatives versus declaratives. *Studies in Second Language Acquisition*, 39(2), 287–317. https://doi.org/10.1017/s0272263116000267

Mora, J. C., & Levkina, M. (2017). Task-based pronunciation teaching and research: Key issues and future directions. *Studies in Second Language Acquisition*, *39*(2), 381–399. https://doi.org/10.1017/S0272263117000183

Nagle, C. (2022). Rethinking pronunciation posttesting. *Journal of Second Language Pronunciation*, *8*(2), 161–167. https://doi.org/10.1075/jslp.22019.nag

Nagle, C., & Hiver, P. (2023). Optimizing second language pronunciation instruction: Replications of Martin and Sippel (2021), Olson and Offerman (2021), and Thomson (2012). *Language Teaching*. Advance online publication. https://doi.org/10.1017/S0261444823000083

Nagle, C. L. (2018). Examining the temporal structure of the perception-production link in second language acquisition: A longitudinal study. *Language Learning*, *68*(1), 234–270. https://doi.org/10.1111/lang.12275

Offerman, H. M., & Olson, D. J. (2016). Visual feedback and second language segmental production: The generalizability of pronunciation gains. *System*, *59*, 45–60. https://doi.org/10.1016/j.system.2016.03.003

Olson, D. J. (2014a). Benefits of visual feedback on segmental production in the L2 classroom. *Language Learning & Technology*, *18*(3), 173–192. http://llt.msu.edu/issues/october2014/olson.pdf

Olson, D. J. (2014b). Phonetics and technology in the classroom: A practical approach to using speech analysis software in second-language pronunciation instruction. *Hispania*, *97*(1), 47–68. https://doi.org/10.1353/hpn.2014.0030

Olson, D. J. (2019). Feature acquisition in second language phonetic development: Evidence from phonetic training. *Language Learning*, *69*(2), 366–404. https://doi.org/10.1111/lang.12336

Olson, D. J., & Offerman, H. M. (2021). Maximizing the effect of visual feedback for pronunciation instruction. *Journal of Second Language Pronunciation*, *7*(1), 89–115. https://doi.org/10.1075/jslp.20005.ols

Perrachione, T. K., Lee, J., Ha, L. Y., & Wong, P. C. (2011). Learning a novel phonological contrast depends on interactions between individual differences and training paradigm design. *Journal of the Acoustical Society of America*, *130*(1), 461–472. https://doi.org/10.1121/1.3593366

Plonsky, L., & Oswald, F. L. (2014). How big is "big"? Interpreting effect sizes in L2 research. *Language Learning*, *64*(4), 878–912. https://doi.org/10.1111/lang.12079

Rato, A., & Oliveira, D. (2023). Assessing the robustness of L2 perceptual training: A closer look at generalization and retention of learning. In A. Ubiratã Kickhöfel & A. Jeniffer Imaregna Alcantara de (Eds.), *Second Language Pronunciation* (pp. 369–396). De Gruyter Mouton. https://doi.org/10.1515/9783110736120-014

Saito, K. (2015). Communicative focus on second language phonetic form: Teaching Japanese learners to perceive and produce English /ɪ/ without explicit instruction. *Applied Psycholinguistics*, *36*(2), 377–409. https://doi.org/10.1017/S0142716413000271

Saito, K., & Lyster, R. (2012). Effects of form-focused instruction and corrective feedback on L2 pronunciation development of /r/ by Japanese learners of English. *Language Learning*, *62*(2), 595–633. https://doi.org/10.1111/j.1467-9922.2011.00639.x

Saito, K., & Plonsky, L. (2019). Effects of second language pronunciation teaching revisited: A proposed measurement framework and meta-analysis. *Language Learning*, *69*(3), 652–708. https://doi.org/10.1111/lang.12345

Sakai, M., & Moorman, C. (2018). Can perception training improve the production of second language phonemes? A meta-analytic review of 25 years of perception training research. *Applied Psycholinguistics, 39*(1), 187–224. https://doi.org/10.1017/s0142716417000418

Sardegna, V. G., Lee, J., & Kusey, C. (2018). Self-efficacy, attitudes, and choice of strategies for English pronunciation learning. *Language Learning, 68*(1), 83–114. https://doi.org/10.1111/lang.12263

Sato, M., & Loewen, S. (2022). The research–practice dialogue in second language learning and teaching: Past, present, and future. *The Modern Language Journal, 106*(3), 509–527. https://doi.org/10.1111/modl.12791

Singmann H, Bolker B, Westfall J, Aust F, Ben-Shachar M (2023). _afex: Analysis of Factorial Experiments. R package version 1.2-1, <https://CRAN.R-project.org/package=afex>.

Solon, M., Long, A. Y., & Gurzynski-Weiss, L. (2017). Task complexity, language-related episodes, and production of L2 Spanish vowels. *Studies in Second Language Acquisition, 39*(2), 347–380. https://doi.org/10.1017/s0272263116000425

Sturm, J. L. (2013). Explicit phonetics instruction in L2 French: A global analysis of improvement. *System, 41*(3), 654–662. https://doi.org/10.1016/j.system.2013.07.015

Suzuki, Y. (2017). The optimal distribution of practice for the acquisition of L2 morphology: A conceptual replication and extension. *Language Learning, 67*(3), 512–545. https://doi.org/10.1111/lang.12236

Suzuki, Y. (2021). Optimizing fluency training for speaking skills transfer: Comparing the effects of blocked and interleaved task repetition. *Language Learning, 71*(2), 285–325. https://doi.org/10.1111/lang.12433

Thomson, R. I. (2012). Improving L2 listeners' perception of English vowels: A computer-mediated approach. *Language Learning, 62*(4), 1231–1258. https://doi.org/10.1111/j.1467-9922.2012.00724.x

Thomson, R. I. (2018). High Variability [Pronunciation] Training (HVPT). *Journal of Second Language Pronunciation, 4*(2), 208–231. https://doi.org/10.1075/jslp.17038.tho

Zhang, X., Cheng, B., & Zhang, Y. (2021). The role of talker variability in non-native phonetic learning: A systematic review and meta-analysis. *Journal of Speech, Language, and Hearing Research, 64*(12), 4802–4825. https://doi.org/10.1044/2021_JSLHR-21-00181

7

RESEARCHING INDIVIDUAL DIFFERENCES

Introduction

Individual differences refer to learner variables such as age of onset of L2 learning, quality and quantity of L2 input and use, aptitude, motivation, and so on. Pronunciation researchers have always been interested in quantifying the extent to which these variables predict pronunciation learning. For instance, in one of the first studies on the topic, Suter (1976) collected information on 20 individual differences and computed correlations between those variables and pronunciation accuracy in English. Early individual differences research, which was heavily influenced by both the Critical Period Hypothesis and the postulates and hypotheses of the Speech Learning Model, was predominantly concerned with examining relationships between age of onset of L2 learning, quantity of L1 and L2 use, and foreign accent in individuals who had immigrated to a country in which the L2 was spoken. Working from the standpoint of the Critical Period Hypothesis, researchers tested very advanced L2 learners to determine if any learner showed completely nativelike L2 performance, especially in the area of pronunciation. The idea was that finding a single L2 speaker who fit this description would be sufficient to falsify the Critical Period Hypothesis. To be clear, there was no doubt that age was one of the most important factors for ultimate attainment in all areas of second language acquisition (SLA), including pronunciation. What was at issue was the relationship between age and attainment, specifically whether the possibility of nativelike attainment declines sharply with age, which would indicate a critical period, or gradually, which would indicate a sensitive period.

DOI: 10.4324/9781003279266-7

220 Researching Individual Differences

During this same period, speech researchers were intensively investigating crosslinguistic influence in speech perception and production, focusing mostly on highly proficient bilinguals who were living in an L2 environment. Studies were centered on individual differences in age of onset, length of residence, and quantity of L1 and L2 use, in part due to the influence of critical period research but also because these variables were important for the bilingual populations examined at the time. Results showed that L2 speakers with earlier ages of onset tended to produce more phonetically nativelike speech and were more likely to be judged to have a nativelike accent. However, an early age of onset did not guarantee nativelike perception and production in the L2, and it also became clear from this work that the L2 had an effect on the L1. Simply put, bilinguals did not seem to perceive and produce L1 sounds like monolingual L1 speakers, nor did they perceive and produce L2 sounds like monolingual L2 speakers. Instead, in most cases, their L1 was somewhat L2-like, and their L2 somewhat L1-like. These findings were the basis of the Speech Learning Model (Flege, 1995; Flege & Bohn, 2021), which was based on the core principle that phonetic learning remains possible throughout the lifespan. Age effects weren't due to a neurobiological critical period for language learning. Instead, they were the result of L1 perceptual attunement. In other words, age was a proxy for the developmental state of the L1. According to the model, the later the onset of L2 learning relative to L1 learning, the less likely it would be for learners to notice and encode subtle, yet important, crosslinguistic differences in sound production. If these differences went unnoticed, then learners would not create a new category for the L2 sound, leading to merged representations and eventually the patterns of crosslinguistic influence (L1-to-L2 but also L2-to-L1) that were being documented in research at the time. Researchers redoubled their efforts to understand how individual differences in age of onset, length of residence, and quantity of L1 and L2 use, among other variables, affected crosslinguistic influence in speech perception and production.

The conceptual focus of this work brought with it certain methodological patterns. With respect to individual difference measures, two analytical approaches were common. In some studies, researchers treated the individual difference as continuous, assessing associations between age of arrival (age of onset of L2 learning) and various dependent variables, including the perception and production of specific vowels and consonants (Flege et al., 1996) and global foreign accent ratings (Flege, Yeni-Komshian, & Liu, 1999). In other studies, researchers constructed comparison groups by dividing continuous measures into categories of early, mid, and late age of arrival, as well as high and low L1 use (Flege, MacKay, & Meador, 1999). Researchers remain interested in individual differences in experiential variables, but their approach to these variables has shifted in several important ways.

For one, there is widespread recognition that age covaries with a range of cognitive and social individual differences that are also important for L2 pronunciation learning, making it difficult, if not impossible, to isolate any unique age effects (Moyer, 2014a). Researchers have also attempted to develop more refined measures of input and experience. For instance, in the revised Speech Learning Model, Flege and Bohn (2021) proposed full-time equivalent, a composite variable based on length of residence and amount of L2 use, as a more sophisticated and appropriate measure of L2 input and use. While such a measure may be sensible for certain populations of L2 learners, such as individuals who have immigrated to an L2 environment, it may not fully capture the diverse experiences of other learner groups (Gorba, 2023). This serves as an important reminder that certain individual difference measures may be more applicable to one learner profile than another (e.g., naturalistic learners who are living in an L2 environment vs. instructed learners whose primary mode of L2 learning is classroom instruction) or more applicable to learners at a certain point in their learning trajectory. Age received special attention in early work due to its relationship with nativelikeness. Although researchers remain interested in age, its importance has been brought into balance with other individual differences because contemporary views of pronunciation learning recognize that nativelike attainment is unlikely for most L2 learners and unnecessary for successful L2 communication.

Whereas early work on individual differences and pronunciation was mostly cross-sectional, examining performance at one point in time (Elliott, 1995; Moyer, 1999), over the past decade pronunciation researchers have increasingly taken a longitudinal approach, examining the variables that predict learning over time. Importantly, these two perspectives (predictors of performance and predictors of learning) are not mutually exclusive, nor do they entail one another. An individual difference variable that predicts performance may not predict learning. Likewise, a variable that predicts learning over one developmental window may not over another, or its relationship to learning may change. Put another way, relationships between individual differences and the rate, shape, and end-state of learning are not static, but rather change as the learning process unfolds over time. A dynamic, interactive, and adaptive view of learning is not new. Moyer argued for "a constellation of influences on accent… [that] do not operate in isolation from one another—the affective and the cognitive go hand-in-hand as one seeks, and consciously utilizes the input available" (2014b, p. 18). Thus, the conceptual framework has not changed. What has changed is the methodological landscape of individual differences research as a whole and its manifestation in the field of L2 pronunciation.

Now, more than ever, researchers are prepared to engage in multi-wave longitudinal work that can speak to the interaction of variables on a variety

222 Researching Individual Differences

of timescales (Nagle, 2021). At the same time, there is a general awareness that understanding the role of individual differences means understanding how the individual differences themselves change and interact and how this process affects learning. I have advocated for a time-varying approach to individual differences, arguing that individual differences research can be most profitably understood as linking two processes of change: change in the individual difference and change in the outcome measure (Nagle, 2023). Individual differences like motivation and effort are inherently dynamic, which means that they are most appropriately measured longitudinally to understand their trait-like and state-like properties. This perspective brings with it conceptual, methodological, and analytical challenges, but I illustrate that it is entirely within reach by building from cross-sectional research to a longitudinal approach, and from a longitudinal approach to a longitudinal time-varying approach, with several concrete examples. It's also worth noting that individual differences research, perhaps more so than any other research area, evolves rapidly, especially on the methodological front. For this reason, as I point out several times in this chapter, researchers interested in doing methodologically robust individual differences research must make a special effort to keep abreast of recent developments in the conceptualization and measurement of the individual differences they study.

Mechanisms and Timelines in Individual Differences Research

An important grounding question for any individual difference study is "What is the mechanism?" That is, by what means does the individual difference affect performance and/or learning? Where early research was concerned with identifying links between a range of individual differences and pronunciation learning outcomes, contemporary individual difference research must go a step further by developing specific hypotheses about how the individual difference works. Darcy et al. (2016) found a link between inhibitory control and vowel discrimination accuracy, which they measured using an ABX discrimination task. They reasoned that "those who demonstrated higher inhibition scores [those who were better at blocking out or suppressing irrelevant or competing information] may have used this ability in the past to support the learning of L2 segmental categories" (2016, p. 764). They went on to hypothesize about the importance of this individual difference in different contexts of learning, reinforcing the idea that individual differences may show context-specific effects insofar as they influence and are influenced by the other individual differences that operate in a given learning environment:

> In the foreign language classroom context, which is characterized by L1 dominance and limited L2 exposure and use, learners' inhibitory control capacity might play a bigger role and make a more important difference

in how accurately L2 sound representations develop than in an immersion setting, where the much larger L2 exposure and use may contribute more fundamentally to L2 phonological development, compared to learners' cognitive skills.

(pp. 766–767)

Their hypothesis could be tested in a longitudinal study comparing L2 phonological learning in classroom and immersion contexts. By establishing a specific, theory-informed perspective on the relationship between the individual difference and the outcome being tested, researchers make a compelling case for studying the impact of that particular variable. Darcy et al.'s (2016) research also highlights the utility of beginning with a cross-sectional perspective. Through a cross-sectional design, which is usually less time- and resource-intensive than its longitudinal counterpart, researchers can identify variables that would be good to target in longitudinal research.

Another excellent example comes from research by Saito and colleagues, who have delved progressively deeper into the role aptitude-related variables play in L2 speech learning. In early work (Saito, Suzukida, & Sun, 2019), their research team operationalized aptitude via the LLAMA aptitude tests, which capture aptitude for language learning across several subconstructs such as grammatical inferencing and phonemic encoding (for a description of the tests, see Meara & Rogers, 2019). In later work, they probed the relationship between different types of aptitude measures (e.g., implicit and explicit aptitude, Saito, Sun, & Tierney, 2018), developing domain-specific tests designed to tap into learners' sensitivity to spectral and temporal differences (Kachlicka, Saito, & Tierney, 2019; Saito, Sun, & Tierney, 2020). They haven't exclusively prioritized one type of aptitude over another, nor have they privileged one approach. Instead, they have examined both domain-general and domain-specific forms of aptitude, and they have done so cross-sectionally and longitudinally, integrating aptitude into research examining a range of other individual differences known to be important for L2 pronunciation learning (Saito, Cui, et al., 2022; Sun, Saito, & Dewaele, 2023; Suzukida & Saito, 2023). Their work has culminated in an auditory precision hypothesis for L2 sound learning (Saito, 2023; Saito, Kachlicka, et al., 2022). This work demonstrates many of the properties of high-quality individual difference research: a combination of cross-sectional and longitudinal approaches, a careful approach to conceptualization and measurement, and integration of the primary individual difference variable with other individual differences. The authors have also done an exemplary job of summarizing the mechanisms through which various forms of aptitude might affect L2 sound learning.

One area for future growth is the length of the window of observation in longitudinal studies. Notably, at the time of writing, Saito and colleagues' longitudinal work has been relatively short-range, insofar as they have investigated the importance of aptitude and other individual differences over a few weeks of pronunciation instruction (Suzukida & Saito, 2023), 4–8 months of immersion (Saito, Sun, & Tierney; 2020; Sun, Saito, & Dewaele, 2023), and an academic year of language instruction (Saito, Suzukida, & Sun, 2019). Thus, an interesting and necessary next step to work on aptitude could be either examining the role these variables play over a longer developmental window, including more data points or recruiting multiple cohorts of learners and tracking those cohorts longitudinally. The first option, a single cohort design, would take longer, but the advantage of that design would be a complete longitudinal data set, where the effect of aptitude could be tracked in the same group of learners over the entire duration of the study. The second option would be an accelerated longitudinal design where all cohorts are studied longitudinally over a shorter period, with the goal of linking several developmental windows via the cross-sectional component. In making these observations, I don't mean to criticize Saito and colleagues' work on aptitude in any way. The fact that they have run several longitudinal studies is noteworthy in and of itself. However, it remains to be seen how aptitude influences long-term learning, promotes long-term attainment, and the periods during which aptitude plays an especially important role.

Consider a few possible studies. To gain insight into the role aptitude plays in learners of varying lengths of residence, research could study a single group of learners from the onset of L2 residence through the 2-year mark, examining the role aptitude plays over the entire period (0–2 years) and over shorter, theoretically interesting subwindows (e.g., 0–6 months, 0–12 months, 12–24 months). Alternatively, researchers could recruit several cohorts of varying length of residence (e.g., recent arrivals with length of residence <1 year, length of residence 1–2 years, length of residence >3 years), tracking those cohorts over, for instance, a year-long period. To make this illustration more concrete, Figure 7.1 provides a visual overview of this example. In this design, length of residence would serve as a proxy for amount of L2 input, albeit a potentially imprecise one, and in the multi-cohort design, the length of residence cohorts would need to be selected with specific criteria in mind. In proposing cohorts of <1 year, 1–2 years, and >3 years of residence as an example, I had in mind Derwing and Munro's (2015) comments on the window of maximal opportunity for pronunciation learning and their longitudinal studies documenting changes over various developmental windows (e.g., seven years in Derwing & Munro, 2013; one year in Munro & Derwing, 2008; ten years in Thomson, Derwing, & Munro, 2023).

A possible rationale for these subwindows could be that aptitude may be particularly important for determining rate of learning at the outset of immersion, but its role might wane over time (effect of aptitude on rate of change in terms of effect size: length of residence <1 year, 1–2 years, >3 years). An alternative hypothesis could be that aptitude might predict sustained learning over time, in which case learners might progress similarly over the initial window of observation, but high-aptitude learners would continue to demonstrate improvement over a longer period (i.e., no effect of aptitude for length of residence <1 year, increasing importance of aptitude for length of residence 1–2 years and >3 years). Whether these hypotheses would be borne out by the data is irrelevant. What I have attempted to illustrate here is the importance of linking concept and method, as well as how research on individual differences can progress conceptually and methodologically.

In considering the two study designs shown in Figure 7.1, some other design choices also deserve commentary. First, in the multi-cohort study, because of the way the cohorts are configured, there would be no data for the year 2–3 period. This is not necessarily problematic, but it could be if we had a conceptual rationale for investigating that period (thus the need to think carefully about how to configure the cohorts vis-à-vis relevant variables of interest). Second, this setup does not describe the frequency of data collection. We could sample relatively infrequently, 1–2 times per year, or we could adopt a much more frequent sampling procedure, collecting data every quarter (four data points per year), every two months (six data points, cf. Munro & Derwing, 2008), or even every month. To determine an appropriate sampling frequency, we would need to think carefully about our hypotheses and the anticipated developmental timeline of the target feature(s) (Nagle, 2021).

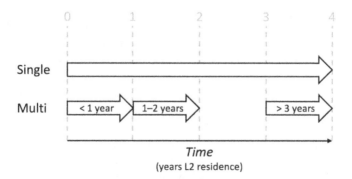

FIGURE 7.1 Illustration of Single and Multi-Cohort Longitudinal Study.

226 Researching Individual Differences

Before we delve into research methods for particular individual differences, I want to give an example of research into another individual difference: motivation. There have been several studies on motivation and pronunciation learning, ranging from research examining concern for pronunciation as a specific subdimension of language learning motivation (Elliott, 1995) to research on general language learning motivation, framed from the perspective of the L2 Motivational Self System (Nagle, 2018; Saito, Dewaele, et al., 2018). There has also been work on beliefs, motivation, and learning strategies (Sardegna et al., 2018). Collectively, this body of work illustrates the diverse ways in which researchers conceptualize motivation and link it to learning behaviors and outcomes. I focus on motivation-behavior-learning links because it seems unlikely that motivation would have a direct effect on learning. Rather, motivation affects behavior, insofar as different types and levels of motivation would be associated with distinct learning behaviors, and those behaviors, in turn, might drive differences in learning. In other words, I'm advocating for the view that the link between motivation and learning is most likely indirect, realized through behavior. Consider an individual who is motivated to achieve a high level of oral proficiency in the L2. That person may decide to pursue additional opportunities to interact in the L2, may request feedback on their speaking skills, and may deploy several pronunciation/speech-related learning strategies to help them improve their pronunciation. This pattern can play out in both a classroom and immersion setting. Motivated classroom learners may ask their instructor for feedback more frequently, may supplement classroom instruction with content that they review and watch at home, and may participate in L2-related activities outside the classroom. Motivated immersion learners may interact with other L1 speakers less frequently, seeking out opportunities for meaningful, extensive L2 use. In short, they may be more willing to communicate in the L2 than their peers, which could have a long-term impact on learning (Derwing & Munro, 2013; Thomson et al., 2023). These vignettes illustrate the potential mechanisms through which motivation may work. The point is not to get bogged down in these examples because these patterns may or may not hold. Rather, this example, like the example for aptitude, is illustrative of the type of thinking required when doing individual differences research. Defining a potential path of influence is a necessary first step toward developing an appropriate set of measures and, in the case of longitudinal work, timing them appropriately. Thinking about the mechanism also helps to prevent a "kitchen-sink" approach, where several individual differences are included in the study at a relatively superficial level (i.e., because they have not been investigated before, which is a weak rationale for the selection of any variable) without consideration of how they operate.

It would be impossible to survey all individual differences in this chapter, let alone provide a methodological guide to doing work on the full range of variables that are the basis of current work. I therefore focus on motivation and L2 use, or experience. I have selected these individual differences because they change over time, are usually assessed via self-report questionnaires, making them latent constructs, and are related to one another: motivation may affect L2 use, insofar as more motivated and engaged learners may show a greater variety and intensity of L2 use that could, in turn, support long-term learning. I want to underscore that doing high-impact individual differences research means understanding the individual difference itself, including its conceptual basis and methodological approaches, including measurement and analysis. In this chapter, I provide targeted information on each area, but for a comprehensive overview of individual differences in SLA, see Li et al. (2022).

Motivation

Motivation, more than any other individual difference, has been a variable of intense focus, and its conceptualization and measurement have undergone several periods of debate and evolution. One of the earliest formulations was the socio-educational model (e.g., Gardner, 2010), a model developed in the context of Canadian bilingualism and grounded in the notion that "the learning of a second language involves taking on features of another cultural community" (Gardner, 2010, p. 2). This definition was crystallized in the construct of integrative motivation. In the first wave of expansion and evolution, researchers aimed to broaden the conceptual basis of motivation research, examining alternative (but not necessarily conflicting) constructs and approaches (Dörnyei, 1994a, 1994b). Eventually, this line of work culminated in the L2 Motivational Self System (Dörnyei, 2009), which has become the dominant model of motivation used in quantitative research. The original formulation of the model included three constructs: (1) the ideal L2 self, which is promotion-focused and describes the individual's hopes, dreams, and aspirations for language learning, (2) the ought L2 self, which is prevention-focused and captures perceived pressures and obligations to learn the L2, and (3) the L2 experience, which represents variables associated with the learning environment such as the instructor's teaching style, the classroom dynamic, and the curricular focus. The ideal and ought L2 selves are conceptualized as future self-guides that orient and direct behavior. According to the model, individuals with a strong ideal L2 self will take steps to reduce the discrepancy between their current self and their ideal self, which might include investing more effort in language learning.

228 Researching Individual Differences

The uptake of this model was swift, resulting in a large number of studies published within a short window. The field quickly reached a saturation point, surpassing the necessary threshold for research synthesis. Boo et al. (2015) synthesized L2 motivation research from 2005 to 2015, and much of that work was grounded in the L2 Motivational Self System. Since then, several other syntheses have emerged, including a scoping review of motivation research on languages other than English (Mendoza & Phung, 2019) and several meta-analyses (Al-Hoorie, 2018; Yousefi & Mahmoodi, 2022). Among other important findings, Al-Hoorie (2018) showed that the ideal L2 self was strongly associated with intended effort, whereas the ought-to L2 self was not. He also found that neither construct was a strong predictor of "objective" outcomes, meaning measures of achievement that were not self-reported. The L2 Motivational Self System model quickly came to dominate motivation research. As an aside, in an interesting example of history repeating itself, one of the primary concerns in early motivation work was precisely the fact that Gardner's model was too dominant: "The main problem with Gardner's social psychological approach appeared to be, ironically, that it was too influential" (Dörnyei, 1994a, p. 273). The L2 Motivational Self System has certainly had a lasting impact on L2 motivation research, but alternative approaches have also flourished (e.g., Dörnyei et al., 2015).

As with any field, intense empirical inquiry brings with it conceptual renewal, so it should come as no surprise that the original formulation of the L2 Motivational Self System has been scrutinized and revised. Papi et al. (2019) developed and tested a model including both motivational focus (ideal vs. ought) and regulatory focus (own vs. other). The 2×2 model showed a better fit to their data than the original model, and, interestingly, the strongest predictor of motivated behavior in their study was the ought L2 self/own. Whereas meta-analytic findings suggested that the ought L2 self had little predictive value, Papi et al. (2019) showed that the revised conceptualization of the ought L2 self/own had the strongest predictive value, at least for their sample of English as a Second Language (ESL) students. At the time I'm writing this book, motivation research is undergoing another round of revision and expansion (Al-Hoorie & Hiver, 2020; Al-Hoorie et al., 2020). An important methodological critique that has arisen is what Al-Hoorie et al. (2020) have described as the "questionnaire curse," which refers to the preponderance of observational studies collecting self-report measures. In making that critique, the authors suggested that motivation researchers should strongly consider interventional studies. I agree with the researchers that more interventional studies would be welcome. I also agree that such studies are much more likely to have clear pedagogical relevance. At the same time, part of the problem with the large body of observational research is, in my view, methodological. Researchers have collected large amounts of cross-sectional data on motivation and other latent constructs (e.g., anxiety), and such cross-sectional data sets are unlikely to yield findings relevant to development. Thus, I believe that examining motivation, behavior, and achievement longitudinally has significant potential to provide novel insight into the variables that regulate learning and the timescales on which they operate. Given the state of motivation research and sustained interest in the topic, I have no doubt that by the time this book is published, a new wave of research will have emerged, so I encourage readers who are interested in doing motivation research to consult the current state of the art, regardless of when they read this book.

I also want to comment briefly on some of the methodological and analytical characteristics of motivation research. First, motivation, however it is conceptualized, is a latent construct composed of many latent subconstructs, such as the ideal and ought L2 selves in the L2 Motivational Self System (or the ideal L2 self/own, ideal L2 self/other, ought L2 self/own, and ought L2 self/other, following Papi et al., 2019). A latent construct cannot be directly observed, so to measure a latent construct like the ideal self, researchers develop banks of items designed to tap into that construct. These items are known as indicator variables, and using those indicator variables, which can be observed, the score on the latent construct can be reconstructed. Analytically, this means establishing a measurement model for the construct, which is most often accomplished using structural equation modeling. And if the construct is analyzed longitudinally, then that measurement model must be shown to persist over time (Nagle, 2023). Thus, a typical study might (1) collect responses to a L2 Motivational Self System questionnaire, such as Papi et al.'s (2019) 2×2 model, (2) use confirmatory factor analysis to determine that the model is a good fit to the data, and (3a) fit a structural equation model to examine relationships between motivation and other study-relevant variables or (3b) fit a longitudinal structural equation model to examine how the constructs change and relate to one another over time.

Most recent motivation studies published in top-tier journals use some form of structural equation modeling. If you are not familiar with this technique, Kline (2023) is an excellent general introduction, Schoonen (2015) provides information on structural equation modeling in SLA, and I have a tutorial on longitudinal structural equation models and measurement invariance (Nagle, 2023). There are also tutorials focusing on specific types of structural equation models, which have been published in *Research Methods in Applied Linguistics* and the methods sections of journals such as *Studies in Second Language Learning* and *Language Learning*. For reasons of space and complexity, I cannot present a full overview of structural equation models here, but having a firm understanding of these models is, in my opinion, necessary for doing methodologically and analytically sound motivation research.

230 Researching Individual Differences

Motivation in Pronunciation Research

To investigate motivation and its impact on pronunciation behaviors and learning, researchers must take care to develop specific, testable hypotheses that are sensible and relevant to the context in which they work. Because of the myriad approaches available to researchers, in this section I formulate a series of questions that you should consider and provide some commentary.

How will you define motivation? Specifically, will you focus on pronunciation-specific forms of motivation, or will you define motivation more generally, via the L2 Motivational Self System or another model of language learning motivation? To answer these questions, you will need to think about the pronunciation outcome measures you have included in your study. If you are interested in studying a specific aspect of pronunciation, then a pronunciation-specific form of motivation is a better candidate for inclusion, whereas more general measures would be better candidates for inclusion in research involving global dimensions of pronunciation. For instance, if you plan on investigating the production of specific L2 sounds, then a measure of motivation tapping into participants' desire to improve their pronunciation of those sounds would be appropriate. If, on the other hand, you plan on investigating fluency, comprehensibility, and accentedness, both general measures of motivation and motivation for pronunciation could be appropriate. Granularity of measurement in motivation should be aligned with granularity in outcomes.

What learning behaviors do you expect to observe in the target learner population? For classroom learners, at-home study time and study strategies, in-class participation, and engagement in extracurricular learning activities such as attending a conversation group, listening to music, or watching television in the L2 could be meaningful markers of motivated behavior. Pronunciation learning behaviors could also be targeted (Sardegna et al., 2018). Immersion learners may engage in some of the same motivated behaviors, but in an immersion context, relevant measures are often related to the proportion of L1 to L2 use, including with whom the learner uses the L2 (Moyer, 2011). Methodologically, many measures of motivated behavior can be collected using the self-report surveys that are common in motivation research, but self-report measures should be triangulated with other measures whenever possible.

In addition to learning behaviors, do you expect learners to demonstrate differences in how they process and respond to the input they receive? And are those differences tied to different forms of motivation? For instance, learners who are especially interested in improving their pronunciation may show greater attention to form and may respond to corrective feedback differently (i.e., requesting detailed and elaborate corrective feedback) than

Researching Individual Differences **231**

their peers with a different motivational profile or focus. These behaviors could be tracked in the lab or observed in the language classroom.

To what extent do you expect motivation to show dynamic properties over the period of observation? To be clear, motivation and learning behaviors are inherently dynamic. Measuring any form of motivation or motivated behavior twice, even over a circumscribed period, is unlikely to yield the exact same results. However, variation can take several forms. On the one hand, it can be stochastic, which means that motivation and learning behavior change, but that change is not necessarily systematic. This can be conceived of as time-specific deviations from the individual's average level of motivation and motivated behavior. On the other hand, change may be systematic, in the sense that motivation and learning behavior themselves can be characterized by a change process. Perhaps motivation is increasing or decreasing over time, or perhaps the individual is investing more and more effort in engaging in meaningful L2 interactions. It's important to approach longitudinal projects with a sense of motivational dynamics, that is, with hypotheses regarding how motivation and behavior might change over time.

What types of behaviors are likely to have an impact on pronunciation learning outcomes? Related, over what time period is this impact most likely to occur? Pronunciation may change rapidly at the outset of learning, when L2 speakers enter a new context of learning (e.g., they immigrate to a location where the L2 is spoken, study abroad for a short period, or enroll in an intensive language course), but outside of these windows of maximal opportunity, pronunciation is likely to change at a slower rate. This means that it's worthwhile to consider collecting data on behavioral changes even if those changes are not immediately accompanied by a change in the pronunciation of a specific feature or global changes in comprehensibility, fluency, or accentedness. That is, as learners become motivated to change their pronunciation, they may begin to develop and deploy a range of learning strategies and behaviors which can, in turn, lead to long-term pronunciation gains, even exceptional outcomes (Moyer, 2014b). The key here is that behavioral changes may be immediate and precipitous as learners test, evaluate, and revise their approach to learning, whereas linguistic gains may only become apparent within a much more comprehensive observational window. One of the challenges for future research is understanding the complexity and time course of these relationships, as they play out over years of L2 instruction and/or L2 immersion (e.g., Derwing & Munro, 2013; Thomson et al., 2023).

What motivational interventions could you implement to boost learners' motivation to improve their pronunciation and speaking ability? Is there an intervention you could implement that might help them understand and appreciate the value of intelligible and comprehensible pronunciation?

232 Researching Individual Differences

What would that intervention look like in your research and teaching context? As Al-Hoorie et al. (2020) observed, there has been a general absence of interventional work targeting motivation, even though such work has the greatest chance of achieving pedagogical relevance.

Experience

Experiential variables have a storied history in pronunciation research. Length of residence and full-time equivalent are macroconstructs that attempt to capture with a single number the totality of the learning experience. Yet, experience is a multifaceted variable that has for decades eluded simple operational definitions. It should come as no surprise then that researchers have endeavored to generate comprehensive lists of potential activities, asking participants to report not just on their quantity of L2 use but also on several quality dimensions such as where the L2 was used, for what purpose, and with whom. For instance, Moyer (2011) gave participants a checklist, asking them to tick the types of use in which they engaged and estimate the number of hours per week for each activity/type. When she examined the relationship between language use and strength of foreign accent in German, she found several medium-to-large correlations with quantity of use (e.g., L1 use showed a large, positive correlation with foreign accent; individuals who reported using the L1 more often tended to have a stronger foreign accent). Interestingly, when quantity of use was subdivided into categories, the variable that showed the strongest relationship of all was the amount of time participants spent interacting in German with friends who were native speakers. Thus, it was not simply total amount of L2 use, but rather L2 use with native speaking friends that was the strongest predictor of accent.

In instructed contexts, such as the language classroom, experience may be operationalized in very different terms. For instructed learners, experience could refer to the number of years they have studied the language or the number of courses taken, both of which would be the instructional equivalent of length of residence. Like length of residence, the number of years of study in and of itself cannot reveal anything about the quality of instruction and the quality of learner engagement. Thus, as is the case for researchers working with naturalistic learners, researchers studying instructed learners have developed a range of instruments to collect finer-grained input and use data. For example, Saito and Hanzawa (2018) asked L1 Japanese learners of English to estimate their total number of hours of input as well as hours spent in form-oriented and content-based classes. They also asked participants to estimate how well they understood the English used in class and how much they spoke in class, both on seven-point scales, to capture information on participants' classroom experience and output. Some researchers have also distinguished between language use inside and outside of class (Saito et al., 2018) as well as previous and current experiences (Suzukida & Saito, 2023). As in Moyer's (2011) study on the type of L2 use (i.e., with whom participants were using the L2), instructed research has attempted to shed light on the types of classroom experiences and extracurricular use that promote pronunciation learning.

Most studies on experience and its correlates have collected cross-sectional data or have asked learners to report on their experience over a couple data points. This approach to data collection renders a relatively flat portrait of language use because it cannot account for the ways in which language use may change over time, nor can it offer detailed insight into the "complex dynamic social realities" learners inhabit (Ushioda, 2011, p. 18). For this very reason, several studies have delved into language use itself in an attempt to understand how the learning context and the learner shape when, how, and with whom speakers interact in the L2. In one illustrative study, Ranta and Meckelborg (2013) asked Mandarin speakers who were pursuing an advanced degree in Canada to complete a language log over a week-long period once per month over six months. Considering the group, language use patterns were surprisingly fixed over the window of observation and were at least partially determined by the academic calendar. Once the academic year ended, participants had fewer opportunities to interact in English in class—one of their primary modes of L2 contact—so their English use decreased. Individual patterns were also revealing. Some participants reported that they were not comfortable interacting in English, which likely contributed to their low levels of interaction. Others indicated a desire to focus on developing their receptive skills rather than their speaking skills, which led the authors to conclude that "learners themselves create the kind of exposure they get" (p. 21). While this is certainly true, many L2 learners may not have the time to interact in the L2.

In a case study on an L2 English speaker (Carita) who was living, studying, and working in Sydney, Benson et al. (2018) described how time and geography shaped the opportunities Carita had for L2 interaction. Briefly stated, Carita lived in a multilingual neighborhood in Sydney, near the language school where she studied, and during the week she had little time outside of studying and working (a necessity for many international students, as Benson et al. pointed out) to engage in leisure activities. Thus, school and work became the primary sites for L2 use, and in those contexts, she predominantly interacted with other L2 speakers. Together, these studies, which combine dense, comprehensive quantitative sampling methods with in-depth interviews, paint a rich portrait of the language use opportunities naturalistic learners have, the social and economic realities they face, and the choices they make. To my knowledge, there has not been similarly detailed work on instructed learners in the language classroom, but there is an abundance of research on input, interaction, and social networks during study abroad (for a methodological overview, see, e.g., Mitchell, 2023).

In summary, then, nearly all research on language use relies heavily on self-report data. Despite this commonality, researchers have taken different approaches to how often they ask participants to report on language use and the type of information they request in that report. We can think of these two methodological features as continuums (Figure 7.2). At this point in the trajectory of language use research, it seems like one-shot designs are unlikely to yield novel insights, even if participants are asked many detailed questions about their patterns of L2 use. Perhaps a cross-sectional study involving several novel learner populations or languages could prove illuminating, but I believe that the field would be much better served by sampling language use longitudinally using appropriately detailed measures. Thus, I advocate for research that falls into the bottom right quadrant of Figure 7.2.

Translating rich, layered language use data into a format suitable for quantitative analysis can be a challenge, but there is reason to believe it's a necessary one if we hope to gain accurate insight into the relationship between use and pronunciation learning. Zielinski and Pryor (2020) carried out a ten-month study focusing on L2 English learners in Australia. Learners reported on various facets of their language use four times throughout the ten-month window, and they were recorded responding to a prompt at the beginning and end of the same period. In one interesting comparison, illustrating the importance of gaining detailed insight into what language use actually entails, the authors analyzed language use and comprehensibility

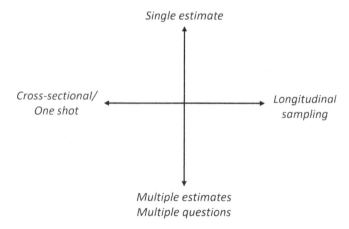

FIGURE 7.2 Illustration of How Researchers Have Approached Measuring Language Use.

data for two learners, Rose and Nina. Nina showed consistently high language use over the study, whereas Rose showed increasing language use. Interestingly, Nina's comprehensibility decreased, despite high language use. When the authors interviewed the learners, they found that Nina predominantly used English to communicate with her husband at home. However, they did not spend much time conversing, preferring instead to watch TV together. Rose, on the other hand, reported expanding contexts of language use. These differences might partially account for Rose's gains in comprehensibility versus the apparent backsliding, or loss of comprehensibility, evident for Nina (see also Derwing & Munro, 2013).

What these studies make clear is that language use is a multidimensional, dynamic construct, and as such should be studied over time and in sufficient detail. Experience sampling could become the gold standard in this area (Arndt et al., 2023a, 2023b). It involves collecting many responses nested within specific windows of time. For example, participants may be prompted to respond to five prompts in one day for three days in a given week, and they may be asked to do so for two weeks over three months. In this example, prompts are nested in days, days in weeks, and weeks in months. This nested structure is advantageous because it can shed light on typical language learning behaviors and, from a statistical standpoint, "because of the larger number of data points per participant, mathematical adjustments can be applied to correct for random error resulting from different interpretations and use of response scales by the respondents" (Arndt et al., 2023a, p. 46). Participants can be prompted to respond based on triggering events or at certain times, and the prompts can be set up to include diverse questions about the interactive context, conversation partners, and the languages used. Arndt et al. (2023b) published a highly customizable app for implementing experience sampling. Once set up, prompts can be sent directly to the participant's phone to ensure rapid, time-locked data collection. Of course, experience sampling is not a panacea for all of the problems of traditional questionnaires. Participants may choose not to respond, may miss a response, or may not respond promptly, all of which could affect data quality. Still, experience sampling, especially app-based techniques that allow participants to respond at any time using their phones, is a significant improvement over traditional methods.

There is no one-size-fits-all approach to experience sampling. Rather, the frequency of sampling and sampling approach must be determined in light of the research questions. Likewise, the types of questions that participants are asked when they are prompted to respond also depend on the research questions and, crucially, on anticipated behaviors for the learner population. The questions asked of naturalistic learners might be quite different than the questions asked of classroom learners, and the schedules on which those learners are prompted might also differ. For example, college-aged participants studying at US institutions typically take courses throughout the morning and early afternoon. Thus, if they are prompted during those times they may be unable to respond, and if they do, their responses may be highly repetitive, dictated by their academic schedule. For a study on classroom learners in a US university context, prompting throughout the afternoon, evening, and into the night might be more likely to shed light on their language learning habits. Alternatively, experience sampling could also be used to collect data during class time, to gain insight into how students respond to particular activities, how willing they are to communicate with classmates, and the languages they use for communication (for an example using pencil-and-paper experience sampling, see Waninge et al., 2014). Experience sampling can therefore be used to tap into constructs far beyond language use. Beyond the time of day, the moments in which participants are prompted must also be considered. For classroom learners, this might mean scheduling responses throughout the semester and potentially anchoring them to key events (e.g., before and after a key assignment or assessment). For instance, two sampling weeks could be scheduled during the first half of the course, before midterm, and two weeks in the second half of the course, after midterm. Regardless of how experience sampling is implemented, what is certain is that it is grounded in a dense sampling procedure that relies on dozens of observations (i.e., dozens of individual responses). In the remainder of this section, I offer some guiding questions and commentary on measuring learning behaviors related to L2 input and use.

What types of language use and behavior do you expect from your participants? Running a pilot study in which participants are asked to freely report when, where, and how they use the L2 may be necessary to generate an accurate and comprehensive list of categories.

Considering the length of the study, how should sampling moments be distributed with respect to time? Will all participants follow the exact same sampling schedule, or will you introduce a certain amount of "jitter" to ensure that sampling moments are more representative? For instance, if participants are prompted during one week per month, will they be prompted on the same week, or will one week be randomly selected such that an equal number of participants respond each week? What are participants' schedules like? Do they have fixed schedules? If so, how can prompting be coordinated with their schedules to avoid data loss and participant frustration (e.g., over not being able to respond when prompted) while simultaneously ensuring that representative behaviors are captured?

What aspects of language use are you interested in capturing? In one study, you may simply be interested in prompting participants to indicate the languages they used in their most recent interaction, where they were, and with whom they were speaking. In another, you may want the same information as well as information on other dimensions of their experience, such as their willingness to communicate, anxiety, and so on. And for classroom learners, you may be more interested in their study habits than their extracurricular language use (which could be quite limited if they are not studying in a location where the target language is spoken outside the classroom).

Considering all of the above, what is the timeframe over which you expect to observe changes in experience, however operationalized? And what predictions do you have about the relationship between experience and language learning? Having clear expectations about change over time and anticipated relationships will help you determine an appropriate sampling schedule and appropriate units of analysis (e.g., days, weeks, months).

Connecting the Dots

As I have implied in the previous sections, motivation, language use, and other emotional and behavioral dimensions of language learning are not necessarily independent but rather covary and influence one another. In fact, in their article on experience sampling, Arndt et al. discussed this point:

> In SLA and in situations like [study abroad] in particular, there are several reasons to believe that the experience and exposure situation are even more dynamic. Learners' social networks develop over time (McManus et al., 2014) and as the learner progresses in linguistic proficiency, more and different activities in the target language become interesting and feasible. Moreover, a perceived successful interaction event may lead to an increased inclination to engage in yet another event (or, conversely, learners who experience difficulties might be less inclined to seek out further interactions in the future).
>
> *(2023a, pp. 41–42)*

It would be difficult, if not impossible, to track motivation, emotion, behavior, and learning dynamically, examining all relevant subconstructs in sufficient detail and specifying the relationships that might exist among them. I'm not advocating for such an approach. Instead, I'm advocating for greater recognition of learner agency and emotion in learning, especially pronunciation learning, given that the way we speak is so personal. I'm certainly not the first to call for such an approach. Individual difference scholars, particularly scholars working within a Complex Dynamic Systems Theory framework (see, e.g., Hiver et al., 2021), have consistently advocated for this approach. I believe that the field is well positioned to begin to

238 Researching Individual Differences

examine these complex relationships because we can collect and store large amounts of data more easily than before and because we have at our disposal a range of statistical techniques specifically designed for complex, latent, time-varying data. In the following section on statistical analysis, I give an example of how language use can be analyzed longitudinally and linked to changes in comprehensibility, and I conclude with an example of motivation, behavior, and comprehensibility in which we examine how changes in all three dimensions are related to one another.

Statistical Analysis

Example 1: Language Use and Comprehensibility

For this example, we'll assume that we've tracked a group of participants' language use and comprehensibility over time while they were living in an L2 environment, such as during study abroad. We'll also assume that we used the experience sampling method to measure language use, asking participants to track their language use during one randomly selected week each month. During that week, we asked them to report on their language use on four randomly selected days, and on each of those days, we prompted them to report whether they had used the L2 in their most recent interaction that was >10 minutes in length (see Derwing & Munro, 2013). In summary, in any given month, each participant responded to 12 language use prompts spread across four days in a randomly selected week. In total, there were up to 36 responses per participant, spread across a total of 12 days, distributed throughout three weeks, with one week per month. At the end of each data collection week (i.e., once per month), when we asked participants to report on their L2 use, we also recorded them responding to a prompt in the L2. From this response, we extracted a 30-second speech sample and presented it to ten native listeners, who evaluated the speakers' comprehensibility on a 100-point scale. Crucially, in this study, the relevant timeframe, or unit of change, is Week, which represents a one-month period. The variables we have for this study are shown in Table 7.1.

As in the other examples presented throughout this book, we begin by computing descriptive statistics and visualizing the data. The descriptive statistics for language use (Table 7.2) indicate that on the whole participants began the study reporting a relatively low amount of L2 use that increased over the three-month window. The pattern of increasing variability in the data, evident in the increasing *SD* month after month, further suggests a fanning-out pattern, which is displayed in the left panel of Figure 7.3. From the left panel, we see that most participants reported using the L2 more frequently as time passed or showed a stable pattern of L2 use. Very few participants reported using the L2 less frequently. Likewise,

Researching Individual Differences **239**

TABLE 7.1 Summary of Study Variables

Variable	Type	Levels/Range
Participant ($n = 60$)	Factor	An index variable that refers to the participants in the study
Week ($n = 3$)	Factor	An index variable that refers to the week when language use data were collected
Day ($n = 12$)	Factor	An index variable that refers to the days on which language use data were collected
Report ($n = 36$)	Factor	An index variable that refers to the reports on language use that were collected
Week.cont	Continuous	The continuous version of the week variable
Day.cont	Continuous	The continuous version of the day variable
Report.cont	Continuous	The continuous version of the report variable
Missing	Factor	A binary variable that can be used to create a data set in which the likelihood of responding to a prompt (i.e., the likelihood of providing a report) decreases as the study progresses
Use	Continuous	A percentage estimate of L2 use
Comp	Continuous	Comprehensibility rating (0–100)
Listener	Factor	An index variable that refers to the listeners in the study

Note. The use and comprehensibility data are stored in separate CSV files.

TABLE 7.2 Descriptive Statistics for Language Use and Comprehensibility by Month

Month	Language Use	Comprehensibility
1	20.63 (8.40)	40.93 (12.40)
2	33.65 (12.78)	46.96 (11.06)
3	46.32 (22.01)	52.64 (14.65)

comprehensibility increased over time, but the change in comprehensibility was more modest, and the amount of variability in participants' initial level of comprehensibility was far greater than the amount of variability in their initial level of L2 use.

Having observed these descriptive trends, we're now ready to analyze the data. First, we fit a mixed-effects model to the language use data in which time is treated as a fixed effect and a by-participant random effect.

```
fm.use <- lmer (use ~ week.cont +
            (1 + week.cont | participant), data = data.use)
```

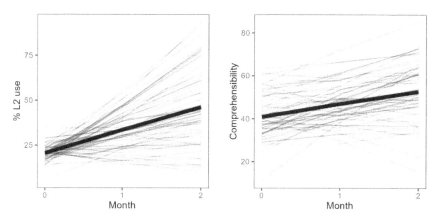

FIGURE 7.3   Language Use and Comprehensibility Trajectories for the Group and Individual Learners.

The statistical assumptions for this model were largely upheld (for code and outcomes, see the R markdown file). The model summary suggests that participants' initial L2 use was 20.69% ($SE = 0.57$, $t = 36.60$, $p < 0.001$). It also suggests that their language use increased by 12.84% per month ($SE = 1.41$, $t = 9.11$, $p < 0.001$) on average. The SD for the by-participant random slopes for time was 10.81, and the slope-intercept covariance was –0.30, which shows that a higher initial amount of L2 use was associated with less change over time.

Now we can extract the by-subject random slopes, which represent estimates of where the individual falls relative to the group, and relate those to comprehensibility. This type of analysis is inspired by much of the work on language use, including experience sampling, where participants are categorized according to their trajectory (e.g., increasing, decreasing) and that trajectory is then linked (usually descriptively) to a linguistic outcome. To extract the random effects, we use the ranef() function, creating a data frame that we then modify to get a streamlined set of estimates.

```
ranef.use <- ranef(fm.use) %>%
  as.data.frame() %>%
  subset(term == "week.cont") %>%
  mutate(participant = grp,
         use.estimate = condval,
         group = ifelse(condval > 0, "above","below")) %>%
  select(participant, use.estimate, group)
```

In the code given above, we also create a new variable, "Group," based on whether each participant's estimate indicated a rate of change that was

Researching Individual Differences **241**

above or below the mean. It bears repeating that random effects are centered on the fixed effect, which is set to zero, so positive scores indicate performance above the mean effect and negative scores performance below the mean effect. This is important because in our data negative scores don't refer to a negative trajectory for L2 use, but rather to a trajectory that was shallower than the group trajectory (but likely still positive).

We're ready to analyze comprehensibility, including the effect of language use on rate of change. In the comprehensibility data, time is within-speakers and within-listeners (because listeners evaluated all learner samples produced at each time point), so we include time as a by-speaker and by-listener random effect. This model is the appropriate unconditional linear growth model for the data.

```
fm.comp <- lmer(comp ~ week +
                (1 + week | participant) +
                (1 + week | listener), data = data.comp)
```

To analyze the effect of language use, we need to incorporate our new Group variable, which refers to whether participants showed a language use trajectory that was above or below the group mean, into the comprehensibility data frame. We can do that by merging the data sets by participant (see the R markdown). Then, we incorporate our Group variable in an interaction term with time (i.e., with Week in our model, which is how time has been specified).

```
fm.comp2 <- lmer(comp ~ group * week +
                 (1 + week | participant) +
                 (1 + week | listener), data = data.comp)
```

When we summarize this model, we see that Group = above has been set as the baseline for model estimates. Therefore, the estimate for week (*estimate* = 9.51, *SE* = 1.60, t = 5.94, $p < 0.001$) refers to the rate of change for learners whose L2 use was above the group mean for L2 use. The estimate for the interaction term, which is labeled as groupbelow:week in our model summary, represents the difference in rate of comprehensibility change for Group = below. The negative estimate (–6.45, *SE* = 1.71, t = –3.76, $p < 0.001$) shows that learners whose L2 use was below the group mean showed a positive, but less pronounced, change in comprehensibility over time. We can compute the estimated rate of change for this group by combining the two terms: $9.51 – 6.45 = 3.06$. As in previous chapters, we could also contrast-code the effect of Group to get the average rate of change in comprehensibility, considering both language use profiles (see the R markdown for this procedure).

242 Researching Individual Differences

In summary, language use showed a significant relationship to the rate of change in comprehensibility. On average, learners who reported using the L2 more often than average showed a rate of change of 9.51 units per month, whereas learners who reported using the L2 less often than average showed a rate of change of 3.06 units per month, corresponding to a difference in rate of change of 6.45 units.

Example 2: Motivation, Learning Behavior, and Comprehensibility

For this example, we'll assume that we have tracked participants' pronunciation motivation, pronunciation learning behaviors, and comprehensibility over three data points spanning a year of language instruction during which time participants also received pronunciation instruction. To measure a construct like pronunciation motivation, we might develop a scale consisting of ten items, asking participants to rate their agreement on a six-point scale ranging from strongly disagree to strongly agree (see, e.g., Sardegna et al., 2018). These ten items are known as indicator variables, and we can use those variables to create a score for each participant on the latent factor. In this case, we would say that the latent construct of pronunciation motivation gives rise to the observed scores on the indicator variables. In longitudinal research, we must establish that the measurement model holds over time. That is, we must ensure that the structure and scale of the model do not change. Otherwise, we cannot know if change in the latent factor is due to true change or is an artifact of a changing measurement model (e.g., because participants interpret the items or scale differently at each time point). This type of analysis is known as a measurement invariance analysis. Normally, this would be the first step in analyzing latent factors longitudinally, but for the sake of this example, we'll assume that we have already checked for and established measurement invariance (for more information on longitudinal measurement invariance, see Nagle, 2023).

The data set for this study is different than the previous data sets we have analyzed (but similar to the structural equation model perception-production data analyzed in Chapter 4). First, instead of responses to individual items, by-participant means are given at each time point. Second, the data are in wide format instead of long format. In wide format, there is no column indicating the time of data collection, rather there is a column for each construct at each time point. This means that there are nine variables in the data set, plus an indicator variable for subjects. Finally, if you inspect the variables, you will see some odd values, such as negative means on motivation. As I mentioned in Chapter 4, when simulating structural equation model data, the model is specified, and data are generated based on the relationships shown in the model (i.e., a data set that is consistent with the model is generated).

Researching Individual Differences **243**

TABLE 7.3 Summary of Study Variables

Variable	Type	Levels/Range
Participant ($n = 286$)	Factor	An index variable that refers to the subjects in the study
mot1	Continuous	Participants' mean motivation score at time 1
mot2	Continuous	Participants' mean motivation score at time 2
mot3	Continuous	Participants' mean motivation score at time 3
bvr1	Continuous	Participants' mean learning behaviors score at time 1
bvr2	Continuous	Participants' mean learning behaviors score at time 2
bvr3	Continuous	Participants' mean learning behaviors score at time 3
cmp1	Continuous	Participants' mean comprehensibility at time 1
cmp2	Continuous	Participants' mean comprehensibility at time 2
cmp3	Continuous	Participants' mean comprehensibility at time 3

In terms of the assumptions I made about the variables, I assumed that participants would respond to motivation items on a six-point Likert scale, that they would report the amount of time they spent practicing their pronunciation in minutes per class day, and that their comprehensibility would be rated on a 100-point scale by many listeners. The variables in our study are given in Table 7.3.

Structural equation modeling is advantageous when the goal is to relate change in one latent construct to change in another. This type of structural equation model is known as a multivariate latent curve model. The model we're trying to fit is shown in Figure 7.4. Following typical structural equation modeling notation, observed variables are shown as boxes and latent variables as circles. Notice that there are six latent variables, a latent intercept and slope for each of the constructs, and these latent variables are defined by the time-specific observed means. In the structural equation model, we allow all latent variables to covary with one another, which is why two-headed arrows appear between them. To avoid visual clutter, I've omitted some of the elements that would be displayed in the full structural equation model (e.g., the factor loadings), and I've made others transparent (e.g., the indicator variables, some of the covariances). The key relationships of interest are the covariances between the latent slopes, which are shown as

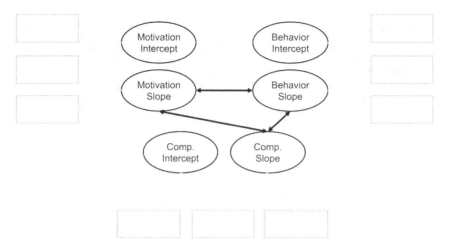

FIGURE 7.4 Simplified Multivariate Latent Curve Model for Motivation, Behavior, and Comprehensibility

bold, black lines in the figure. These represent the extent to which changes in motivation covary with changes in behavior and comprehensibility and the extent to which changes in behavior covary with changes in comprehensibility. Put another way, are changes in motivation accompanied by changes in behavior, and are changes in behavior accompanied by changes in comprehensibility?

To fit a structural equation model in R, the *lavaan* package (Rosseel, 2012) is used. The basic procedure is to specify the model, fit the specified model to the data, and then assess model fit and model parameters. As usual, we could summarize the data by computing time-specific means for each construct, but for the sake of space, I'll skip that step.

We first need to define the model. This means we need to specify the latent intercepts and slopes for each construct. Latent variables are defined using an equal size and a tilde (=~). The name of the latent variable goes to the left, and the indicator variables that make it up go to the right. Latent intercepts are defined by premultiplying the time-specific means by 1, and latent slopes are defined by premultiplying them by an increasing number, starting with 0. The entire model must be given between quotation marks, and spaces and notes (#) can be introduced for the sake of readability.

```
mbl.model <- "
# motivation
mot.int =~ 1*mot1 + 1*mot2 + 1*mot3
mot.slp =~ 0*mot1 + 1*mot2 + 2*mot3
# behavior
```

```
bvr.int =~ 1*bvr1 + 1*bvr2 + 1*bvr3
bvr.slp =~ 0*bvr1 + 1*bvr2 + 2*bvr3
# comp
cmp.int =~ 1*cmp1 + 1*cmp2 + 1*cmp3
cmp.slp =~ 0*cmp1 + 1*cmp2 + 2*cmp3
"
```

Once the model is defined, we simply use the growth() function, specifying the model and the data. We also indicate that what goes into the model are the means of the observed variables by including the meanstructure argument.

```
mlcm.fit <- growth(mbl.model, data.mbl, meanstructure = T)
```

Now, we have a fit object that is similar to the model objects that are created when we fit a mixed-effects model. We can request a summary of the fit using the summary() function with a few additional arguments specific to structural equation models (e.g., requesting standardized estimates).

```
summary(mlcm.fit, fit.measures = T, estimates = T, standardized = T)
```

This will produce a long output consisting of several chunks of information: fit indices, latent variables and factor loadings, covariances, intercepts, and variances. For our purposes, we will consider the fit indices, intercepts, and covariances. In general, indicators of acceptable fit for a structural equation model are root mean square error of approximation (RMSEA) and standardized root mean squared residual (SRMR) < 0.05 and comparative fit index (CFI) and Tucker-Lewis index (TLI) > 0.95. Based on our model fit indices (CFI $= 0.999$, TLI $= 0.997$, RMSEA $= 0.02$ and its 90% CI $= [0.00, 0.06]$, and SRMR $= 0.02$), we can conclude that our model is a good fit to the data. The estimated values for the latent intercepts and slopes, which are reported in the "Intercepts" portion of the model, are given in Table 7.4. All these estimates are highly statistically significant, and the positive values for the latent slopes indicate that participants' pronunciation motivation, pronunciation learning behavior, and comprehensibility increased over

TABLE 7.4 Summary of Latent Intercept and Slope Estimates

	Motivation	Behavior	Comprehensibility
Latent intercept	2.99	12.10	59.98
Latent slope	0.86	9.93	8.98

246 Researching Individual Differences

time. The fact that the estimates vary in magnitude is simply a function of the distinct scales on which each construct was measured (i.e., simulated).

Finally, we turn to the most critical piece of information: the covariances. We could inspect all covariances to determine the strength of the association (1) between the latent intercept and slope for each construct (e.g., motivation intercept and slope), (2) among the latent intercepts (e.g., motivation intercept and behavior intercept), (3) between the latent intercepts and slopes across constructs (e.g., motivation intercept and behavior slope), and (4) among the latent slopes (e.g., motivation slope and behavior slope). Of these, we're especially interested in (4) because our primary goal is to determine if the rate of change in learning behavior is tied to the rate of change in motivation and if the rate of change in comprehensibility is tied to the rate of change in behavior. We're also interested in the relationship between the rate of change in motivation and the rate of change in comprehensibility, but we assume that this relationship is likely non-significant (because motivation predicts behavior and behavior comprehensibility).

To get the standardized estimates, we look at the "Std.all" column. The motivation slope shows a medium, positive correlation with the behavior slope ($r = 0.39$, $p < 0.001$) and a small, positive, non-significant correlation with the comprehensibility slope ($r = 0.04$, $p = 0.579$). The behavior slope, in turn, shows a small, positive, and significant correlation with the comprehensibility slope ($r = 0.23$, $p = 0.001$). We can therefore conclude that motivation and behavior grow together, as do behavior and comprehensibility, albeit to a lesser extent considering the size of the correlation coefficients.

Summary and Recommendations

In this chapter, we have surveyed the individual differences landscape in L2 pronunciation research, focusing intensively on motivation and language experience and use. I have made a case for engaging in longitudinal research on the relationship between individual differences and pronunciation learning, considering the mechanisms through which and the timeframe over which individual differences operate. I have also argued that to do robust individual differences research entails developing expertise in the individual difference itself, including how it is conceptualized, measured, and analyzed.

- Think carefully about the mechanism. It's not enough to demonstrate a relationship between an individual difference and a measure of pronunciation performance or learning. The mechanism by which that individual difference works is critical for understanding its influence.
- Related to the previous point, think about whether the individual difference will show a direct relationship to pronunciation learning or whether

the relationship is more appropriately conceptualized as indirect. Some individual differences, such as language use, could have a direct impact on pronunciation development, whereas others, such as motivation, may operate indirectly, by influencing learning behaviors which could then, in turn, drive development.

- When engaging in longitudinal research, consider how both the individual difference and the dimension of L2 pronunciation under investigation might change over time. Calibrate the window of observation and the frequency of data collection with anticipated developmental timelines.

Chapter Questions

1. What is the "questionnaire curse" in motivation research? Look at a recent motivation study using a self-report questionnaire. What items are included in the questionnaire? What are the strengths and weaknesses of the approach?
2. Pick an individual difference that you're interested in. How has it been measured and analyzed? What are some considerations that would be important to keep in mind when designing a study to measure the relationship between that variable and pronunciation learning?
3. Based on (1), look up two studies examining that individual difference that were published in the last two years. What sorts of research questions did the authors ask, and what predictions did they make? How did they approach the measurement of the individual difference?
4. In this chapter, we examined simulated data in which the pronunciation variable was comprehensibility, a global, listener-based construct. In what ways might individual differences influence the production of specific target structures, such as individual sounds and contrasts?
5. Based on your answer to (2), reflect on individual differences in L2 speech perception learning. Would the same individual differences you listed for production also be important for perception? Why or why not? What predictions would you make for individual differences and L2 perception learning?
6. For the first data example, we worked with a complete data set, assuming that participants responded to all of the language use experience sampling prompts. Use the "missing" variable to subset the data to a data set consisting of non-missing data (missing == "no"). Then, reanalyze the data when some missingness is assumed. What problems do you encounter? How might you surmount them? Once you've completed the analysis, compare the analysis without and with missing data. How do the results differ?

248 Researching Individual Differences

References

Al-Hoorie, A. H. (2018). The L2 motivational self system: A meta-analysis. *Studies in Second Language Learning and Teaching*, *8*(4), 721–754. https://doi.org/10.14746/ssllt.2018.8.4.2

Al-Hoorie, A. H., & Hiver, P. (2020). The fundamental difference hypothesis: Expanding the conversation in language learning motivation. *SAGE Open*, *10*(3). https://doi.org/10.1177/2158244020945702

Al-Hoorie, A. H., Hiver, P., Kim, T.-Y., & De Costa, P. I. (2020). The identity crisis in language motivation research. *Journal of Language and Social Psychology*, *40*(1), 136–153. https://doi.org/10.1177/0261927x20964507

Arndt, H. L., Granfeldt, J., & Gullberg, M. (2023a). Reviewing the potential of the Experience Sampling Method (ESM) for capturing second language exposure and use. *Second Language Research*, *39*(1), 39–58. https://doi.org/10.1177/02676583211020055

Arndt, H. L., Granfeldt, J., & Gullberg, M. (2023b). The Lang-Track-App: Open-source tools for implementing the experience sampling method in second language acquisition research. *Language Learning*, *73*(3), 869–903. https://doi.org/10.1111/lang.12555

Benson, P., Chappell, P., & Yates, L. (2018). A day in the life: Mapping international students' language learning environments in multilingual Sydney. *Australian Journal of Applied Linguistics*, *1*(1), 20–32. https://dx.doi.org/10.29140/ajal.v1n1.21

Boo, Z., Dörnyei, Z., & Ryan, S. (2015). L2 motivation research 2005–2014: Understanding a publication surge and a changing landscape. *System*, *55*, 145–157. https://doi.org/10.1016/j.system.2015.10.006

Darcy, I., Mora, J. C., & Daidone, D. (2016). The role of inhibitory control in second language phonological processing. *Language Learning*, *66*(4), 741–773. https://doi.org/10.1111/lang.12161

Derwing, T. M., & Munro, M. J. (2013). The development of L2 oral language skills in two L1 groups: A 7-year study. *Language Learning*, *63*(2), 163–185. https://doi.org/10.1111/lang.12000

Derwing, T. M., & Munro, M. J. (2015). *Pronunciation fundamentals: Evidence-based perspectives for L2 teaching and research*. John Benjamins.

Dörnyei, Z. (1994a). Motivation and motivating in the foreign language classroom. *The Modern Language Journal*, *78*(3), 273–284. https://doi.org/10.2307/330107

Dörnyei, Z. (1994b). Understanding L2 motivation: On with the challenge! *The Modern Language Journal*, *78*(4), 515–523. https://doi.org/10.2307/328590

Dörnyei, Z. (2009). The L2 motivational self system. In Z. Dörnyei & E. Ushioda (Eds.), *Motivation, language identity and the L2 self*. Multilingual Matters.

Dörnyei, Z., MacIntyre, P. D., & Henry, A. (Eds.). (2015). *Motivational dynamics in language learning*. Multilingual Matters.

Elliott, A. R. (1995). Field independence/dependence, hemispheric specialization, and attitude in relation to pronunciation accuracy in Spanish as a foreign language. *The Modern Language Journal*, *79*(3), 356–371. https://doi.org/10.1111/j.1540-4781.1995.tb01112.x

Flege, J. E. (1995). Second language speech learning: Theory, findings, problems. In W. Strange (Ed.), *Speech perception and linguistic experience: Issues in cross-language research* (pp. 233–277). York Press.

Flege, J. E., & Bohn, O.-S. (2021). The revised speech learning model. In R. Wayland (Ed.), *Second language speech learning: Theoretical and empirical progress* (pp. 3–83). Cambridge University Press.

Flege, J. E., MacKay, I. R., & Meador, D. (1999). Native Italian speakers' perception and production of English vowels. *Journal of the Acoustical Society of America*, *106*(5), 2973–2987. https://doi.org/10.1121/1.428116

Flege, J. E., Munro, M. J., & MacKay, I. R. A. (1996). Factors affecting the production of word-initial consonants in a second language. In R. Bayley & D. R. Preston (Eds.), *Second language acquisition and linguistic variation* (pp. 47–73). John Benjamins.

Flege, J. E., Yeni-Komshian, G. H., & Liu, S. (1999). Age constraints on second-language acquisition. *Journal of Memory and Language*, *41*(1), 78–104. https://doi.org/10.1006/jmla.1999.2638

Gardner, R. C. (2010). *Motivation and second language acquisition*. Peter Lang.

Gorba, C. (2023). Is full-time equivalent an appropriate measure to assess L1 and L2 perception of L2 speakers with limited L2 experience? *Languages*, *8*(1), 56. https://www.mdpi.com/2226-471X/8/1/56

Hiver, P., Al-Hoorie, A. H., & Evans, R. (2021). Complex dynamic systems theory in language learning: A scoping review of 25 years of research. *Studies in Second Language Acquisition*, 1–29. https://doi.org/10.1017/s0272263121000553

Kachlicka, M., Saito, K., & Tierney, A. (2019). Successful second language learning is tied to robust domain-general auditory processing and stable neural representation of sound. *Brain and Language*, *192*, 15–24. https://doi.org/10.1016/j.bandl.2019.02.004

Kline, R. B. (2023). *Principles and practice of structural equation modeling* (5th ed.). Guilford Press.

Li, S., Hiver, P., & Papi, M. (Eds.). (2022). *The Routledge handbook of second language acquisition and individual differences*. Routledge.

Meara, P. M., & Rogers, V. E. (2019). *The LLAMA Tests v3*. Cardiff: Lognostics.

Mendoza, A., & Phung, H. (2019). Motivation to learn languages other than English: A critical research synthesis. *Foreign Language Annals*, *52*(1), 121–140. https://doi.org/10.1111/flan.12380

Mitchell, R. (2023). Researching study abroad: Tracking social networks. In C. Pérez-Vidal & C. Sanz (Eds.), *Methods in study abroad research: Past, present and future* (pp. 345–372). John Benjamins.

Moyer, A. (1999). Ultimate attainment in L2 phonology: The critical factors of age, motivation, and instruction. *Studies in Second Language Acquisition*, *21*(1), 81–108. https://doi.org/10.1017/S0272263199001035

Moyer, A. (2011). An investigation of experience in L2 phonology: Does quality matter more than quantity? *The Canadian Modern Language Review*, *67*(2), 191–216. https://doi.org/10.3138/cmlr.67.2.191

Moyer, A. (2014a). What's age got to do with it? Accounting for individual factors in second language accent. *Studies in Second Language Learning and Teaching*, *3*, 443–464. https://doi.org/10.14746/ssllt.2014.4.3.4

Moyer, A. (2014b). Exceptional outcomes in L2 phonology: The critical factors of learner engagement and self-regulation. *Applied Linguistics*, *35*(4), 418–440. https://doi.org/10.1093/applin/amu012

250 Researching Individual Differences

Munro, M. J., & Derwing, T. M. (2008). Segmental acquisition in adult ESL learners: A longitudinal study of vowel production. *Language Learning, 58*(3), 479–502. https://doi.org/10.1111/j.1467-9922.2008.00448.x

Nagle, C. (2018). Motivation, comprehensibility, and accentedness in L2 Spanish: Investigating motivation as a time-varying predictor of pronunciation development. *The Modern Language Journal, 102*(1), 199–217. https://doi.org/10.1111/modl.12461

Nagle, C. L. (2021). Assessing the state of the art in longitudinal L2 pronunciation research. *Journal of Second Language Pronunciation, 7*(2), 154–182. https://doi.org/10.1075/jslp.20059.nag

Nagle, C. L. (2023). A design framework for longitudinal individual difference research: Conceptual, methodological, and analytical considerations. *Research Methods in Applied Linguistics, 2*(1), 100033. https://doi.org/10.1016/j.rmal.2022.100033

Papi, M., Bondarenko, A. V., Mansouri, S., Feng, L., & Jiang, C. (2019). Rethinking L2 motivation research. *Studies in Second Language Acquisition, 41*(2), 337–361. https://doi.org/10.1017/s0272263118000153

Ranta, L., & Meckelborg, A. (2013). How much exposure to English do international graduate students really get? Measuring language use in a naturalistic setting. *The Canadian Modern Language Review, 69*(1), 1–33. https://doi.org/10.3138/cmlr.987

Rosseel, Y. (2012). "lavaan: An R Package for Structural Equation Modeling." *Journal of Statistical Software, 48*(2), 1–36. https://doi.org/10.18637/jss.v048.i02.

Saito, K. (2023). How does having a good ear promote successful second language speech acquisition in adulthood? Introducing auditory precision hypothesis-L2. *Language Teaching.* Advance online publication. https://doi.org/10.1017/S0261444822000453

Saito, K., Cui, H., Suzukida, Y., Dardon, D. E., Suzuki, Y., Jeong, H., Révész, A., Sugiura, M., & Tierney, A. (2022). Does domain-general auditory processing uniquely explain the outcomes of second language speech acquisition, even once cognitive and demographic variables are accounted for? *Bilingualism: Language and Cognition, 25*(5), 856–868. https://doi.org/10.1017/s1366728922000153

Saito, K., Dewaele, J.-M., Abe, M., & In'nami, Y. (2018). Motivation, emotion, learning experience, and second language comprehensibility development in classroom settings: A cross-sectional and longitudinal study. *Language Learning, 68*(3), 709–743. https://doi.org/10.1111/lang.12297

Saito, K., & Hanzawa, K. (2018). The role of input in second language oral ability development in foreign language classrooms: A longitudinal study. *Language Teaching Research, 22*(4), 398–417. https://doi.org/10.1177/1362168816679030

Saito, K., Kachlicka, M., Suzukida, Y., Petrova, K., Lee, B. J., & Tierney, A. (2022). Auditory precision hypothesis-L2: Dimension-specific relationships between auditory processing and second language segmental learning. *Cognition, 229*, 105236. https://doi.org/10.1016/j.cognition.2022.105236

Saito, K., Sun, H., & Tierney, A. (2020). Domain-general auditory processing determines success in second language pronunciation learning in adulthood: A longitudinal study. *Applied Psycholinguistics, 41*(5), 1083–1112. https://doi.org/10.1017/s0142716420000491

Saito, K., Sun, H. U. I., & Tierney, A. (2018). Explicit and implicit aptitude effects on second language speech learning: Scrutinizing segmental and suprasegmental sensitivity and performance via behavioural and neurophysiological measures. *Bilingualism: Language and Cognition*, *22*(5), 1123–1140. https://doi.org/10.1017/s1366728918000895

Saito, K., Suzukida, Y., & Sun, H. (2019). Aptitude, experience, and second language pronunciation proficiency development in classroom settings. *Studies in Second Language Acquisition*, *41*(1), 201–225. https://doi.org/10.1017/s0272263117000432

Sardegna, V. G., Lee, J., & Kusey, C. (2018). Self-efficacy, attitudes, and choice of strategies for English pronunciation learning. *Language Learning*, *68*(1), 83–114. https://doi.org/10.1111/lang.12263

Schoonen, R. (2015). Structural equation modeling in L2 research. In L. Plonsky (Ed.), *Advancing quantitative methods in second language research*. Routledge.

Sun, H., Saito, K., & Dewaele, J.-M. (2023). Cognitive and sociopsychological individual differences, experience, and naturalistic second language speech learning: A longitudinal study. *Language Learning*. https://doi.org/10.1111/lang.12561

Suter, R. W. (1976). Predictors of pronunciation accuracy in second language learning. *Language Learning*, *26*(2), 233–253. https://doi.org/10.1111/j.1467-1770.1976.tb00275.x

Suzukida, Y., & Saito, K. (2023). Detangling experiential, cognitive, and sociopsychological individual differences in second language speech learning: Cross-sectional and longitudinal investigations. *Bilingualism: Language and Cognition*, *26*(4), 762–775. https://doi.org/10.1017/S1366728922000700

Thomson, R. I., Derwing, T. M., & Munro, M. J. (2023). How long can naturalistic L2 pronunciation learning continue in adults? A 10-year study. *Language Awareness*. Advance online publication. https://doi.org/10.1080/09658416.2023.2227559

Ushioda, E. (2011). Motivating learners to speak as themselves. In G. Murray, X. Gao, & T. Lamb (Eds.), *Identity, motivation, and autonomy in language learning* (pp. 11–24). Multilingual Matters.

Waninge, F., Dörnyei, Z., & De Bot, K. (2014). Motivational dynamics in language learning: Change, stability, and context. *The Modern Language Journal*, *98*(3), 704–723. https://doi.org/10.1111/modl.12118

Yousefi, M., & Mahmoodi, M. H. (2022). The L2 motivational self-system: A meta-analysis approach. *International Journal of Applied Linguistics*, *32*(2), 274–294. https://doi.org/10.1111/ijal.12416

Zielinski, B., & Pryor, E. (2020). Comprehensibility and everyday English use. *Journal of Second Language Pronunciation*, *6*(3), 352–379. https://doi.org/10.1075/jslp.20011.zie

8

CONCLUSION

L2 pronunciation research has reached a critical inflection point. The critical threshold of studies needed for meta-analysis has been reached in several subfields, and there is no sign that progress will slow. As the field continues to move forward, the questions asked and methods used will continue to evolve, providing increasingly nuanced perspectives on how L2 speech perception and production capacities develop, how bidirectional (L1-to-L2 and L2-to-L1) crosslinguistic influence manifests in the perception and production patterns of diverse bilingual populations, and how pronunciation instruction can be optimized. Research models are also evolving and will continue to do so in the coming years. Traditionally, individual researchers have produced scholarship, and review and promotion committees have prioritized single- and first-authored publications. Single-authored publications won't go away, nor should they. Individuals should have the option to work independently if they choose to do so. At the same time, single authorship should be viewed as one viable option among many. Co-authorship is increasingly recognized and valued, and science is moving toward larger-scale, multisite studies because that research model has the greatest chance of producing highly rigorous, meaningful, and impactful work. In short, research models now range from independent scholarship to small-scale and large-scale national and international collaborations.

Each approach comes with its own challenges and opportunities, but all of them should be informed by a core set of methodological principles, particularly an emphasis on replication, reproducibility, and slow, incremental, and open science (Marsden & Morgan-Short, 2023). Research syntheses have repeatedly revealed considerable diversity in study findings. Certainly,

DOI: 10.4324/9781003279266-8

some of this diversity is to be expected, even among highly methodologically similar studies. Yet, the current methodological reality is that studies rarely differ in one or two design decisions. Instead, they often prove orthogonal to one another because although they investigate the same topic, they do so using radically different methods. In fact, if two studies investigating the same topic are selected at random, it's more likely than not that they will differ in most substantive aspects of methodology. It's not surprising, then, that one study reports an effect where another does not, making it difficult to know how reliable findings are. Design decisions, considered within the context of each individual study, are sensible, but when these decisions are projected out and varied across several, if not dozens of studies, then it becomes difficult to see the forest for the trees. In the conclusion to this book, rather than focusing on specific topics for future research, I'd like to focus on how research can be conducted, including the types of studies that are likely to have a positive impact on the field, referencing the methodological principles listed above.

Replication can help us take a more systematic approach to understanding variability in effects (see, e.g., McManus, 2022). L2 pronunciation as a field is in the perfect position to engage in serious replication research. Take, for instance, research on pronunciation instruction. Meta-analyses point to moderate-to-large positive effects, subject to a range of moderator variables, especially concerning learning contexts and measurement choices (Lee et al., 2015; Saito & Plonsky, 2019). Yet, we still lack a clear understanding of how specific instructional techniques can be optimized. Close and approximate replications of existing experimental studies can provide key insight into how minor modifications to study characteristics and procedures can affect results, and this information can be leveraged to enhance pronunciation pedagogy (Nagle & Hiver, 2023). Furthermore, replication studies can be a sensible entry point into research for junior scholars who want to gain experience in research methodology and reporting while making a meaningful contribution to the field. Replication studies are not necessarily easier to carry out than traditional empirical studies because replication demands careful consideration of what to replicate, why, and what to modify. However, done correctly, they offer detailed insight into the relationship between concept and method, and their results provide information on the stability of a finding.

Another tool that we have at our disposal for probing the stability of effects is multisite research, which can be carried out with a small group of collaborators or in large teams (see, e.g., Moranksi & Zalbidea, 2022). In a multisite study, the same research instruments and protocol are used to collect data from two or more site-specific samples. This approach is valuable because the data from each site can be analyzed together or separately,

254 Conclusion

and in mixed-effects models, site can be treated as a fixed or random effect, for the purpose of quantifying the variability in effects across sites. This approach is especially valuable for pronunciation because it's easy to imagine how variability in geography could affect study findings. For one, learners in different areas could be exposed to different dialects, and at a more local level, learners located in rural and urban communities may have different opportunities for L2 interaction. To make this point more concrete, L2 Spanish learners who are living in Texas are likely exposed to far more Spanish than L2 Spanish learners in some other parts of the US, and even the passive exposure Texas learners receive could have a measurable impact on their perception and production abilities. Moreover, there are many bilinguals living in Texas, especially in Southern Texas, which means that Spanish and English are often in contact with one another, which could lead to subtle yet important differences in the phonetic characteristics of local varieties of English and Spanish. Put another way, English may take on some of the characteristics of Spanish, and Spanish may take on some of the characteristics of English. If the English and Spanish to which learners are habitually exposed are markedly different from the English and Spanish to which learners in other parts of the US are exposed, then it seems perfectly reasonable to hypothesize that these community-level variables could have an impact on learners' pronunciation. Researchers have yet to leverage multisite studies to examine these types of differences, which present an exciting avenue for future research. As Flege and Bohn (2021) argued, the unit of analysis can be narrowed to the individual speaker, but it can also be widened considerably to the community or geographic region where speakers study, live, and work. In describing the rationale for their multisite project, Moranski and Zalbidea made a conceptually similar argument: "Our definition of scalability focuses not only on lateral expansion of a method (e.g., different language courses or modalities within the same program), but also no vertical expansion within hierarchical structures, such as schools within districts or universities within a region" (2022, p. 48). Pronunciation researchers are prepared—and the field as a whole is primed—to engage in this type of work.

Last but certainly not least, there is also an opportunity to participate in big-team speech science (e.g., Coretta et al., 2022). In this research model, dozens of teams of researchers come together to tackle a project. This model can be traced back to the Center for Open Science (https://www.cos.io/) and specifically the Many Labs project, which sought to replicate several core findings in psychology (see, e.g., Klein et al., 2014). Currently, in speech research, Coretta et al.'s (2022) study is one of the few studies highlighting researcher degrees of freedom in speech analysis. Where Klein et al. (2014) examined how variability in research modality and context affected replication findings, Coretta et al. (2022) focused on the methodological garden of forking paths, investigating how the decisions the research teams made regarding acoustic and statistical analysis affected their findings. Simplifying the punchline from Coretta et al. (2022), measurement decisions matter. By crowdsourcing measurements from many teams who used many different approaches, the authors were able to estimate mean effects, controlling for the individual decisions that were made. This approach is especially valuable because it allows for abstracting away from individual studies and idiosyncratic approaches toward a more global understanding of how an effect varies. Klein et al. (2014) were concerned with replicating psychology findings and Coretta et al. (2022) with researcher degrees of freedom, but big-team speech science can be used to address a range of compelling pronunciation "problems." For instance, longitudinal data collection and analysis can be logistically and financially challenging. Yet, at the time of writing, there is at least one publicly available online corpus of longitudinal L2 speech data: the LANGSNAP project (Mitchell et al., 2017). Individual researchers or small groups of individuals could examine pronunciation learning in L2 French and Spanish, but a more profitable approach might be to formulate a research question that many teams would attempt to answer using the LANGSNAP data. In this way, rather than one or two studies on pronunciation learning, it might be possible to generate many more research reports, accelerating the pace of discovery. It would also be possible to examine methodological differences and their impact on findings, in the spirit of Coretta et al. (2022). Big teams of researchers could also be brought together to develop a common research protocol and collect data at many sites. Thus, there are several ways teams can work together, and several stages at which teams can be formed, to generate findings that are more impactful and generalizable than what any single individual or small group could produce on their own.

Before closing, I'd like to highlight one additional area for continuing work: research on research methods themselves. As the field of vision of second language acquisition has expanded, the types of research products have expanded as well. Methodological issues have come to the forefront of L2 research. As early as 2013, Byrnes, the editor of *The Modern Language Journal* at the time, described a "methodological turn" in L2 research. Since then, numerous journals have added methodological article categories, such as the *Studies in Second Language Acquisition* Methods Forum and the *Language Learning* Methods Showcase. The year 2022 also saw the inauguration of *Research Methods in Applied Linguistics*. L2 pronunciation researchers have examined methodological issues, and they have also proposed and validated new methods. I fully expect work in this area to continue, and it's essential that it does. Without sound methods, we cannot

256 Conclusion

have confidence in our findings. Thus, there will always be a need for work scrutinizing the means by which we obtain and analyze pronunciation data. Notable recent examples are Gallant's (2023) examination of typed transcription as a dual measure of comprehensibility and intelligibility and the special issue of the *Journal of Phonetics* dedicated to emerging data analysis in phonetic sciences (Roettger et al., 2019).

The future of L2 pronunciation research, and indeed, the future of L2 pronunciation research methods, shines brighter than ever. There are many ways to engage in meaningful, high-impact L2 pronunciation research, both individual and group- or team-based. In this conclusion, rather than focusing on particular research topics, which are dictated by complex individual, institutional, and contextual priorities, I have focused on the means by which we go about doing research and the broad types of research we conduct. I look forward to seeing and learning from what the future brings.

References

Byrnes, H. (2013). Notes from the editor. *The Modern Language Journal, 97*(4), 825–827. https://doi.org/10.1111/j.1540-4781.2013.12051.x

Coretta, S., Casillas, J. V., Roessig, S., Franke, M., Ahn, B., Al-Hoorie, A. H., Al-Tamimi, J., Alotaibi, N. E., AlShakhori, M. K., Altmiller, R. M., Arantes, P., Athanasopoulou, A., Baese-Berk, M. M., Bailey, G., Sangma, C. B. A., Beier, E. J., Benavides, G. M., Benker, N., BensonMeyer, E. P., ... Roettger, T. B. (2022). Multidimensional signals and analytic flexibility: Estimating degrees of freedom in human-speech analyses. *Advances in Methods and Practices in Psychological Science, 6*(3), 25152459231162567. https://doi.org/10.1177/25152459231162567

Flege, J. E., & Bohn, O.-S. (2021). The revised speech learning model. In R. Wayland (Ed.), *Second language speech learning: Theoretical and empirical progress* (pp. 3–83). Cambridge University Press.

Gallant, J. (2023). Typed transcription as a simultaneous measure of foreign-accent comprehensibility and intelligibility: An online replication study. *Research Methods in Applied Linguistics, 2*(2), 100055. https://doi.org/10.1016/j.rmal.2023.100055

Klein, R. A., Ratliff, K. A., Vianello, M., Adams Jr, R. B., Bahník, Š., Bernstein, M. J., Bocian, K., Brandt, M. J., Brooks, B., Brumbaugh, C. C., Cemalcilar, Z., Chandler, J., Cheong, W., Davis, W. E., Devos, T., Eisner, M., Frankowska, N., Furrow, D., Galliani, E. M., ... Nosek, B. A. (2014). Investigating variation in replicability: A "many labs" replication project. *Social Psychology, 45*(3), 142–152. https://doi.org/10.1027/1864-9335/a000178

Lee, J., Jang, J., & Plonsky, L. (2015). The effectiveness of second language pronunciation instruction: A meta-analysis. *Applied Linguistics, 36*(3), 345–366. https://doi.org/10.1093/applin/amu040

Marsden, E., & Morgan-Short, K. (2023). (Why) Are open research practices the future for the study of language learning? *Language Learning*. Advance online publication. https://doi.org/10.1111/lang.12568

McManus, K. (2022). Replication research in instructed SLA. In L. Gurzynski-Weiss & Y. Kim (Eds.) *Instructed second language acquisition research methods* (pp. 103–122). John Benjamins.

Mitchell, R., Tracy-Ventura, N., & McManus, K. (2017). *Anglophone students abroad: Identity, social relationships and language learning.* Routledge.

Moranski, K., & Zalbidea, J. (2022). Context and generalizability in multisite L2 classroom research: The impact of deductive versus guided inductive instruction. *Language Learning, 72*(S1), 41–82. https://doi.org/10.1111/lang.12487

Nagle, C., & Hiver, P. (2023). Optimizing second language pronunciation instruction: Replications of Martin and Sippel (2021), Olson and Offerman (2021), and Thomson (2012). *Language Teaching,* 1–14. https://doi.org/10.1017/S0261444823000083

Roettger, T. B., Winter, B., & Baayen, H. (2019). Emergent data analysis in phonetic sciences: Towards pluralism and reproducibility. *Journal of Phonetics, 73,* 1–7. https://doi.org/10.1016/j.wocn.2018.12.001

Saito, K., & Plonsky, L. (2019). Effects of second language pronunciation teaching revisited: A proposed measurement framework and meta-analysis. *Language Learning, 69*(3), 652–708. https://doi.org/10.1111/lang.12345

INDEX

Note: **Bold** page numbers refer to tables and *italic* page numbers refer to figures.

Abrahamsson, N. 69, 74
accentedness 68, 139–140, 230–231; described 144–145; descriptive statistics for **152**; development of 150–157; group changes in *152*; and IELTS and TOEFL tasks 140; of L2 speakers 134; linguistic predictors of 135; nativelikeness of speech 134; and rhythm and word stress 136; Spaghetti plot of changes in *153*
afex package 15, 51, 88, 205
Amazon Mechanical Turk 145
American Statistical Association 12
Amrhein, V. 13
analysis of variance (ANOVA) 46–47, 49–53, 55, 57, 60–63, 82, 84, 87–88, **90**, 122, 184, 204–206, 210
anova() function 92, 93
aov_car() function 51, 53, 55, 88, 205
aov_ez() function 51
Arndt, H. L. 235, 237
Audacity (computer software) 40

Baayen, H. R. 47
Baese-Berk, M. M. 119
balancing practical and statistical significance 12
Benson, P. 233

blocking 179–181, 195–197; by context 179–181; formats **180**; stimuli 179; by talker 179–180
Boersma, P. 31, 33
Bohn, O.-S. 114, 121, 221, 254
Bongiovanni, S. 74
Boo, Z. 228
Brauer, M. 11, 13, 92–93, 100, 154

Casillas, J. V. 115, **116,** 126
coding/analyzing: data 80–82; production data 79–82
Colantoni, L. 74
Comma Separated Values (CSV) file 43–44
Comparative Fit Index (CFI) 129
comprehensibility: descriptive statistics for **152**; development, and study abroad 157–163; development of 150–157; group changes in *152*; individual differences 242–246; language use and 238–242; and learning behavior 242–246; and motivation 242–246; Spaghetti plot of changes in *153*
confint() function 54
contrast coding Vowel 101–102
contrast() function 54, 90, 208

260 Index

controlled production 68, 77, 85, 115, 199

Coretta, S. 254–255

counterbalancing 38, 63

COVID-19 pandemic 145

Crowther, D. 140, 142–143

current approaches: to perception-production link 113–116

Curtin, J. J. 11, 13, 92–93, 100, 154

Darcy, I. 222–223

data: collection 79–80; missing 3, 47, 59, 98, 104, **105, 151,** 159, 164, 210, 247; production 79–82; structures 15, 59, 83, 104, 128, **151,** 210

Davies, R. A. I. 7, 9, 13

Derwing, T. M. 59, 70, 82–84, *83,* 90, 97, 135–136, 144, 149, 191, 224

Derwing, Tracey M.: *Pronunciation fundamentals* 1

description of hypothetical study/ simulated data 47–48, 59–60

designs/designing: integrated/ complex 211–212; perception task 34–44; rating task 146–149; stimuli 34–39

DHARMa package 15, 102–103, 185

Discovering statistics using R (Field and Miles) 5

discrimination task 32, 35–36, 41–42, 44–45, 63, 222

Earle, F. S. 77

Eefting, W. 30

emmeans() function 206, 207, 210

emmeans package 15, 53, 61, 89, 102, 156, 162–163, 187, 206

emtrends() function 162, 187

Escudero, P. 31, 33

evaluation: preparing speech for 142–143; sampling speech for 139–142

experience, and individual differences 232–237

experimental manipulation 194–198

Face, T. L. 74

Field, Andy: *Discovering statistics using R* 5

Field, Zoë: *Discovering statistics using R* 5

Flege, J. E. 10, 30, 32, 77, 114, 121, 221, 254

fluency: descriptive statistics for **152**; development of 150–157; group changes in *152*; Spaghetti plot of changes in *153*

Foreign Language Acquisition (FLA) 29

Fouz-González, J. 180

Gallant, J. 256

Gass, S. 135

generalization 35–36, 138, 172, 176, 178, 182, 192, 196, 199, 212

ggplot2 package 15–16

glmer() function 55

global features: comprehensibility/ fluency/accentedness 150–157; overview 134–137; preparing speech for evaluation 142–143; production of 134–164; rating task, designing 146–149; researching 134–164; sampling listeners 143–146; sampling speakers 137–139; sampling speech for evaluation 139–142; statistical analysis 150–163; study abroad and comprehensibility development 157–163; validating L2 speech ratings data 149–150

Gorilla (computer software) 43, 80

group_by() function 48

growth() function 129, 245

A guide to doing statistics in second language research using SPSS and R (Larson-Hall) 5

Hanzawa, K. 232

high variability phonetic training (HVPT): goals of 178–180; logistic mixed-effects model fit to HVPT training data **186**; as perception training paradigm 172; shape of learning during 182–187; variables/ experimental groups in simulated HVPT data **183**

Hirschi, K. 146

hist() function 52, 89

Hiver, P. 202

Al-Hoorie, A. H. 213, 228, 232

Huensch, A. 139

Hyltenstam, K. 69

hypothetical study 47–48, 59–60

identification task 32–34, 42, 43, 47, 60
individual differences: and
comprehensibility 242–246;
connecting the dots 237–238;
experience 232–237; language
use/comprehensibility 238–242;
and learning behavior 242–246;
mechanisms/timelines in research
222–227; motivation 227–229; and
motivation 242–246; motivation in
pronunciation research 230–232;
overview 219–222; researching
219–247; statistical analysis 238–246
individual differences research:
mechanisms in 222–227; timelines
in 222–227
install.packages ("lme4") 17
integrated/complex designs 211–212
International English Language Testing
System (IELTS) 140
International Phonetic Alphabet (IPA)
42, 181
International Picture-Naming
Project 40
intraclass correlation coefficient
(ICC) 149–150
Isaacs, T. 136, 147
Isbell, D. R. 140, 142–143

Jia, G. 114
Judd, C. M. 9, 10

Kang, O. 146
Kim, D. 30
Klein, R. A. 254–255
Kline, R. B. 130, 229

language use/comprehensibility
238–242
Larson-Hall, J. 4, 52, 88; *A guide to
doing statistics in second language
research using SPSS and R* 5
lavaan package 15, 128, 244
learning: beyond training 212–213;
shape of, during HVPT 182–187
learning behavior: and
comprehensibility 242–246;
individual differences 242–246; and
motivation 242–246
Levis, J. M. 1
Li, S. 227
library() function 17

linear mixed-effects model fit **95, 161**
LinguaPix database 40
lme4 package 15–17, 154
lmer() function 16
lmerTest package 13, 15, 91
logistic mixed-effects model fit **57, 58,
62, 101, 186**
longitudinal data analysis 3, 47–48,
122, 224, 255
longitudinal measurement 242
longitudinal research methods 3–4
longitudinal studies 4, 70, 90, 104,
114, 126, 223–224
Luke, S. G. 9

MacKay, I. R. 31
measuring learning: perception training
176–178; production training
198–200
mechanisms, in individual differences
research 222–227
Meckelborg, A. 233
Meteyard, L. 7, 9, 13
Miles, Jeremy: *Discovering statistics
using R* 5
Milin, P. 47
missing data 3, 47, 59, 98, 104, **105,
151,** 159, 164, 210, 247
mixed-effects model fit **94**; linear **95,
161**; logistic **57, 58, 62, 101, 186**
mixed-effects model/modeling 8–11,
55–59, 60–63, 83, 122–126
model comparisons 12, 92, **101**
model/modeling: mixed-effects 8–11,
55–59, 60–63, 83, 122–126;
statistical significance and 11–13
Mompeán, J. A. 180
Moorman, C. 112, 119, 174, 178
Moranski, K. 254
motivation: and comprehensibility
242–246; individual differences
227–229, 242–246; and learning
behavior 242–246; in pronunciation
research 230–232
Moyer, A. 221, 232–233
Multilingual Picture Database 40
multivariate latent growth curve model
126–130
Munro, M. J. 59, 70, 82–84, *83,* 90,
97, 135–136, 144, 147, 149, 224;
Pronunciation fundamentals 1
Myers, E. B. 77

262 Index

Nagle, C. L. **116,** 119, 136–137, 139, 142, 202

Offerman, H. M. 194, 199, 201–203
Olson, D. J. 190, 192, 194, 199, 201–203
online recruitment 145
Oswald, F. L. 130

Papi, M. 228–229
perception data: analyzing 44–47; and binary trial-level responses 63; binomial distribution of 63
perception, measuring 31–34
perception-production link: current approaches to 113–116; mixed-effects model 122–126; multivariate latent growth curve model 126–130; overview 110–113; perception-production measurement issues 116–118; researching 110–131; statistical analysis 122–130; systematic approach to 118–122
perception-production measurement issues 116–118
perception summary 181–182
perception task: designing 34–44; designing the procedure 41–44; designing the stimuli 34–39; design worksheet **43**; recording and preparing the stimuli 39–41
perception training 171–187; developing training procedure 179–181; measuring learning 176–178; perception summary 181–182; picking a topic 171–176; shape of learning during HVPT 182–187; statistical analysis 182–187
Perceptual Assimilation Model (PAM) 27–28, 111
Perrachione, T. K. 171–172
phonological sieve 23–24, 26
phonotactic constraints 74
Plonsky, L. 79, 130
poly() function 91, 93
Praat (computer software) 40–41, 81, 143, 193
preliminary steps 48–59; stop consonant perception over time 48–59; vowel perception over time 60–63

preparing speech for evaluation 142–143
production data: analyzing 79–82; coding 79–82; collecting 79–82
production of global features: comprehensibility/fluency/accentedness 150–157; overview 134–137; preparing speech for evaluation 142–143; rating task, designing 146–149; researching 134–164; sampling listeners 143–146; sampling speakers 137–139; sampling speech for evaluation 139–142; statistical analysis 150–163; study abroad and comprehensibility development 157–163; validating L2 speech ratings data 149–150
production of specific features: collecting/coding/analyzing production data 79–82; overview 68–70; researching 68–105; speech production tasks and stimuli 77–79; statistical analysis 82–103; target structures 71–77
production summary 200–201
production training 187–211; designing the intervention 193–194; measuring learning 198–200; picking a topic 187–193; production summary 200–201; retention over time 201–211; selecting variables for experimental manipulation 194–198; statistical analysis 201–211; visual feedback training 201–211
Prolific 145
Pronunciation fundamentals (Derwing and Munro) 1
pronunciation research, motivation in 230–232
pronunciation training and instruction: integrated and complex designs 211–212; learning beyond training 212–213; overview 169–171; perception training 171–187; production training 187–211; researching 169–214
Pryor, E. 234
PsychoPy (computer software) 43, 80

random effects 84
randomization 42, 63, 179, **180**

ranef() function 240
Ranta, L. 233
rating task, designing 146–149
recording/preparing stimuli 39–41
reliability 146, 148–150
researching: individual differences 219–247; perception-production link 110–131; production of global features 134–164; production of specific features 68–105; pronunciation training and instruction 169–214; speech perception 22–64
residuals() function 52
retention 175, 177, 178, 182
Root Mean Square Error of Approximation (RMSEA) 129
R Operators **16**
Rose, M. 74

Saito, K. 79, 82, 117, 136, 190, 193, 232
Sakai, M. 112, 119, 174, 178
sampling: listeners 143–146; speakers 137–139; speech for evaluation 139–142
scale() function 93
Schertz, J. 30, 34
Schoonen, R. 130, 229
simulated data 47–48, 59–60
simulateResiduals() function 102
sjPlot package 15, 56, 101
Sonsaat-Hegelheimer, S. 1
specific features: collecting/coding/analyzing production data 79–82; overview 68–70; researching 68–105; speech production tasks and stimuli 77–79; statistical analysis 82–103; target structures 71–77
Speech Learning Model (SLM) 1, 4, 27–28, 69, 111, 114, 121, 220–221
speech perception: analyzing perception data 44–47; designing the perception task 34–44; measuring perception 31–34; overview 22–27; researching 22–64; research topics 29–31; statistical analysis 47–63
speech production tasks and stimuli 77–79
speech rating tasks 149–150
spontaneous production 79, 104, 163, 199

Standardized Root Mean Squared Residual (SRMR) 129
statistical analysis 47–63; individual differences 238–246; perception-production link 122–130; perception training 182–187; production of global features 150–163; production of specific features 82–103; production training 201–211; shape of learning during HVPT 182–187; stop consonant perception over time 47–59; visual feedback training: retention over time 201–211; vowel perception over time 59–63
statistical significance 11–13; balancing practical and 12; and model/modeling 11–13
statistical significance and modeling 11–13
Steele, J. 74
stimuli: designing 34–39; recording/preparing 39–41
stimulus design 36
Stölten, K. 82
stop consonant perception over time 47–59; ANOVA 51–55; hypothetical study/simulated data 47–48; mixed-effects model 55–59; preliminary steps 48–59
stop consonant production over time 84–97
stop consonants 71, 76
study abroad, and comprehensibility development 157–163
summarize() function 48
summary() function 51, 88, 129, 155, 245
SuperLab (computer software) 43
Suter, R. W. 219
Suzuki, Y. 175, 197
systematic approach: to perception-production link 118–122

tab_model() function 56, 101
target structures 26, 71–77
Tees, R. C. 33
TextGrid (computer software) 81
Thomson, R. I. 70, 147, 178, 182, 192
timelines in individual differences research 222–227

264 Index

training: learning beyond 212–213; perception 171–187; production 187–211
Trofimovich, P. 136
Trubetzkoy, Nikolai 23–24
Tucker–Lewis Index (TLI) 129

validating L2 speech ratings data 149–150
van Poeteren, K. 82, 117
Varonis, E. M. 135
visual feedback training 201–211
voice onset time (VOT) 71–73, 82, 85, *86, 87,* 115, 204

vowel intelligibility over time 97–103
vowel perception over time 59–63; ANOVA 60–63; hypothetical study/ simulated data 59–60; mixed-effects model 60–63; preliminary steps 60–63

Waninge, F. 236
Werker, J. F. 33

Zalbidea, J. 254
Zhang, X. 169, 172
Zielinski, B. 234